1000
COOKS' HINTS

First published in Great Britain in 1985 by
Octopus Books Limited

This edition published in 1991 by
Treasure Press
Michelin House
81 Fulham Road
London SW3 6RB

© 1985 Hennerwood Publications Limited

ISBN 1 85051 678 2

Printed and bound in the United Kingdom by The Bath Press

Illustrations by Patricia Capon / Joan Farmer Artists
              Ch ' en Ling

1000 COOKS' HINTS

Margaret Coombes
Cordon Bleu Cookery School (London) Ltd
Cassandra Kent
Mary Meredith
Daphne Metland
Rosemary Wadey

TREASURE PRESS

#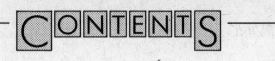

PLANNING

1

FEEDING THE FAMILY

Make a list: Organization is really the key to success when feeding a family. Plan the meals a week at a time. Write down all the main courses and desserts, then pin the list up in the kitchen. This will both make shopping easier and allow you to ensure that the diet is well balanced. It should also avoid last minute panics and frantic searches in the freezer for something for tea.

Get ahead: Once a week spend an hour or so doing all the routine jobs in the kitchen. Refill storage jars and the salt and pepper mills; make up a salad dressing and keep it in the fridge; half make pastry by rubbing the fat into the flour, then store the crumb mixture in the fridge. This keeps well for a week or two and can be used straight from the fridge, simply add water and roll out. Biscuits can be made too and frozen or stored in tins. Alternatively make refrigerator biscuits which keep raw in the fridge in a long sausage shape; when you need biscuits simply cut a few slices off the roll and bake.

Eat today and tomorrow: Arrange menus so that some of the food needed for the next day can be precooked on the preceding day. For instance if cooking rice to serve hot one day, cook enough to make a rice salad for lunch the following day. If making a white sauce to use in a chicken pie one day, make enough to serve with cauliflower the next day. A little careful planning will cut down the time spent preparing meals considerably and reduce the unintentional leftovers.

Cook in: Batch-baking will save time and energy; both the sort you pay for and your own. Have a baking afternoon and make enough cakes, biscuits and pies or crumbles to last a week or two. Freeze the results and there will always be a good supply of desserts and baked foods available. It is a good way to use seasonal gluts like soft fruits, apples and plums too. Even without a freezer most cakes and biscuits will keep for several days in an airtight tin and desserts, such as crumbles and pies, for two or three days in the fridge, see 'Pastry items' page 342.

Family favourites: It is useful to know that the family will finish the meal with no waste when you serve their favourite dishes, but also worthwhile trying to introduce new flavours and dishes. Do this gradually by adding at least one new dish each week, so that menus do not become boring, then increase it to two a week and so on, if you really enjoy cooking.

Diet change: This slow introduction of different dishes is also a good way to change the family's diet and introduce vegetarian or whole-food dishes. Taken gradually the family is not so likely to rebel and the cook has time to experiment with new foods and get used to cooking them, so that in time they too become family favourites.

Double take: If you have a freezer it is well worth cooking double quantities of most dishes and freezing the spare: it is almost as quick to cook two casseroles as one. Make sure you store them in separate containers though, or everyone may simply eat twice as much!

Lunch boxes: Packed lunches for a whole family can mean frantic mornings of making sandwiches and filling lunch boxes. Minimize this by cooking some foods for the lunch box while cooking the evening meal. Pop a scone-based pizza in the oven along with the evening meal; bake some cornish pasties when making shepherds pie; or cook some chicken drumsticks alongside a roast chicken or a few extra sausages to eat cold for lunch.

MENU PLANNING

We eat with our eyes: Food well presented and colourful will impress the eye and stimulate the appetite. Take care to choose vegetables that will brighten up a neutral main course. The best garnishes are simple rather than fussy. Mix different vegetables such as carrots and peas in one serving dish, or sweetcorn and button onions to give colour contrasts.

Seasons best: Plan menus to take advantage of seasonal foods, which are usually plentiful, cheap and in prime condition. If you use traditional menus for seasonal foods you will often find that they match the weather conditions too: so warm winter puddings will help keep the cold out while making best use of autumn plums, apples, pears and so on.

11

A little bite: Contrast in texture and style of dishes matters. Smooth creamy desserts, such as fools and mousses, really need crisp biscuits served with them for contrast. Croûtons with soup, or crisp salads with rich pasta dishes do the same thing.

Watch your shape: The shape and size of food are important. Avoid a complete meal made up of small bitty foods; risotto and fruit salad, pasta shells and rice pudding, etc.

Once a meal: One golden rule worth following is not to use one sort of food more than once in a meal; so only use one pastry dish, use rice as a vegetable or dessert, not both. The same is true of sauces, avoid repeating a sauce similar in taste or texture on the starter and the main course.

Rich and spicy: Flavours matter, of course, but so too do the richness and spiciness of food. In very formal dinners with six or seven courses, it is traditional to serve a sorbet between courses to cleanse the palate. Not many people want to go to those lengths when entertaining at home, but the basic idea is worth following. Try to serve something light and refreshing after a rich main course.

Currying favour: Curry and other highly spiced dishes often affect the taste of foods served immediately afterwards, so opt for something quite strong tasting but refreshing as a dessert, such as lemon soufflé or a citrus sorbet.

First and foremost: Starters or first courses are meant to stimulate the appetite, so are best kept light and small. Foods such as fresh or smoked fish, piquant salads or well-flavoured soups are ideal and so are fruits like tomato, grapefruit and melon.

Filling the gap: More complicated and filling starters are useful where the main course itself is quite simple. Of course there are occasions when a filling first course is useful to make the main course go further. Yorkshire pudding was originally used for this purpose. Cooked under the meat so the drippings collected in it, the pudding was served with plenty of gravy before the main course. This effectively blunted the appetite, thus making the joint go further. This is a useful idea to copy when having to feed rather more people than the meat was intended for.

Warming meals: If the weather looks changeable, try to plan meals so that at least one course can be served hot or cold. A soup that can be chilled or served warm depending on the sun or a hot sauce to pour over a cold dessert when a chill has set in will be most welcome. Add a few baked potatoes or some hot herb bread to a salad meal on a cold day.

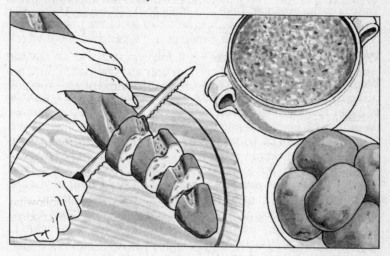

SPECIAL OCCASIONS

Advance planning: Entertaining friends and family can be most enjoyable, but requires a little forethought. Try to plan meals that can be prepared well in advance with little effort needed at the last minute. One course hot, one course cold and one prepared in advance is a good rule.

Ringing the changes: Keeping a record of what dishes are served on which occasions will allow you to ring the changes or to be sure of serving people's favourite dishes. If you also note down any strong dislikes or allergies, you can be sure of pleasing most of the people most of the time. A dinner party log book of this kind should list the date, the occasion, who was present and what food and wine was served. In another section of the book keep a list of friends and note down their likes and dislikes.

13

Pots and pans: Consider what sort of cooking pans and serving dishes the food will need. Equipment can often be borrowed or hired, but some things will need particular pans or dishes; whole fish will need a fish kettle, asparagus a steamer, soufflés a soufflé dish, etc.

Time is of the essence: Take into account the time available. If you do not have unlimited time, it is better to serve simple food well cooked and presented, than attempt a complicated meal which needs a great deal of attention.

Weekend guests: Having guests for the weekend means careful planning of all meals and as much advance preparation as possible to avoid spending too much time in the kitchen. Choose simple desserts such as cheese and fresh fruits or a home-made icecream or sorbet that can be served straight from the freezer. Keep main meals filling and simple with salads and vegetable dishes that are quick and easy to put together at the last minute. Plan a few extra snack type meals as well, just in case guests stay longer or you are all extra hungry late at night. Keep a few store cupboard standbys to hand, such as a packet of breadmix that can be made up into a pizza or good tinned soup that can be dressed up with a little cream to make an impromptu lunch dish (see also page 324 for more information on what to keep in store).

A light touch: Avoid making meals too heavy, especially if you enjoy lively conversation! Pace the courses, so that there is time between them for the food to settle and conversation to take over. The French have the right idea with their two-hour lunch breaks! This applies particularly to the dessert. Offer something simple like fresh fruit or sorbet as an alternative to a heavy pudding.

The right style: Plan a meal to suit the occasion – supper after a firework party, for instance, will be very different from supper after the theatre or a concert. Firework party food should appeal to children as well as grown-ups and be the type of thing that can be eaten standing up; after theatre suppers should feature light but elegant food. Special occasions usually make menu planning simpler as the sort of food needed is obvious.

Cause for a party: If you have no particular event to celebrate, then it provides a conversation point if you choose a theme for the evening. Have an American-style Thanksgiving meal, or a midsummer barbecue. Entertain quite cheaply by having a pizza party or a harvest supper with a casserole and plenty of baked apples. You can follow through the theme with suitable drink and decorations to complete the evening.

Back to basics: Cut time and effort when entertaining by making sure that all the basics are made well in advance. Sauces, biscuits, bread, pastry, breadcrumbs, etc, can all be made up and frozen or stored in the fridge or larder. Write a list of everything you are going to eat, not forgetting little extras like herb butter, and tick them off as they are prepared.

On the side: A sideboard is useful when entertaining. It allows some food and most dishes to be put out before the meal so there is extra room in the kitchen. Many items, such as biscuits to serve with desserts, butter balls or curls, biscuits and bread for cheese, or the coffee tray, can be prepared and placed in the dining room in advance. A heated tray helps too, as vegetable dishes and plates can be kept near to hand during the meal.

A clever creation: If you don't have a sideboard, a coffee table, small desk, or cupboard will do and can be covered with a tablecloth to protect or disguise it.

Tried and tested: For very special occasions have a dummy run. Try out the dishes and make sure you have enough saucepans, serving dishes, cutlery and glasses. Sort out garnishes and vegetable accompaniments with an eye to colour combinations so that the finished dishes will look attractive.

A day out: When entertaining after being out all day, it is important to make sure that the food will require a minimum of last-minute attention. Casseroles are ideal; they can be precooked the day before and reheated or left to cook on an oven auto-timer or in a slow cooker. An alternative is to leave food to marinate, so that it only requires some finishing touches when you get home. Kebab meat can be left soaking in a spicy sauce, chicken breasts can be put in a mixture of wine and oil. They can then be grilled when needed and served with a simple salad.

Sunday roast: When serving roasts with various vegetables, persuade someone to carve at the table. This will then leave the kitchen clear for you to sort out the gravy, vegetables, etc., so that by the time the meat is carved, everything else will be ready as well.

Fast food: If time is limited when entertaining, make up a large platter of cold foods that can be bought ready to eat. For a predominantly fish dish, arrange piles of prawns, crab, smoked salmon and such on a large tray and serve with rye bread, pumpernickel and other unusual breads. Another idea is to choose a variety of delicatessen products, such as cold meats and pâtés or a selection of unusual cheeses. Some supermarkets sell party platters already made up, which can be very useful if you have no time to prepare the food yourself.

If your guests have offered to bring a bottle of wine, let them know your menu in advance, so that they have a chance to match their wine to the food.

Super soufflés: Soufflés make impressive desserts or lunch dishes but you do need punctual guests as the soufflé will not wait. Since soufflés are cooked quite quickly (about 40-45 minutes on average) it is worth making the basic sauce in advance, then whisking the egg whites and completing the dish only when the guests arrive. You will have about three-quarters of an hour to have drinks or eat the main course and then serve the soufflé immediately it is cooked.

Simple supper: Curry makes a good supper dish, since it can be cooked in advance and it can be served simply with rice, or dressed up with a wide variety of side dishes. Add dishes of natural yogurt, sliced bananas, chopped onions, mango chutney, raita (grated cucumber mixed with yogurt), or sliced tomatoes. It can also be eaten with a fork, away from the table, which makes it ideal for parties, too.

Salad days: Hot summer days are perfect for entertaining, since friends can spill out into the garden. Keep the main course simple, cold or barbecued meat, and go to town on the salads. Serve a selection of different types and experiment with the ingredients. Try mixing nuts, beans or dates with more traditional salad foods. Moulded salads look attractive; set tomatoes, cucumber or beetroot in aspic in a ring mould or make a rice salad, add the dressing then press into a ring mould and chill. A variety of salad dressings can also be served, so that people have a choice.

Pitta pockets: Lunchtime foods should be simple and light. When feeding several people try pitta pockets. Buy fresh pitta bread, white or wholemeal varieties, and serve warm. Put out little dishes of a variety of cooked foods and salads and let people make up their own pitta pocket. Try chopped, fried bacon; mushrooms cooked in a little butter; onions lightly fried, hard-boiled eggs sliced in mayonnaise, tomatoes, sweetcorn and other salad foods. Make good use of whatever is in the fridge.

▓SERVING QUANTITIES

Getting it right: Buying and preparing the right amount of food is important for two reasons, it eliminates waste and avoids the more embarrassing alternative of not having enough food. Remember to

17

allow for varying appetites though; if the members of your family have spent the morning swimming or have been for a brisk walk, they are likely to eat far more than they would after an afternoon spent lazing in the garden.

Soups: When serving soup as a first course, allow about 200 ml (⅓ pint) for each person plus enough for one or two people to have second helpings. When serving soup as a lunch-time main course, allow about 300 ml (½ pint) for each person.

Sauce for the goose...: When making savoury sauces and gravies to be served in a separate sauce boat make about 50 ml (2 fl oz) for each person.

Good game: Since so much of the weight of poultry and game is made up of the carcass, it is not easy to gauge the amount of meat that a cooked bird will provide. Turkeys have a large carcass, so bigger turkeys have a better ratio of meat to total weight. For this reason allow 225 g (8 oz) for each person (for a family of four you will need a 3.5 kg (8 lb) turkey).

Lean but rich: Game is very rich, so less meat is needed, but it lacks the plumpness of chickens which have been bred for the table.

Counting on game: A wild duck will generally only feed two people at best. Pheasants are slightly more meaty, so that one will feed two or three people. A brace of pheasants consists of a cock and a hen bird. The cock pheasant looks bigger but actually contains the same amount of meat as a hen. Grouse and other small birds should be served one for each person. Venison has very small bones and little fat and so will serve more per pound than beef; allow about 100 g (4 oz) for each person.

Meats: Allow at least 100 g (4 oz) for each person when serving meat together with a selection of vegetables in casseroles and other meats in sauces but remember to take into account the amount of fat on the meat. After trimming, as much as 50-75 g (2-3 oz) on each 450 g (1 lb) can be lost. Allow 175-225 g (6-8 oz) for each person for roast meats and chops, but for special occasions, or when serving steak, you may wish to allow more meat. A generous steak will often weigh 350 g (12 oz).

Vegetable medley: The quantity of vegetables to be served will depend on the type and how many are being served at once. Allow about 225 g (8 oz) of leafy vegetables, such as cabbage and spring greens, for each person, and about 100 g (4 oz) of root vegetables, which include potatoes, carrots, turnips and such. Allow 100 g (4 oz) of sweetcorn, peas, etc. When serving two or more vegetables reduce the overall quantities slightly.

Stews and casseroles can be made with the less expensive cuts of meat. If using beef, chuck or shoulder steak, clod or skirt cuts are best. For mutton or lamb, choose middle neck, double scrag, scrag or fillet end of leg. Breasts, knuckle and shoulder cuts are the most suitable for veal, and rabbit either whole or jointed is very good. If the particular cut chosen contains a fair quantity of bone, remember to allow more weight per person than with a boneless cut.

Sweet sauce: People generally like more custard and sweet sauces on puddings, so allow about 85 ml (3 fl oz) for each person.

Packets of pastry: Bought ready made pastry has its weight printed on the wrapping, but remember that this refers to the total weight. When a recipe calls for 225 g (8 oz) of shortcrust pastry, it usually means pastry made with 225 g (8 oz) flour plus the weight of the fat and the other ingredients. Bought ready made pastry that weighs 225 g (8 oz) is likely to be equivalent to 150 g or 175 g (5 or 6 oz) of home-made pastry. To assess how much ready made pastry you need, take into account that shortcrust pastry is generally made with half as much fat as flour i.e. for 225 g (8 oz) pastry you need 350 g (12 oz) total weight. Flaky pastry is generally made with three portions of fat to four portions of flour i.e. for 225 g (8 oz) pastry you will need to buy 400 g (14 oz) of ready made pastry. Puff pastry is made with equal quantities of fat to flour i.e. 225 g (8 oz) requires 450 g (1 lb) ready made pastry.

▓RECIPE BASICS

Waste not: Most of us don't look up a recipe for familiar dishes, such as apple pie or quiches, and often make too much pastry as a consequence. To avoid wastage it's worth noting that 100 g (4 oz) shortcrust pastry will line a 15 cm (6 inch) flan ring; 150 g (5 oz) pastry will line an 18 cm (7 inch) ring; 200 g (7 oz) pastry will line a 20 cm (8 inch) ring; 250 g (9 oz) pastry will line a 23 cm (9 inch) ring. To cover a 1.6 litre (2¾ pint) dish or make the top and bottom for a 20 cm (8 inch) pie plate, 225 g (8 oz) pastry will be needed. This quantity will also make 12 mince pies or 20-24 jam tarts.

Sausage rolls: To make 8 medium or 12 small sausage rolls make up 175 g (6 oz) flaky pastry, using 175 g (6 oz) flour and 100 g (4 oz) fat. Buy 225 g (8 oz) sausagemeat for the filling. If using frozen puff pastry, buy a packet weighing 300-350 g (11-12 oz).

Cake bakes: A Victoria sandwich mixture is the base for many cakes. The basic recipe of two eggs, 100 g (4 oz) flour, 100 g (4 oz) sugar and 100 g (4 oz) margarine will fill two 18 cm (7 inch) sandwich tins. For a deeper cake use 15 cm (6 inch) tins. Increase the quantities to three eggs and 175 g (6 oz) of all other ingredients for 20 cm (8 inch) sandwich tins. When baking this mixture in one deep cake tin, the smaller quantity will fill an 18 cm (7 inch) cake tin, the larger a 20 cm (8 inch) cake tin. The 2 egg mixture will also fill a Swiss roll tin (you can cut up the rectangular cake into fingers and ice them), or the same amount will make 12-16 queen cakes.

Daily bread: Home-made bread fills the house with an appetizing smell and most people cannot wait for it to cool before trying a slice. 25 g (1 oz) fresh yeast is enough to raise up to 1.5 kg (3 lb) of bread dough. If using dried yeast, allow 15 g (½ oz) but remember to mix it with sugar and warm liquid and stand it aside for 20 minutes or so until it foams. For rolls allow about 50 g (2 oz) dough for each roll: 450 g (1 lb) of bread dough will make about eight rolls. Fancy dinner rolls can be smaller and will give about 12-16 for each 450 g (1 lb). Weigh the pieces of dough to ensure they are even in size.

Fast flans: Biscuit-based flans are quick and easy to prepare. Digestive biscuits are the type most commonly used, but ginger biscuits and even chocolate digestives can be used too. Allow 175 g

(6 oz) biscuits and half as much butter or margarine to line a 20 cm (8 inch) flan ring. Chill for 30 minutes before filling.

Set and match: Gelatine is used in many desserts as a setting agent. Take care to soften the gelatine before use by sprinkling the gelatine powder over three to four tablespoons of the liquid. Do not add liquid to the dry gelatine as this makes it go lumpy. Warm the gelatine in a bowl over a pan of hot water and leave without stirring until dissolved. It goes clear as it dissolves. About 15 g (½ oz) gelatine is enough to set 600 ml (1 pint) liquid. Keep the dissolved gelatine warm over the pan of hot water until needed.

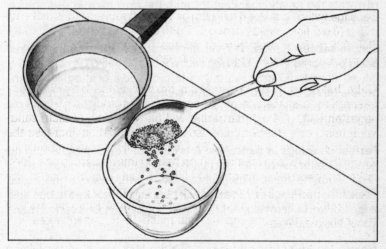

Pouring gelatine: Pour rather than spoon the dissolved gelatine into the mixture to be set. And if adding to cream, pour the gelatine in a thin stream from a height. This allows the gelatine to cool a little but not so much as to make it stringy.

Even gelatine: When using gelatine always soak the granules before use in cold liquid so the gelatine absorbs the moisture and melts quickly and evenly when warmed.

Complete soaking: Use a sufficient quantity of water or fruit juice to soak the gelatine completely. Do this in a small receptacle. A little more liquid, if needed, will not spoil the recipe.

Never boil: When warming gelatine in a liquid never allow it to boil as this will make it tough and rubbery and stop it mixing evenly through the mixture.

Never stir: Melted gelatine should pour freely, like water, into the mixture. Never stir it on melting but make sure that all of it leaves the pan.

Prevent sinking: When gelatine is added to a creamy mixture to set it, such as a soufflé or mousse, before moulding the mixture needs to be stirred in a pan with ice packed round it until it thickens. This prevents the gelatine sinking through the mixture and setting in a solid layer at the bottom of the dish or mould.

Simple sauces: Sauces vary in thickness according to their uses. Basic proportions for a pouring sauce would be 15 g (½ oz) fat, 15 g (½ oz) flour to 300 ml (½ pint) of liquid. For a coating sauce, increase this to 25 g (1 oz) fat/flour to each 300 ml (½ pint) of milk and for a thick binding sauce allow 50 g (2 oz) fat/flour to each 300 ml (½ pint) of liquid.

Perfect puddings or pancakes: A traditional Yorkshire pudding tin needs a batter made with 300 ml (½ pint) of milk, one egg and 100 g (4 oz) flour, to fill it. This same mixture will make 6 individual Yorkshire puddings or 12 very small puddings, if cooked in bun tins. It is also worth knowing that the same recipe can be used to make about six pancakes.

Well covered: Almond paste is quite expensive but it is important to allow sufficient to cover the cake well or the icing will not remain smooth. An 18 cm (7 inch) cake requires about 450 g (1 lb) of almond paste. For larger cakes add 225 g (8 oz) of paste for each extra 2.5 cm (1 inch) cake; so for a 20 cm (8 inch) cake allow 750 g (1½ lb) and so on.

Royal finish: Final icing with royal icing will require about 450 g (1 lb) icing for an 18 cm (7 inch) cake and an extra 100 g (4 oz) for each extra 2.5 cm (1 inch) of cake i.e. for a 20 cm (8 inch) cake allow 500 g (1¼ lb) icing, for a 23 cm (9 inch) cake allow 750 g (1½ lb), etc. A two-tier cake with a 30 cm (12 inch) base and a 25 cm (10 inch) top will cut into about 100 pieces.

▓ACCOMPANIMENTS

Hot bread: Garlic or herb bread is a popular accompaniment to soups, salads and barbecues. Allow 75 g (3 oz) butter and a clove of garlic to each small French loaf. For the large sticks allow 150-175 g (5-6 oz) butter and two small cloves of garlic. Alternatively use herbs instead, allowing one-two tablespoons of finely chopped herbs to mix with the butter.

Well sliced: Sandwiches are a good standby for packed lunches, picnics and elegant afternoon teas. Most standard sliced loaves have between 20 and 24 slices and will make 10-12 rounds of sandwiches which, cut into small triangles, will give 40-48 small sandwiches. Allow four-six of these for each person for afternoon tea or picnics where other food is offered. At least eight will be needed for packed lunches. About 75 g (3 oz) of well-softened butter will be needed to spread each loaf of bread. If making a great number of sandwiches, mix half butter and half margarine to make spreading easier and more economical. When using very moist fillings take care to spread the bread generously with the butter to prevent the sandwiches becoming soggy.

Finger food: For canapés and other small snacks served with drinks allow six-eight for each person. Allow fewer if they are to precede a meal, but if they are meant to replace lunch, allow about 12 for each person. Ensure that the canapés are small enough to be eaten in one bite and that they will not fall apart when picked up.

A jug of wine: Calculating the amount of drink to be allowed for a party is difficult as this can vary with the occasion. Sherry is generally served in small glasses and one bottle will provide about 16 glasses. Spirits provide about 32 shorts to the bottle and each small bottle of mixer will provide 2 or 3 glasses, so allow about 10 mixers for each bottle of spirits. A 75 cl bottle of wine will contain about six glasses and a litre bottle eight. Champagne usually provides five glasses to the bottle.

Coffee and cream: A cup of freshly-made coffee is a good end to a meal or a party. Allow two-three teaspoons of ground coffee for each cup or, if making it in large quantities, weigh out 50 g (2 oz) for each 600 ml (1 pint); it is easier to weigh than to count out 20 or 30 spoonsful. Each pint will give four-five cups of coffee. Serve it black and offer milk or cream, allowing about 25 ml (1 fl oz) for each cup. For French style café au lait use about 150 ml (¼ pint) of hot milk and add 50-75 g (2-3 oz) strong black coffee. This type of coffee is usually served in a larger cup.

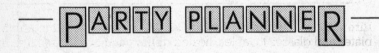

ORGANIZATION

Enjoy yourself: Giving parties is often so much hard work for the host and hostess that the following morning, faced with the clearing up, they vow 'never again'. Advance planning, simple food and plenty of post-party help make the whole business much more pleasant.

Lists of lists: Begin by making lists of things to do, people to invite, food to serve and so forth. Decide on the number of guests, taking into account how many people you can fit comfortably into your home and how many people you can afford to feed. Send out invitations or telephone friends about four weeks in advance and allow for a few people who will be unable to come. Make sure you give details of the date and time and some indication of the kind of party you are giving.

Disposables: Another alternative is to use disposable plates and plastic glasses, which have the enormous advantage of eliminating the washing up. Many are attractive and robust and they are ideal for outdoor events such as barbecues, picnics and summer parties in the garden.

Cordon Bleu

TIPS

If organizing an informal buffet party for a number of people, it is simplest to plan one big dish and a variety of accompanying salads. Bear in mind that the food should be easy to eat with a fork while standing or sitting. It should also be simple so that guests can easily help themselves. In cold weather or if the party is likely to go on late into the night, a hot soup is always a welcome sustainer.

Hire it: Local hire shops should be able to supply anything from plates and glasses to tables, heated trolleys and even sometimes a complete marquee. It may be well worth the cost of hiring equipment, if only to prevent your own glasses and crockery being broken. Replacing parts of a dinner service can be expensive and for large parties it is best to put away your own valuable pieces and hire a selection instead.

Temporary tables: A buffet table should be long and narrow, so that as many people as possible can help themselves at any one time and plenty of food can be placed on it. Steady paste tables or trestle tables (which can be hired) are ideal and once covered with tablecloths look presentable. Sometimes village and church halls have folding tables and stacking chairs which can be borrowed in return for a small donation.

Space matters: Avoid crowding a buffet table. Try to have napkins, cutlery, drinks and glasses on another table nearby (see page 15). Wrap a napkin around knives and forks so that each guest simply has to pick up one parcel rather than find separate knives and forks.

Double bill: For large buffet parties have two of each of the salad and vegetable dishes and place one at each end of the buffet table. Place the main meat dishes in the centre, so that two queues of people can be formed to work their way from the sides to the middle to collect their food.

Floral art: Flower arrangements for buffet tables need to be stable, so that they are not knocked over. Keep them flat and sit them at the back of the table where they will not prevent people reaching the food. Avoid flowers that are likely to drop petals into the food or are strongly perfumed.

Within easy reach: Try to arrange food so that everything is easy to reach. Dishes which require serving spoons are best placed at the front of the table, while foods that can be picked up, such as sausage rolls, can go further back. On a wide dining room table make a raised section at the back by putting stout boxes under the tablecloth, so that all the dishes can be seen and reached. It's a good idea to put an old blanket on the table first to protect the table and stop the boxes slipping.

Help yourself: Buffet parties are the easiest to organize for large numbers. Everyone can help themselves to food and drink and eat standing up if there are not enough chairs. Try to choose fork and finger food, so that it is easy to cope with, and provide plenty of paper napkins and large plates.

Twice as nice: Always expect some guests to have two desserts if there is a choice of dessert. Also if offering fruit or cheese remember that some people will have both!

Individual approach: Serve individual dishes where possible. Although these take longer to prepare, they do speed up serving and avoid a long queue at the table. Cold meats and poultry should be served sliced for the same reason. Cut butter into cubes or make butter curls and slice the bread.

Portion control: When guests are to help themselves it's best to mark the portions to act as a guide. Use the decorations such as whirls of cream or lines of piping on desserts and cut quiches and other savoury dishes into portions but leave them arranged as a whole for an attractive appearance.

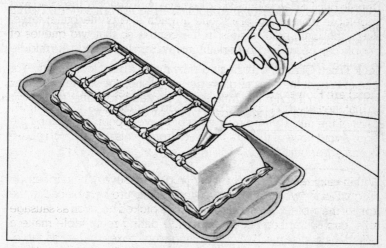

Cool it: Wine that needs to be served chilled can be kept cold in a bucket half full of water with ice cubes floating in it. This is the quickest way to chill wine and ensures that the fridge is kept free for storing food. Return half-full bottles to the bucket to keep them cool until needed.

Driver's friend: Offer water with wine and/or a non-alcoholic fruit cup for those who prefer not to drink and for drivers. Try using cartons of fresh fruit juices mixed with lemonade or bubbly mineral water for a quick and refreshing soft drink.

Ice and easy: Make up plenty of extra ice cubes in advance, so that you do not run out on the night. One easy way to do this is to fill plastic egg cartons with water and freeze until hard, then tip the cubes into plastic bags and refill the cartons to make more. If you don't have time to freeze lots of ice cube trays, freeze a shallow layer of water in plastic boxes then break up the ice by turning it out on to a clean tea towel and hitting it with a rolling pin.

Frozen fruits; For drinks freeze slices of lemon, orange or limes in advance. Lay the cut slices on non-stick baking trays and freeze until hard before placing them in plastic bags. They can be added to drinks quickly to chill and flavour as they melt. For a large bowl of summer punch, freeze some water in a pretty jelly mould with chopped glacé cherries and angelica arranged in a pattern. Tip this into the punch, so that it keeps the drink chilled all evening while looking attractive.

Jack Frost: Glasses with frosted rims make drinks look pretty. You can also frost the rims of glass dessert dishes for serving ices and sorbets. Dip the rim in a little lightly beaten egg white, then into a saucer or plate of sieved icing sugar or caster sugar.

Ice by the pound: If short of freezer space or time, ice cubes can be bought from some supermarkets, off licences and a few freezer centres. The ice cubes can be kept solid for several hours in a freezer box filled up with newspaper.

Early coffee: If you need more coffee than your filter coffee maker can provide, make it up in advance and reheat when needed, or make it just before guests arrive and pour it into a vacuum flask ready to use later. The same method can be used for sauces and soups if you are short of space or saucepans.

Roll out the barrel: If serving beer from the cask, organize it the day before if possible, since it needs some time to settle before it is drunk. Make sure the cask is level and leave it to stand before using.

Decanters need careful cleaning after use. Rinse them thoroughly and leave to drain completely. If your decanter is narrow-necked, it will need to be supported while it is draining, so stand it upside down in a sturdy jar or vase. Return to store unstoppered but covered with a piece of tissue paper secured with a rubber band. This will keep the inside clean and fresh.

The morning after...: The morning after the party no-one ever feels like clearing up. Bribe overnight guests with the promise of plenty of fresh hot coffee and croissants, or employ local teenagers on an hourly rate to cope with the worst mess. Distribute plenty of bin liners and trays in each room or around the garden and work systematically, throwing away rubbish and collecting glasses.

Getting washing-up organized: Stack all the dirty things on one side of the sink and put out trays covered with tea towels to hold the clean things. Wash up in stages.

Clearing the decks: During a party have a regular round up of glasses and plates and remove them to the kitchen. This will avoid too many breakages and help minimize the amount of clearing up to be done at the end of the evening.

Instant bins: Cover some cardboard boxes with wallpaper and put one in each room tucked in a convenient corner before the party, so that rubbish like paper plates, paper napkins and plastic cups and glasses can be deposited straight into them. At the end of the evening, go round and collect the boxes ready to take out to the dustbin. Have a couple of spare ones, so that you can put them out during the evening should the existing boxes become full.

Quick rescue: Keep an emergencies box handy during parties, so that if drinks are spilt or plates dropped you can cope with the minimum of fuss. In a cardboard box keep a dustpan and brush, plenty of kitchen towels, some old white cotton rag for blotting up drinks from carpets and upholstery, and add tissues, plasters and safety pins just in case.

Large parties: For large parties food needs to be good but simple. Make sure there are plenty of filling breads, potatoes or other carbohydrates to help absorb the alcohol. Choose mostly dishes that can be frozen or prepared in advance, so that on the day all you have to do is serve the food and arrange the rooms.

▮IMPROVIZATION

An inventive mind: Necessity is said to be the mother of invention and this is true when it comes to providing food for large numbers of people. Regular party givers might find it well worthwhile to buy particular pieces of equipment or extra chairs and tables, but for most of us this is not practical. Some lateral thinking will often allow you to use existing equipment at little or no extra cost.

Serving dishes: For extra serving dishes use trays, with paper napkins on them; these are ideal for sausage rolls and similar foods and easy to clean afterwards as you simply throw away the napkins. Baking trays can also be used, covered with foil to make them look less functional; and so too can squares or rounds of strong card also covered with foil. Large mixing bowls can be used for salads or a party punch, and small glasses and tumblers can be used for extra desserts, such as mousses or fools. Wicker baskets are cheap and useful for holding sandwiches, rolls, biscuits and fresh fruits.

Extra platters: A large kitchen chopping board, scrubbed clean, makes an ideal cheese board. A short off-cut of worktop leftover from a kitchen installation will do the same; or an old marble slab of the kind originally used on dressing tables and washstands can be trimmed and used for a cheeseboard as well.

Ashtrays: Small foil baking tins make useful ashtrays and it is worth having plenty of these about the house, placed somewhere heat-proof, as even people who don't usually smoke, occasionally have a cigar or cigarette at a party. If using them outside, weight them with a small pebble to prevent them being blown away.

Party lights: A barbecue or summer party in the garden needs to be well lit. Garden lights can be made using jam jars with night lights inside. Paint the outside of the jar with a little coloured poster paint and allow to dry, then stand the night light inside. Place the lights along a wall or on the edges of paths to prevent people stepping off into the flower beds. Alternatively place a bucket or large dish of water on a patio and float several night lights in it. Take extra care if children are around.

Tablecloths: Old sheets or curtains make good tablecloths and are often large enough to cover the table completely. If tablecloths have become stained or worn in the middle, put them on the table, then cover with a smaller cloth used as an overcloth.

Be seated: Floor cushions make good extra seats. Another solution is to place a stout piece of wood between two chairs which have been stood against a wall. Cover the wood with an old blanket and/or small cushions.

Child's play: If there are children around, give them their own picnic outside if the weather is fine, or let them picnic at a desk or a coffee table.

SHOPPING

2

SHOPPING SENSE

▓CAREFUL PLANNING

Can you cope?: Go for a glut of cheap fresh food only if you know you can cope with it quickly. Fresh fruit and vegetables should be frozen, bottled or otherwise preserved within hours of getting them home or they will start to deteriorate.

Where will you put it?: Think about storage before embarking on a major bulk-buying expedition for canned or packet goods. These need to be stored in a cool, dry place, which rules out such areas as a damp garage or the top shelf of the airing cupboard. You may need to set aside special cupboards or shelves for storage. Make sure they are sufficiently accessible (not stuck up in a loft reached by a ladder you keep in the shed) otherwise you'll find it easier to visit the corner shop rather than go on an expedition to find the home stores.

Share a car: Consider transport costs when planning major shopping expeditions. If you can take turns sharing a car into town with a neighbour, it will halve petrol and parking costs.

Balancing out the cost: If you don't have a car it might even be worth taking a taxi home, say once a month. Buying a large amount of goods in one go would be far more economical than having to go into town twice a week on the bus for small loads.

Counting the cost: Shopping around for bargains makes sense only if you have the time and if the transport costs are not increased thereby. There is little point in tracking down the cheapest brand of custard powder in your area if you have had to drive between shops and possibly incur parking charges. You will save more money by buying a dearer brand in the shop you first visit.

Time can be money: If you work from home or if you could do without a cleaning lady for the housework by spending less time shopping, it makes sense to buy from a convenient outlet, even if it isn't the cheapest.

Lifestyles: Plan shopping expeditions according to your particular lifestyle. If you live alone and have limited food storage facilities, you may find it easiest to pick up small quantities of fresh food each day as you need it.

Regulate your shopping: Where large families are catered for, shopping should be planned with care. It's best to organize one major shop for non-perishable foods – weekly, fortnightly or monthly depending on the cash, transport and storage space available. To maintain maximum freshness, perishable foods can be bought once or twice a week and stored (see pages 76 to 91).

Not in front of the children: Try to avoid shopping with very small children. It's boring for them and distracting for you. Leave them with a neighbour if possible and do the same for her in turn. Older children (seven and upwards while willing) are useful for helping to pack your bags and nipping around for things you've forgotten, while you stand in the checkout queue.

Shopping reminders: Make lists before you go shopping. You don't need to stick to them slavishly if you see a bargain but it will ensure that you don't forget the essentials. If you're familiar with your supermarket layout, then organize your shopping list accordingly.

The golden rule: When shopping for food, eat before you shop. If you're consumed by hunger pangs in a supermarket, everything will seem that much more desirable and you'll probably end up buying things you don't want or need.

Don't always scrimp: Saving pennies on a bargain is not always worthwhile. With meat, for example, buying a lean tender cut that costs more than a scraggy fatty one could save you a lot of preparation time. And when you've removed the edible parts from the cheap meat you could find that weight for weight you haven't saved anything. When you want the best it's worth paying for it rather than for something that is recognisably second-rate.

Read the labels: Food labels get ever more informative; many now carry nutritional advice as well as a list of ingredients. Bear in mind that in an ingredient list the items are in the order of quantity. There is most of the ingredient at the head of the list and least of the one at the bottom. Additives are listed by E numbers. For an explanation of these you need a copy of the free leaflet 'Look at the Label' from the Ministry of Agriculture, Fisheries and Food.

▥ BULK BUYING

A lot goes a long way: Catering packs can be good value but be cautious. Money saved on their purchase may not be worth it: the family may go off the taste of a packet soup halfway through a giant drum. Conversely, such packs may increase your spending if the family like it so much that they consume it in larger quantities than they have done previously.

Be realistic: Even though some bulk item represents a real saving in money terms, nothing is a bargain if you and your family don't really like it. It's never worth stocking up on foods which aren't popular, however cheap they may be.

From large to small: Where possible, repackage catering size containers into smaller ones. Foods like instant coffee will go stale quickly if left in a large tin which is opened frequently and should be decanted into clean, empty jars and sealed well. A vast can of baked beans or tomato purée should be divided into suitably-sized portions and frozen.

Bulk discounts: Supermarket multi-buys are often good value and you usually only need to purchase three or four samples of a product in order to benefit from the discount.

Important dates: Check sell-by dates carefully when buying in bulk. The bargain price may reflect the fact that the goods are nearly at the end of their shelf life. And in any case you need to be sure that you will consume them within the appropriate period.

Club together: Co-operative bulk-buying makes sense in some communities, particularly in rural areas where shops are some distance away and transport not readily available. Get together with neighbours or friends and approach butcher, fishmonger and greengrocer to see what quantities they are prepared to offer a discount on.

Shop at the local: It's even worth approaching a local corner shop (which might otherwise not get the volume of trade) to see whether the shopkeeper is prepared to offer a reduction in cost if you buy things like cat food or cooking oil by the crate. Before entering into the agreement though, check carefully that the prices offered are lower than those in the supermarkets.

A job for everyone: Share the workload on a co-operative bulk-buying system. Those with transport who go to pick up goods should not also be the ones to weigh them out into the required quantities and collect the money from members.

At the end of the day: Fresh food bargains can be found in supermarkets at the end of the morning before early closing and on Saturday afternoons. There's usually a crush of people waiting to seize them, as the prices are marked down, but if you can face this, there are real savings to be made on things like cream, yogurt, delicatessen and fresh meat.

Weekend closing: Visit the greengrocer before it closes for the weekend and see what bargains are to be had. You may find very ripe fruit and vegetables on offer. These are fine provided they are used instantly in a fruit salad or a soup. They will otherwise be thrown out as they will be rotten by Monday, so the shop will think it's had a bargain too!

Midweek shopping: Fruit and vegetable stalls in markets have cheaper produce in the middle of the week. On Mondays and Fridays prices tend to be higher.

Watch out: Check that the sell-by date hasn't been passed on market stall produce, particularly with dairy produce and delicatessen foods. In addition to being past its best, the food is unlikely to have been refrigerated. It might seem a bargain but you could end up with food poisoning.

Apples and pears: If you can beg some of the shaped packing material for fruit from your greengrocer when buying in bulk, it makes excellent storage for apples and pears, as the indentations prevent the fruits from rolling against each other.

Meat and fish: Bulk-bought meat and fish are often good value at certain times of the year but need to be prepared for the freezer quickly. If you are freezing either product without first cooking it, it is worth asking your butcher or fishmonger to prepare it according to the cuts or portion quantities you require and to bag it up for you. They often have vacuum sealing machines which ensure a good airtight seal and may well do a better job than you could at home. Don't forget to label each package before you freeze it. See also pages 262 to 264 for more freezing hints.

Muesli, pulses and flours: There are good savings to be made when buying large quantities of foods sold loose, such as muesli, pulses and flours. However, be sure to buy them from outlets with a quick turnover and in places where strict hygiene regulations are observed. A bargain sack of flour is entirely wasted if you find it is full of weevils halfway down.

Cordon Bleu
TIPS

If stocking up on almonds, buy them whole with their skins on. They retain their oil better like this and when blanched to remove the skins they are juicier.

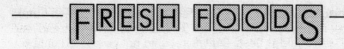

▓FRUIT

Home grown: The UK produces only about 30% of the fruit it consumes; the rest is imported. Transport and storage methods have improved over the years so that quite delicate fruits can now be moved considerable distances and arrive in good condition.

Know your seller: Not all fruit sold is in good condition and a well-kept supermarket is often a better source of fresh fruit than a greengrocer with a poor turnover. Different fruits require different degrees of temperature and humidity to remain in good condition and it can be difficult for any one outlet to achieve this.

Be firm: Some greengrocers and, in particular, market traders have the reprehensible habit of having sound fruit on display but filling your bag with produce of less good quality. Complain about this if you are given inferior fruit and don't buy there again if the situation doesn't improve.

Take advice: A reliable greengrocer will know his stock and his market so that he will not buy over-priced fruit that he won't be able to sell. Ask his advice on what is currently good value.

Buy as you need: Fruit tends to deteriorate fast in centrally heated homes, so it's best to buy little and often.

Know your apples: Different varieties of apples ripen at different times of the year, so that there's always some kind available. If you're faced with an unfamiliar variety, ask the greengrocer about the taste and texture.

Apricot skins: When choosing apricots make sure the skin is smooth and free of wrinkles.

Avocado ripeness: Press the narrow end of an avocado gently with your forefinger. If it gives slightly, it is ready to eat. If it is still firm consider storage, see page 76.

Banana store: Bananas are ripe to eat when the skins have turned from green to yellow. Black-skinned bananas are overripe and tend to have wet, squidgy flesh. Bananas should not be peeled until you intend to use them, as exposure to air darkens their flesh, see also page 76 for storing under-ripe bananas.

Blackberry choice: Fresh blackberries vary astonishingly in flavour depending on whether they are cultivated commercially, grown naturally in gardens or grown completely wild and untended. The commercial variety tend to be sweet and the wild ones tart, though there is no difference in appearance. They should be black all over; any red sections are unripe and will taste sour.

Cherry ripe: Colour is no indication of ripeness, since different varieties may be white, red or black when ripe. Ripe cherries should have a softish feel. Most cherries can be eaten raw but some varieties are sour even when ripe and should be used in preserves.

Citrus crosses: Many citrus fruits have been crossed with each other to produce new varieties. In addition to oranges, tangerines and grapefruit try things like pomelo, tangelo (ugli fruit), minneola, ortanique, kumquat, satsuma, and clementine for a change. Choose heavy fruits. Satsumas are loose-skinned but should not be too loose.

Coconut shy: Shake a coconut to see if it is in good condition. You should be able to hear the milk sloshing around inside.

Date lore: Ready-stoned dates are not as good quality as those with their stones in. Without the stones the dates lose their shape and dry out more quickly. Use them in cooking.

Fig colour: Fig skins may be white, green, purple or black. Fresh figs are usually eaten raw, while dried ones are used in cooking. When ripe the skins have a fresh bloom and the flesh feels soft.

Good gooseberries: Choose plump, fairly firm gooseberries. The larger they are, the sweeter they will be.

Grape skins: There are two basic types of grape: white (which is in fact a greenish yellow colour) or black (dark purple). Flavours vary according to the type. The grapes should be fresh-looking, with a

40

bloom on the skins. There should not be many brown-skinned grapes in the bunch.

Kiwi know-how: It's hard to judge the ripeness of a kiwi fruit unless you can touch it. The brown hairy skin should give a little but not be soft and squashy. To eat raw at table provide sharp knives and table napkins or encourage people just to cut it in half and eat the flesh with a spoon. Kiwi fruit are also known as Chinese gooseberries.

Lemons and limes: Select fruit with clear unblemished skins which have a slight shine. All parts of the fruit from zest (for flavouring foods) to pips (for helping set jams) can be used. Limes have a stronger, more unusual flavour than lemons but can be used to replace them in virtually all instances.

Loganberries: These look similar to raspberries but are larger and darker. They are raspberries crossed with blackberries. They have a stronger taste than raspberries.

Lychee look: Lychees have brown, knobbly, hard skins which makes it difficult to tell when they are ripe. Their delicious white flesh tastes like grapes.

Make the most of mangoes: Look for smooth, unblemished skins, which can be green or yellow and red. When ripe they should yield to gentle pressure.

Melons big and small: Size is no indicator of sweetness with melons as they range from a size you can cup in your hands to the vast water melon globes. Judge the ripeness of a melon not by how soft it is but by its smell, which should be sweet and distinctive. Charentais melons have golden sweet flesh and a delicate scent. Honeydew melons have pale green sweet flesh, while Galia melons have darker green flesh. Ogen melons have very sweet yellow-green flesh. Water melons have pink flesh with black seeds and are of a watery texture, which is very refreshing.

Substitute a nectarine: Nectarines can be used in place of peaches in any recipe as their flavour is similar although they have smooth shiny skins rather than soft furry ones. They should be unblemished and just soft to the touch.

Made for marmalade: Bitter oranges are usually called Sevilles and are not sweet enough to eat. They are used for making marmalade and sometimes in cooked dishes and are only available in the UK in January and February.

Perfect papayas: Papayas are ripe when the skin has turned from green to yellow. They can be eaten raw or cooked.

Peach choice: Peaches fall into two main categories, although there are thousands of varieties: some have golden flesh and some white but the main difference is whether or not the stone adheres to the flesh. The golden-fleshed peaches tend to have rosier, more golden skins than the white-fleshed ones, which have paler, whiter skins. Freestone peaches are good for eating, while clingstones are suitable for cooking. Whichever type of peach you are buying, avoid those with green patches.

Pear appearance: Pear skins vary in colour according to type. They become overripe quickly, so are best bought in the quantities needed and eaten quickly. Buy pears which feel hard to the touch and let them ripen in the fruit bowl.

Pineapple scent: You can tell when a pineapple is ripe as the scent of the flesh will come through the skin. Choose ones which have stiff leaves that are not blackened or soggy.

Plum varieties: There are many varieties of plums. Some plums can be eaten, others are too sour and need to be cooked. They should all have firm, unblemished skins and give when touched. Damsons are small purple plums that are always cooked. Greengages have green skins and are very sweet when ripe. They should be eaten when soft to the touch.

Ready rhubarb: Buy firm, crisp sticks. The thinner stems will be more tender and will need less cooking. Remember to cut off any leaves, as these are poisonous.

Strawberry fair: Try to buy strawberries which still have their hulls on as they will keep better. Buy in the quantities you need and eat quickly as strawberries do not keep well once ripe. As a general guide to stage of growth, the more scented the flesh is, the riper the berries are.

VEGETABLES

Small is best: Vegetables that are just to be cooked lightly – steamed, boiled or stir-fried – should be small for maximum flavour. With most vegetables large size does not indicate a better flavour. Large vegetables are best used in soups or stews or as purées.

Little and often: Buy vegetables in the freshest condition you can find them, bearing in mind that a supermarket with a good turnover is likely to have on sale fresher goods than a greengrocer who does not have a lot of trade.

Grow your own: Even the smallest garden can grow a few vegetables provided you are not hidebound by the idea that flowers and vegetables should not be mixed. There's no reason for not growing a few quick salad crops, such as lettuce, radish and spring onions amongst the roses and some vegetables, such as globe artichokes and sweetcorn, can be positively ornamental. If you live in a flat with just window boxes or a kitchen windowsill, grow your own fresh herbs, which can be used to add freshness and flavour to shop-bought vegetables.

Think fresh when shopping: Ask your greengrocer about what's in season. He should be able to guide you to what's freshest and cheapest at any one time. Don't be rigid about choice. If you meant to buy carrots but find good, small new turnips, buy them instead.

Artichoke choice: Globe artichokes should have green, tightly packed leaves. Small leaves have more flavour than large. Avoid those with dry or cracked edges.

Jerusalem artichokes: These knobbly vegetables are among the most difficult to peel, so buy the smoothest you can find.

Asparagus tips: Avoid brown, woody stems and go for those which are green and straight. Don't worry about choosing the plumpest heads, smaller ones often have better flavour. Thin, ragged asparagus, called sprue, often tastes excellent but is best used in savoury flans or other dishes, as its limpness makes it difficult to dip into melted butter or other sauce.

Aubergine gleam: Aubergines – also called egg plants, especially in American recipes – should be shiny with smooth, unblemished deep purple skins.

Broad bean pods: These should be as small as you can find them. Really young broad beans can be cooked and eaten pod and all. Otherwise shell them and cook the beans. Tough, large, hairy pods contain big beans which take long cooking to tenderize and have a rather overpronounced flavour.

French and runner beans: Look for slim, crisp beans rather than large flabby ones.

Sprouting beans: Bean sprouts, alfalfa and pea sprouts are easily grown at home either in jam jars or in a specially purchased kit. They are nicest when small and crisp and should be cooked as soon as possible after picking or buying.

Beetroot blood: The size of beetroot is not as significant as with other vegetables, although smaller ones are more tender and sweet. Buy those with undamaged skins or they will bleed into the cooking water and lose a lot of their flavour and goodness.

Heading for broccoli: Look for firm heads with lots of leaf and a good crisp stalk. Most people prefer the flavours of purple and green broccoli to the more common and coarser white.

Brussels sprouts: These definitely deteriorate in flavour as they get larger and are also more difficult to cook evenly, even with a good deep cross cut on the base. Buy the smallest, most tightly-curled heads you can find. They should be bright green in colour, rather than yellow-green.

Year-round cabbage: All types of cabbage should feel heavy for their size and have crisp undamaged leaves. Different cabbages come into season as the year passes. In general they are more delicately flavoured in spring and summer and develop a heartier, coarser taste as the year wears on.

The age of the carrot: These really are at their best when small and young; if you grow your own don't fail to eat the thinnings. When buying look for carrots which are brightly coloured and have smooth skins; young ones just need topping and tailing while large older ones should be pared and chopped.

Weighing up celeriac: Choose roots which are heavy for their size – there is little advantage in buying small unless you only want a little.

A good head of cauliflower: Avoid discoloured heads, cauliflowers should be white or yellow with firm tightly-packed florets and fresh-looking leaves.

Head for celery: Choose celery with fresh-looking leaves. Beware of short stalks which have possibly been over-trimmed.

Chicory choice: When buying chicory, look for white leaves, green parts indicate a bitter flavour. It should be firm, and not wilting.

Chinese leaves: These should have a fresh appearance with leaves that are tightly packed around a heavy head.

Courgette check: These are best bought small and tender-skinned. The large ones tend to be tougher, though they can be used for stuffed courgette recipes.

Cucumber cunning: Look for an evenly green skin and a small size. Don't buy discoloured or soft ones. The flavour is the same whether the cucumber is curved or straight.

Endive varieties: These may be straight or curly-leaved. Choose those without any wilt and with pale green leaves.

Fennel facts: Look for white or pale green bulbs without any blemishes when buying fennel and avoid dark green coloured bulbs as this indicates bitterness.

Kohl rabi: Avoid large pieces of kohl rabi as these tend to be tough and difficult to tenderize. The best specimens are less than 5 cm (2 inches) in diameter.

Leek loss: These tend to have more wastage than many other vegetables since the white part is the most flavoursome and tender. Small young leeks have a better flavour than large ones which are tougher. They should be fresh looking with really white bases and bright green tops.

Lettuce lore: Buy lettuce with fresh-looking leaves without any rotten parts. Lamb's lettuce (also called corn salad) and rocket are similar to lettuce and should be bought when small and crisp.

Many a mushroom: Cultivated mushrooms come in a variety of sizes from closed-up buttons to wide-open flats. Oyster mushrooms, which are more strongly flavoured, are now becoming more widely available. When buying mushrooms, look for white, firm ones and avoid any that are brown and wrinkled.

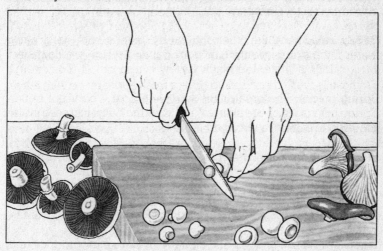

Okra (ladies' fingers): Do not buy any which have damaged ridges or brown parts. Okra is only tasty when fresh.

Know your onions: The skins should be dry and papery and the onions feel firm to the touch. Do not buy any which are sprouting.

Purchasing parsnips: Buy those which are small and firm without side shoots. Older large parsnips have a pronounced flavour and a thick core which reduces the amount of usable vegetable.

Peas please: Fresh peas have only a short season but are available processed in various ways throughout the year. If buying fresh look for pods which, when held up to the light, show small peas with spaces between. Thickly crammed pods tend to hold tough peas.

Pick a pepper: Whether green, red, yellow or even black, peppers should have shiny skins and feel firm to the touch. Wetness indicates that they are past their best.

Potato performance: The selection of different types of potato now available means you can buy particular varieties to suit particular cooking methods. If you are not familiar with a variety on sale, ask the greengrocer how it performs. New potatoes do not keep well, so should be bought in small quantities; old potatoes keep well if stored correctly (see page 83).

Salsify selection: Like beetroot, salsify bleeds into the cooking water if the skin is pierced, so don't buy any which are damaged. Most salsify is white; the black variety is also called scorzonera.

Spring onions: The greater the white – edible – part, the better. Spring onions which are slim taste mild, as the bulbs increase in size the flavour becomes stronger.

Seakale: Seakale or Swiss chard, as it is sometimes known, should have firm stalks with no discoloration or signs of wilt.

Shopping for spinach: Look for bright green, fresh-looking leaves – lighter shades in summer than in winter. Remove any yellow areas.

Small swedes are best: The smaller swedes are easier to cook until tender. Very large swedes are tough and even long cooking does not tenderize them. Choose roots with whole skins.

Sweetcorn colouring: Sweetcorn is past its best when golden. It is freshest and sweetest when pale in colour. Choose cobs which have a good covering of corn and are not ragged at the end. If the cobs are still encased in leaves, these should be pale green.

Tomato tones: Unless they are to be used for cooking, buy firm, light red tomatoes. Once the colour deepens they are too ripe to be sliced easily for use in salads.

Turn to turnips: When young these should have green and white skins and be small and round. As they get older, the skin turns creamy and the flavour becomes coarser.

Fresh watercress: Look for fresh, crisp bunches with dark green leaves and no yellow or brown sprigs. Check the centre of the bunch to make sure that all the leaves are fresh.

▓DAIRY PRODUCE/MILK

Freshest in Europe: The Milk Marketing Board claims that milk sold in the UK is the freshest in Europe. The bacterial count has been reduced from 100,000 per ml in 1981 to 20,000 per ml in 1984. A sample from all the farms producing milk is tested each week and the price paid to the farmer is reduced if the standard is not met.

Doorstep delivery: Although the milk floats which deliver to your home are not refrigerated, the massed bank of bottles keeps the milk cool.

Shop storage: Check where fresh milk is stored in a corner shop or supermarket and put your hand on the bottle or carton to make sure it is adequately cold. If not, micro organisms will develop and the milk will deteriorate.

Take it in: Milk left standing on a doorstep will lose its valuable Vitamin C through the action of light. It may also rise in temperature and develop micro organisms. Take it in as soon as it is delivered and refrigerate it at once (see page 85).

Shop buying: If you leave for work before milk is delivered, it will have deteriorated on the doorstep, particularly in warm weather, before you get home. It is better to buy from a shop on the way home. Properly stored milk should last a good week from the time it is bottled before a stale flavour develops.

Untreated milk: This is sometimes sold directly from farms but is not generally available to the public. Because it has not been pasteurized, there is some risk that disease from the cattle will be transmitted to the consumer. Untreated milk in a bottle can be recognized by its green or green and gold-striped top.

Pasteurized milk: This has been heat-treated to kill bacteria and has a slightly reduced vitamin content. It is sold in silver-topped bottles.

Homogenized milk: This has been pasteurized, then processed to break up the fat globules, so that there is no cream line. The nutritional value is similar to that of pasteurized. It is sold in a red-topped bottle.

49

High cream milk: This is made from milk of Jersey, Guernsey and South Devon cows. It is usually pasteurized, has a minimum butterfat content of 4%, a marked cream line and similar nutritional value to pasteurized milk. It is sold in gold-topped bottles.

Sterilized milk: This is homogenized milk which is heat-treated in the bottle and vacuum sealed. It is sold in metal-topped bottles.

Skimmed and semi-skimmed milk: These are milks from which half or all of the fat content has been removed. They are popular with slimmers but cannot be used in all types of cooking (they are no good for junket, for example). Skimmed milk is sold in blue-topped bottles and semi-skimmed in red and silver-topped bottles.

Long life milk: This has been ultra heat-treated (it is often called UHT milk). The very high temperatures used give it long keeping qualities – up to two years. The carton does not need to be refrigerated until opened, after which it should be treated as ordinary milk.

▓ DAIRY PRODUCE/CREAM AND YOGURT

Container check: Make sure that cream in a shop is stored in a chilled cabinet, unless it is the long life variety. Check that the lid of the carton is not damaged; if air gets into it the cream will go off.

Fat content: The butterfat content of different types of cream varies and affects its ability to be whipped or piped. Clotted cream has a butterfat content of 55-60% and is too thick to whip. Pasteurized whipping cream (35-42%) and double cream (48%) can be whipped. Pasteurized single cream (18%), soured cream (18%) and homogenized half cream (12%) can only be poured. Whipped cream (35-42%) is sold ready whipped.

Crème fraîche: Much used in nouvelle cuisine because of its low fat content, this is not strictly speaking a cream, as it is fermented to allow lactic acid to develop.

Read the label: Yogurt may be fresh or long life. The former should be sold from a chilled cabinet and refrigerated as soon as possible. Long life yogurt does not need refrigeration but is nicer if chilled before eating. Read the sell-by dates on the labels of both types.

Soured cream: This is cream into which a culture has been introduced to produce a soured effect.

Fat content: Check the fat content before you buy yogurt if you're worried about your calorie intake. Some yogurts are low or reduced fat; others are not. Note that if the low fat variety is fruit-flavoured it will still be quite high in calories.

Drinking yogurt: This is a thinned-down version of yogurt, which is designed for drinking rather than spooning or cooking. Consume by its sell-by date and keep refrigerated until then.

Yogurt culture: This is available in some health food shops and delicatessens. It is used to turn milk into home-made yogurt. A cheaper, more readily available substitute is a tablespoonful of natural yogurt.

How live?: Some cartons of yogurt state that it is live. In fact all yogurt is live. If you are concerned about how good it is for you, check the ingredients list for additives. The fewer the better.

Cordon Bleu

TIPS

If using chocolate for cake decoration, for example, to make chocolate caraque or to coat florentines, buy a good quality plain block chocolate that is not too sweet. 'Couverture' is a special chocolate used by professional patissiers.

DAIRY PRODUCE/BUTTER AND CHEESE

Butter types: Butter may be unsalted, slightly salted or salted. Unsalted butter keeps less well (salt acts as a preservative) so should be bought as fresh as possible and used quickly.

Block vote: Don't assume cheese cut from a block is fresher than pre-packed. It depends on the shop's turnover. Look at the block before you buy a piece from it. If there are little bits flaking off the surface, drying out has begun and the cheese will stale quickly.

Check packaging: Avoid butter which is oozing out of its wrapping (which means the storage has been too warm) or has a tear in the pack (damaged in transit). It may be rancid if it has not been kept chilled or contaminated if the packet is torn.

The smell test: Butter which has turned rancid has a distinctive, unpleasant smell. Refrigerated fresh butter should not have any particular smell.

How salty?: As a rough rule of thumb, butter is likely to be more salty if it has been imported from some distance, e.g. New Zealand, than if it is made reasonably locally.

Dry vacuum: Vacuum-packed cheese tends to dry out more quickly than film-wrapped, so buy the latter if you want to keep cheese a few days before eating it.

Date lore: Read the best before date on pre-packed cheese and buy according to when you want to eat it.

Avoid contaminating cheese: Cheese can attract micro organisms if kept near fresh meat without being covered. It can also pick them up from a chopping board which doubles as a cheese board. Scrub boards well before putting cheese on them.

Special purchase: Specialist cheese shops are increasing in number and stock a wider range of different cheeses than supermarkets and delicatessens. Not all may be in peak condition though, as those varieties which don't sell well may remain in the shop too long. Take advice from the expert on which cheeses are in good condition (tactfully ask him what he sells a lot of to find out what's likely to be at its best).

Little and often: Buy cheese only in small quantities and try to eat it within two or three days. If you spot a real bargain and want to buy a lot you can, of course, freeze it. Bear in mind that freezing stops the enzyme action which matures and eventually deteriorates cheese and that thawing will not start it off again as the enzymes will be dead. Freeze cheese therefore in the condition in which you want to eat it. Pack it in small quantities, so that it can be consumed quickly when thawed, see also page 264.

Grated cheese: Some shops sell ready-grated cheese. This is usually cheese grated from the ends of blocks or rounds. It is past its best for eating fresh but perfectly good for cooking. A bag of grated cheese will keep in the refrigerator for up to a week or can be frozen and used when needed.

The age of maturity: Cheddar cheese may be mild, medium or mature. Mild Cheddar has been matured for only 3 months, medium for 6 months and mature for 12 months. Cheese graders decide which Cheddars are suitable for maturing to the full and which need to be sold earlier, depending on the amount of moisture in each individual cheese.

Parmesan piece: Parmesan cheese, essential for an authentic Italian flavour with pasta and other regional dishes, will keep for ages if sold in the piece and grated when required. Ready-grated Parmesan stales quickly, so should be bought in small quantities and used up fast.

Processed cheese: This has a bland flavour and rubbery texture. It is made by heat processing cheeses, which are not suitable to be sold fresh. Processed cheese slices are useful for making toasted sandwiches and the mildness of flavour often appeals to children, who do not care for strong cheeses.

Vegetarian cheese: This is made by curdling the milk with plant extract rather than with the usual rennet. It is available in specialist cheese shops, some supermarkets and health food shops.

▓EGGS

Look for freshness: The date on the egg box will tell you when the eggs were packed, which should be within a day or so of being laid. When buying loose eggs from a farm shop or other outlet you will have to rely on the word of the seller.

Buy fresh: Only buy eggs from shops that have a brisk sale, so that you are getting eggs that have not been kept in the shop for too long.

Avoid the float test: You can check for freshness by putting an egg in water (stale eggs float, fresh ones sink) but it's not a good idea, since once the shell is wetted it allows micro organisms to enter. Only try it if you're going to break the egg and use it immediately.

Look at the white: Another way of seeing how fresh an egg is before use is to crack it on to a plate and look at the way the white spreads. Older eggs have thinner whites which spread quickly; fresh eggs spread more slowly in a thicker layer.

Cracks mean contamination: If an egg is cracked it may well have been contaminated by micro organisms. If you're using an egg you have cracked accidentally in the kitchen, break it into a clean container first to see if it is off.

Smell as a guide: The smell of an egg will tell you if it is off, when it will have a sulphurous smell. But remember that eggs can pick up flavours from items which are stored near them (see page 86).

Know your class: Class A eggs are fresh (they should be sold within eight days of being laid) with firm whites and yolks in the centre. They have clean shells and when measured for classification have an air space at the end of no more than 6 mm. They should have been stored at not less than 10°C. Class B eggs may be slightly older or may have been stored at below 8°C for transport in chilled lorries. Class C eggs are used only in manufactured foods. They are not allowed to be sold to the public.

Weight grading: Eggs are also graded according to their weight. When using recipes check what size is specified, since this may affect the finished result, for instance in a cake. Size 1 eggs weigh more than 70 g each. Size 2 weigh 65-70 g. Size 3 weigh 60-65 g. Size 4 weigh 55-60 g. Size 5 weigh 50-55 g. Size 6 weigh 45-50 g. Size 7 weigh less than 45 g.

Free range eggs: Free range eggs are those laid by hens which have access to outside runs, have reasonable space in their sheds, have not been fed antibiotics or hormones and have not had their beaks trimmed. If you want to be sure of buying eggs which are truly free range, look for the FREGG symbol. This is the mark of the Free Range Egg Association (FREGG) which is at 37 Tanza Road, London NW3 2UA.

More unusual eggs: You can now buy a variety of eggs laid by birds other than hens. Commercially produced duck eggs are reared in hygienic conditions and can be used in place of hens' eggs, particularly in baking. Non-commercial duck eggs may be contaminated and should only be used in cooked dishes and not eaten boiled, fried, poached or scrambled as the cooking process is not long or hot enough to kill any micro organisms present. Goose, gull, partridge, pheasant, quail and turkey eggs are also produced commercially. Buy only from outlets which have a quick turnover and serve hard-boiled.

BREAD

Slice squeeze: Sliced bread in a wrapper should carry a 'best before' date, which will give you an indication of its freshness. To check its condition, squeeze it gently. If it is moist and soft it will yield, then spring back into shape.

Use your eyes: When buying crusty, unwrapped breads look for a dry, crackly crust. Once home you can check freshness by applying the squeeze or pressure test above.

Spotting staleness: You can tell that bread is stale when the moisture has left the crumb and moved into the crust. The flavour of the bread will change when this occurs, as the volatile oils evaporate and the moisture leaves the bread.

Whole grains: Wholewheat and wholemeal bread are made from the whole wheat kernel with nothing removed. They contain plenty of the bran (fibre), also vitamins and minerals.

Go for granary: Granary bread is made from a special type of flour which is malted and contains pieces of whole cereal.

Refined white: White bread is made from refined white flour from which most of the bran and wheatgerm have been removed. As this process also removes vitamins and minerals, these are by law added to all white bread made in the UK.

Dark rye: Rye bread is dark in colour and rather heavy and sticky in texture. It has a distinctive flavour and is often sold ready sliced to use as a base for canapés.

Pitta pockets: Pitta bread is unleavened and sold in flat oval shapes, which can be cut in half and opened up to form pockets from which to eat kebabs, salads and foods, which would otherwise require a knife and fork.

▓▓ FISH

A matter of taste: The freshness of fish is to some degree a personal affair. Those who live near the sea and who eat fish straight from it will have the freshest fish and become familiar with its flavour. Inland dwellers whose 'fresh' fish has had to travel to them will accept their usual flavour as fresh and may well find the taste of fish fresh from the sea strange.

Sea-fresh: Really fresh fish tastes of the sea: a slightly salty flavour which gradually disappears over a period of four days. After this fish has virtually no flavour and needs to be cooked in sauce or with other ingredients to give it taste.

Off flavours: Fish which is more than six or seven days old develops a sour taste, which is hard to disguise by cooking. Over 12 or so days old it becomes inedible.

A well-iced slab: Once fish is killed it ceases to be sterile and so becomes vulnerable to invasion by micro organisms. It should be gutted, washed and stored in ice, not touching other fish. Check that your fishmonger keeps a clean and healthy slab. It doesn't matter if the ice melts a bit, as this keeps the fish well washed.

Full up: Where fish is left ungutted in order to preserve its shape, as for example a whole salmon, smell it carefully before buying. The internal organs will deteriorate before the outer flesh.

The nose test: Once fish starts to smell 'fishy', it is beginning to go off. The ideal place to check for this is under the gills but most fishmongers are unlikely to let you do this.

The touch test: The best indicator of the freshness of fish is the resilience of the flesh. It should spring back into shape when pressed. As fish ages the flesh develops a putty-like texture. Really fresh fish has a slimy skin which dries as it ages. Red patches along the backbone of small fish definitely indicate staleness.

The eye test: The most likely way that you will be able to judge the freshness of fish – unless you have an exceptionally obliging fishmonger – is to look at its eyes. In recently killed fish these are convex and clear. As a fish ages they sink and become opalescent.

Smoked fish: It is more difficult to tell how fresh smoked fish are, because they have been subjected to a smoking (and in some instances dyeing) process. Depending on type, the colour will range from pale straw through bright yellow and brown to red. The best ways to judge are to look at the storage conditions, which should be the same as for fresh fish, and to check that the skin is moist and firm.

Seasonal goodness: Some fish, such as coley, plaice and sole, are available all year round but others have their seasons and are best at certain times of year. The close season is usually the spawning period which allows the species to restock itself.

Deep sea fish: More deep sea fish e.g. monkfish, gurnard, are becoming available on fishmongers' slabs. Some of these fish are very large and ugly and not all of the carcass is good to eat. If your fishmonger sells things like monkfish and garfish, ask his advice on how much to buy and how to cook.

Make friends with a fishmonger: Reap the benefit of your fish-monger's knowledge about what is good value and how to prepare it. If you are short of time or unfamiliar with fresh fish, ask him to do things like scale, gut and fillet fish for you. His professional quality knives will mean he can do the job quickly with good-looking results. He should also be able to supply you with quantities of fish bones (from filleting for other people) and heads usually at a low price, so that you can make your own fish stock in useful or freezable quantities.

Watch out for shellfish: Shellfish should be very fresh otherwise they can cause food poisoning. They are usually sold live or ready cooked. Live shellfish should be stored in ice or actually in sea water, although crustaceans, such as lobster and crab, will keep perfectly well (if more convenient) wrapped in damp newspaper in a refrigerator for 24 hours. Cooked shellfish should be refrigerated. Do not buy shellfish that smells high. Be sure to buy it as near to its cooking time as possible, transport it home quickly – preferably in an insulated container, and consume it as quickly as possible and definitely within 24 hours. Oysters to be eaten raw should always be bought from a reliable source with a good turnover, as they are more likely to cause food poisoning if they're not. If you persistently suffer from 'food poisoning' after eating shellfish, check whether you are allergic to them – the symptoms are similar.

▨POULTRY

Boiling fowl: These tend to be rather scraggy and tough as they are older birds than those sold for roasting. If you are buying them from a farm they are likely to be old laying birds. Boiling fowl are cheaper than other poultry, weight for weight. The size of bird is immaterial as the flesh tastes the same whether small or large. They should not be roasted or grilled but boiled or cut up and casseroled for a long period at a low temperature. They make excellent stock but the flesh is fairly tasteless and needs to be used in dishes like curry or with a strongly flavoured sauce.

Roasting chicken: Virtually all the chickens sold for roasting are reared under controlled conditions designed to produce as much tender, tasty flesh in as short a time as possible.

Look for a roaster: The flesh of a fresh bird should look plump and well padded.

Foot mark: Young birds for roasting have small feet with no coarse scales on them. Their spurs are short.

Smell guide: Fresh poultry has no smell. If possible sniff the flesh before you buy. If it is not fresh it will have a distinctive scent and the skin will be slimy.

Packaging material: Some people with sensitive palates can taste certain types of packaging used for poultry. In any case it is advisable to remove the packaging from fresh or chilled poultry and cover the bird loosely before storing in the refrigerator. If your scales don't weigh large amounts or are not a suitable shape for weighing poultry be sure *not* to destroy the slip which gives the bird's weight or you will not be able to calculate the cooking time accurately.

Butcher's skill: Unless you are expert, it is sensible to ask a butcher to draw poultry for you. Be sure to take the giblets home though. Chicken livers can be frozen individually (see page 263) until you have enough to make a pâté or other dish with them. The rest of the giblets can be used to feed pets or to improve the flavour of stock made from the chicken carcass.

Keep cool: Don't buy a fresh or chilled chicken and leave it in a warm car for hours. Micro organisms develop quickly in poultry, so it is important to keep it cool. Make the journey between refrigerated store and your home refrigerator as fast as possible.

Intensive rearing: Most of the chickens on sale in the UK are reared under intensive conditions and sold either frozen or chilled. You will get more meat from a chilled chicken than a frozen one, because there's more water in a frozen one. Frozen birds should be thawed according to the instructions on the wrapper before cooking.

Maize-fed yellow: Chickens which are fed on maize have a distinctive yellow colour and taste quite different from those intensively reared on a diet of fish meal. Maize-fed chickens are usually French and lighter in weight than most British-reared chickens. They can be bought fresh in some supermarkets.

Free-Range Chicken: There is no legal definition as yet of free-range chicken, but it is generally understood that free-range chickens have access to the open air and are free to run around and feed at will. They are usually slaughtered at 8-10 weeks old, though larger, older birds are sometimes available at Christmas. Free-range chickens are usually sold fresh, though a few supermarkets now sell frozen birds. They are more expensive, because of the extra rearing and maintenance costs, as opposed to those reared by intensive methods, but it is agreed that the taste and texture of free-range chicken is much superior.

Smoked out: Smoked chicken is increasingly available. It can be carved straightaway without further cooking or it can be incorporated into cooked dishes.

Piece by piece: Chicken pieces tend to work out more expensive than buying a whole bird and jointing it yourself. However, if you want several pieces of a particular cut, such as breast or drumsticks, it is better to buy them ready jointed. Butchers which have plenty of restaurant trade may be prepared to sell you the less popular cuts cheaply.

Turkey talk: Fresh turkeys cost more than frozen ones but tend to have a better flavour. Although today they are fattened much faster than formerly, avoid very large birds as they tend to have tough, dry flesh. Frozen turkeys are always tender because they are killed and processed while still young and relatively small.

Go for hens: Turkey hens have more tender and plumper breast flesh than turkey cocks. Ask your butcher for the turkey hen.

A turkey nose: Fresh turkeys have particularly bloody giblets and a pronounced smell in the body cavity. This does not indicate that they have gone off; it is perfectly natural. Wipe the bird's inside with a damp cloth before cooking it.

GAME

Know your seasons: Game is the word used to describe wild birds and animals, which may be hunted and killed for food only at certain times of year; the remaining period is to allow them to breed in order to maintain the species.

Game birds: Traditionally in the UK, game is hung to make it high before it is eaten. If you are given or buy freshly shot game, you will have to hang it yourself or ask the butcher to do it. How high you allow it to become is a matter of personal taste and something that you can find out only by trial and error. In hot weather or warm surroundings a bird should be hung for a shorter time than in the depths of winter. Plucking and drawing game is again something you may prefer a butcher to do for you. It does not take long if you are experienced but can take ages at first.

Rabbits and hares: Rabbits should be cleaned within hours of killing and eaten soon after. Hare is usually hung for a week or so to produce a more gamy flavour in the flesh.

Old for flavour: Venison is the name for meat from deer. It is dark red and has a gamy flavour more reminiscent of hare and pheasant than the beef which it resembles. It should be well hung and preferably from an older beast; meat from young deer lacks flavour. Venison needs to be marinated to make it tender and add flavour.

▓MEAT

Know your butcher: And he will know you. If you become a regular and valued customer, your butcher will take the trouble to tell you what is good value at a particular time, give a discount if you buy in quantity for batch cooking and spend time preparing special cuts for you – for example by barding it, see page 64.

Give notice: If you need a particularly unusual cut, some kind of special preparation or a large quantity of meat, let the butcher know in advance. Butchers tend to be busier towards the weekend, so make special requests early in the week.

Cordon Bleu **TIPS**

Try something different for a change. Not all experiments need to be with expensive foods, oxtail for instance, makes a delicious, economical dish, whether braised or made into soup. An average-sized oxtail will serve four people. Look for one that has an equal amount of meat to bone. The fat should be white and the meat bright red.

In hot weather: Avoid a butcher with meat on display, even in a refrigerated cabinet. It should be kept in cold storage and brought out only on request.

Supermarket choice: Many large supermarkets have a butcher permanently on the premises preparing the meat for sale. If you telephone with a special order, it will be cut for you.

Seeing red: Some shops attempt to make meat appear more attractive by shining red light on to it. Take this into account when buying.

Colour guide: The colour of meat is not necessarily an indication of its freshness. Exposure to air darkens meat without affecting flavour. A slimy appearance and off smells indicate staleness.

Vacuum packing: This makes meat go a purplish colour and look unappealing, although storage life is increased. Gas-packed meat remains red and also has a good storage life.

Homework: You'll get better value meat if you know what parts of the animal the various cuts come from, then you'll know what can be substituted if a particular cut isn't available.

▓ MEAT/BEEF

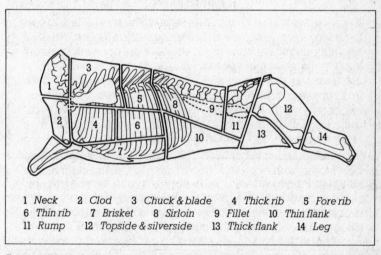

1 Neck	2 Clod	3 Chuck & blade	4 Thick rib	5 Fore rib
6 Thin rib	7 Brisket	8 Sirloin	9 Fillet	10 Thin flank
11 Rump	12 Topside & silverside	13 Thick flank	14 Leg	

Storing Meat: It is important to prevent transfer of bacteria from raw meat to other foods in the kitchen. Always wash hands, knives and other utensils after handling or preparing raw meat. Keep both raw and cooked meats covered and store well apart in the refrigerator, avoiding all contact.

How old?: Prime beef is from cattle between 2 and 3 years old. The flesh should be firm, well marbled with white fat (unless from Guernsey, Jersey or South Devon cattle in which case the fat will be yellow). A layer of gristle between the muscle and outer fat indicates an older animal, which will have tougher flesh.

Cuts classified: Cuts of beef are described as prime, medium and coarse. Prime cuts include fillet, rump, sirloin and wing rib, which are suitable for grilling or open roasting. Medium cuts include fore, top and back ribs, topside and aitchbone and are cheaper but tougher. They can be open roasted at lower temperatures than prime cuts and are also good pot-roasted or braised. Coarse cuts, such as brisket and silverside, are much less tender and need to be cooked, ideally in liquid, for long periods at low temperatures.

Cordon Bleu TIPS

If you have decided to buy steak, you will have a variety of cuts to choose from. Rump steak has a marvellous flavour but must be well hung to be properly tender. Sirloin or entrecôte if cut thinly becomes a minute steak. A T-bone steak is a whole slice cut from the sirloin including the bone. Porterhouse comes from the wing rib. A fillet steak is the most tender and most expensive, with tournedos also being considered a great delicacy. Chateaubriand, a thick cut from the heart of the fillet is generally dry-fried or grilled.

Adding fat: Prime cuts tend to be very lean and benefit from being cooked with added fat to keep the flesh moist. Ask the butcher to lard or bard the meat for you (see page 62 for advance warning). Larding is done by threading strips of bacon fat through the meat, using a special larding needle. Barding involves wrapping the meat in a coating of protective fat (which may be rashers of bacon) and tying it with string.

MEAT/VEAL

Fresh veal: This should be light coloured. It is known as 'white' meat, along with chicken and turkey. Look for fine texture and pink, moist flesh but avoid wet, flaccid-looking meat.

Boning up: Always take home veal bones which the butcher has cut out for you. They make excellent jellied stock.

MEAT/LAMB

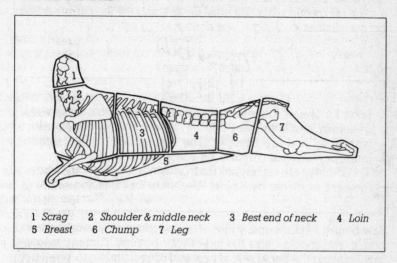

1 *Scrag*   2 *Shoulder & middle neck*   3 *Best end of neck*   4 *Loin*
5 *Breast*   6 *Chump*   7 *Leg*

Young and tender: The best, most tender lamb is very young and called spring lamb. It is slaughtered when just a few months old.

Mutton from lamb: Mutton is the meat produced when the sheep is slaughtered over one year of age. It is hard to find nowadays, since most sheep are killed young to produce lamb meat. It is less succulent but has a more pronounced flavour which goes particularly well in casseroles.

Colour know how: Fresh spring lamb should be pale pink with a light marbling of fat and an outer layer of smooth, supple, papery skin. Older lamb has redder flesh and more fat.

Mutton colour: Mutton cuts are, for obvious reasons, larger and heavier than lamb. The meat is darker, firmer and more fatty. Mutton for roasting should not be more than two years old. If any older, it should be casseroled or braised.

Leave fat on: Don't ask the butcher to remove fat from lamb or mutton for roasting. It is essential for keeping the flavour in and can be cut off after cooking if you don't want to eat it.

Cordon Bleu

TIPS

Look for lambs' kidneys still encased in their suet. This will generally mean they are English, as imported ones are sold without fat and are cheaper. The casing not only keeps the kidneys moist but can also be rendered down for dripping. The kidneys are usually sold individually, although sometimes they are available by weight. Use them for grills and sautés.

Saw bones: Because many cuts of lamb contain awkwardly-shaped bones, you should enlist the aid of your butcher. *Chining* involves sawing along the backbone of best end of neck or loin to free it from the rib bones. Once cooked you can lift out the bone to make the meat easier to carve. *Chopping through the backbone* between the ribs on best end of neck or loin makes it easier to carve into individual portions after cooking.

Chopping the knuckle bone: This is usually essential with a leg or shoulder of lamb in order to be able to fit the joint into a roasting tin. A butcher should do this without asking.

Skinning: This is necessary if you want to cook the meat with a glaze, so that its flavour penetrates the flesh, or if you want to crumb coat or cook it in pastry.

▓ *MEAT/PORK*

Specialist sellers: Unlike beef and lamb, pork should be eaten fresh. Buy, if possible, from specialist pork butchers who usually keep their meat in optimum condition.

Cold store: Because pork tends to go off more quickly than either beef or lamb, it should be purchased only from a refrigerated display or cold store.

Colour choice: Young pork should have a firm, dry meat, which is pink and fine-grained. The fat should be cream-coloured and the rind smooth and flexible. Freshly-cut surfaces should be moist.

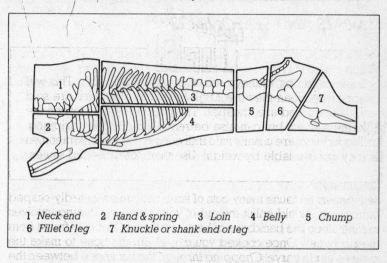

1 *Neck end*   2 *Hand & spring*   3 *Loin*   4 *Belly*   5 *Chump*
6 *Fillet of leg*   7 *Knuckle or shank end of leg*

Older pork: This has a darker-coloured flesh than the young pork. Avoid meat with fat which seems flabby or too thick and rind which is coarse and hairy.

Crisp crackling: Buy pork with the rind on and ask the butcher to score it deeply and closely in a criss-cross or diamond pattern. The cuts should go right through the rind into the fat below.

Rind extra: If you intend to cook pork without the rind, ask the butcher to remove it for you but take it with you and cook it in the roasting pan with the meat to improve the flavour of the gravy.

Also known as: Fillet of pork is sometimes called tenderloin – and vice versa.

Cheap trotters: Pigs' trotters are usually inexpensive to buy. They add flavour as well as acting as a gelling agent in stocks and casseroles. The meat on them, although small in quantity, and difficult to get off, is very tasty.

67

▓MEATS AND SEASONINGS

Pick a pâté: Choose a pâté that looks moist and has no dry edges. If you are having a chunk cut from a large bowl ask to taste it first. Some commercially-made pâtés have little flavour or an overriding taste of monosodium glutamate.

Charcuterie choice: Charcuterie is correctly used to refer to products containing pork. A shop calling itself a charcuterie will stock a good selection of pâtés, terrines, galantines and sausages.

Salami style: Most cold sausages, wherever they come from, are referred to as salami, although this term should correctly be used only for those from Italy. Saucisson is the word used for French 'salami', and wurst the German one. Whatever their provenance, these cold sausages consist of uncooked meat and fat which is minced to varying degrees of fineness, mixed with seasoning and compressed into a natural casing. They are air dried for periods ranging from a week to several months (depending on size and content) before being offered for sale and will keep for ages if stored in a dry atmosphere.

Nice slices: If you like your sausage finely sliced it is best to get the shop to do this – that way you can select the thickness you like – or alternatively buy it ready sliced in a vacuum pack. Vacuum-packed salami tends to be greasier than that cut from the whole sausage.

Piece perfect: When buying salami off the piece avoid any that is soft in the middle or which smells strongly acidic. Because the meat is not cooked it is important that the salami is made and dried correctly to avoid it being a health hazard.

Air-dried ham: There is no health hazard associated with this or with air-dried beef, since the meat is brined before drying to preserve it and is left whole until ready to slice. These air-dried meats need to be sliced to paper thinness and are best bought in slices, as near as possible to the time when you want to eat them.

Smoke signals: Many varieties of sausage are sold smoked, which imparts a distinctive flavour to the meat. Most are eaten raw but can be cooked and incorporated into dishes, such as cassoulet. They are usually sold under a variety of names. If you cannot find a shop that will let you taste first, try small quantities of different types to find out what you enjoy.

Salad selection: Ready-made salads in cartons save hours of preparation even if you do have a food processor. They are particularly useful if you just want a small quantity of a particular type or if you want to offer guests a variety of tastes and texture. Be wary of those which contain onion, as its flavour tends to permeate the whole salad if not eaten soon after purchase. Add a little bottled mayonnaise or yogurt if you find the salad dressing is too tart.

Know your oils: Different oils have markedly different flavours, ranging from the unobtrusive sunflower and corn to the positively pungent walnut. Those with a marked flavour can enhance or complement the ingredients of a salad, while those with less distinctive tastes are best used in cooking. Sesame seed oil is widely used for stir frying because of its particular flavour.

Cholesterol counts: For people concerned about their cholesterol intake, it is worth noting that sunflower, safflower, grapeseed and olive oils are lower in cholesterol than peanut and palm.

Olive oil mystique: Olive oil has a distinctive taste and there is a lot of gourmet mystique attached to it. Because it is expensive, it is sometimes worth mixing it with a cheaper, flavourless oil when you need a large quantity of salad dressing. The olive flavour will still predominate. Virgin olive oil is deemed the best and is made by pressing the best olives without applying any heat. Oil made by this method is thick and greenish. Other grades of olive oil are cheaper because they are made by a quicker method which involves heat. They have a less sweet taste but, unless you are a particular connoisseur, this is unlikely to be evident when mixed with other ingredients, as in a vinaigrette.

Vinegar variety: As with oils there is a wide variety of vinegars. The main choice lies between malt and wine. Malt vinegar is the traditional British accompaniment for fish and chips and is also used in chutneys and preserves. Its strong, distinctive taste does tend to overpower other ingredients when used in vinaigrettes and sauces; a wine or cider vinegar will give a better flavour. Wine vinegars may be white or red and have varying strengths of flavour. French wine vinegar made by the Orleans method is thought the best. Colour is not important except where it affects the appearance of the finished dish. Unusual flavours are created by adding herbs, such as mint or tarragon, or fruit, such as raspberries or black-currants, to white wine vinegar. Sherry vinegar has a strong mellow flavour and is widely used in Chinese and some French cookery. It is always worth paying extra for good quality vinegar, as the flavour of cheaper ones is often very acidic.

Salt of the earth: Salt may come from earth or sea. Rock salt is mined or pumped from salt deposits in the earth. Sea salt is evaporated from the sea, as is bay salt, which is usually greyish in colour. Coarse salt has a stronger taste than the free-flowing variety, which has added chemicals to make it flow easily. Because coarse salt is difficult to use at table, it is best to put it in a salt mill, so that it can be reduced to finer particles. Flavoured salts are mixed with herbs and spices, such as garlic or celery seed.

Ubiquitous msg: Monosodium glutamate is not, in fact, a salt, al-though it is commonly believed to be so. It is a mineral. It will bring out the flavour of other ingredients it is mixed with. It is widely used in commercially-prepared foods but its main use in home cooking is as a meat tenderizer; indeed it is sometimes sold under that name.

Pick your pepper: White pepper comes from ripe berries of the pepper vine. Black pepper comes from unripe berries, which are picked when green and left to dry in the sun. Green peppercorns are unripe berries, which may be dried artificially but are more usually sold canned or bottled in brine. Their soft texture makes them suitable for adding whole to cooked dishes or crushing into butter or sauces. White and black pepper are sold either as whole peppercorns or powdered. Black pepper has a more definitive flavour than white but the latter creates a better appearance in pale dishes and sauces, which would be marred by black specks. Beware of anything sold as pink peppercorns. These are not from a pepper vine but are the berries of Florida Holly and are harmful eaten in any quantity.

Mustard mixtures: Mustard comes as white, brown or black seeds and the different varieties available include various combinations of them, either in ground (flour) form or just coarsely crushed, as in Moutarde de Meaux. As liquid brings out the flavour of mustard, many of the ready-made varieties use different vinegars, wines and flavourings, such as herbs and honey to produce different tastes. English mustard made from mustard powder is the strongest variety, French mustards are milder, German and Austrian ones are both mild and sweet and American mustards generally have a completely different, creamy, spreading texture with a mild sugary flavour. All mustards can be cooked with or served plain but Dijon is probably the best to cook with.

▨ BUYING ABROAD

Resist seduction: Many foods which taste marvellous when accompanied by blazing sunshine, an après-ski atmosphere or the excitement of a foreign way of life lack the same flavour when transported to home climes. Don't think that foods which thrill when abroad will necessarily evoke the same sensation at home.

Weigh it up: Canned and bottled foods take up a disproportionate amount of weight (in aeroplane terms) and bulk (in carrying terms) compared to their value. Don't drag home a 10-litre tin of olive oil or anchovies unless you're sure they're a real bargain compared with what you can buy at home.

Long hauls: If you're determined on bulk importation consider cutting down your outgoing luggage before you set off – even taking an empty suitcase with you. Alternatively leave the car boot as uncluttered as possible.

Home checks: Make sure that you have some idea of what certain foods cost at home before deciding they're a bargain abroad. So many previously unobtainable foods can now be bought in the UK that it doesn't make sense to go through the hassle of bringing them back if, for a small cost more, you can pick them up on a trip to the local delicatessen.

Homesick foreigners: If you're particularly addicted to a foreign delicacy which you haven't been able to find on sale here, it's worth making some inquiries. Homesick immigrants, short-stay overseas personnel and diplomats may well have their source of foods which you don't find in your local shops. Write to the commercial attaché at the embassy of the relevant country and ask if there is an importer or other source of the goods. Some items are imported for restaurant use and never reach shops; provided you are prepared to buy in sufficient quantity you may be able to have a share of a special consignment.

Rural reality: City dwellers have, on the whole, better access to unusual foods than those living in rural areas. Mail order purchase of unusual foods could be easier than bringing them back from abroad. Study small ads in national newspapers for unusual foods and – as above – write to embassies enquiring about particular specialities.

Plan with care: Don't bring back perishable goods from abroad unless (a) customs regulations permit, see right, (b) the journey from the original refrigerated cabinet to your home refrigerator is short enough to permit safe storage and (c) you are using an insulated container.

Homework first: Before you visit a foreign country find out what its food specialities are. Guide books are usually helpful as are cookery books dealing with the country's cuisine. And of course ask people when you get there. Try things before you buy. It's always a good idea to eat local specialities when abroad.

Keep the law: Don't fall foul of customs regulations when bringing back food from abroad (and, conversely, check with the embassy before taking some British delicacy to overseas friends). Customs regulations about what you can bring in change fairly frequently, so check before you leave.

Eye appeal: Part of the attraction of many foods abroad is the way they are packed, particularly things like chocolates and confectionery. A small, well-presented gift of food makes a good gift on return from holiday for people such as neighbours who have looked after your home or fed your cat.

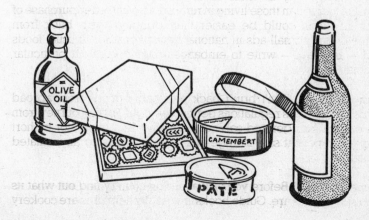

STORING

3

PERISHABLES

▍STORING FRUIT

The fruit bowl: Warm temperatures hasten the ripening process and cause apples to lose their crispness and tangy flavour very rapidly. Only put a day's supply at a time in the fruit bowl. Keep reserve supplies in a polythene bag in the refrigerator.

Garden fresh: One of the easiest ways to store quantities of cooking apples (or eaters that store) is in strong polythene bags loosely sealed with a twist-tie. This aids retention of natural carbon dioxide. To produce just the right environment, pierce the bag with a darning needle once for each pound of fruit. Only store fruit that is perfect and keep different varieties separately. Hidden bruising is one of the greatest reasons for apples failing to keep, so always handle them with care.

Cool bags: Store the bags away from frost in a cool, slightly damp and dark place. A container of water near to the apples keeps the temperature moist. Avoid the garage or a centrally-heated area as fluctuating temperatures don't help. Remember to inspect the apples from time to time.

Let them ripen: Unless you want a ripe avocado to eat the same day, buy firm fruit and let them ripen at home in one to three days. Ripening time can be shortened by placing the fruit in a paper or polythene bag slightly closed and keeping it at room temperature (a kitchen drawer is a good place for this). For slower ripening, keep avocados in the refrigerator (but not in the freezing compartment) for up to a week.

A tip to remember: The avocado stone placed in a purée or avocado dip mixture delays discoloration.

To refrigerate or not?: The wise shopper selects bananas that are not quite fully yellow. They will be firm and more resistant to bruising when taken home. At home they will continue the ripening process if kept at room temperature. Once they have reached the stage of ripeness best suited to the individual taste, they can be placed in the refrigerator and held for three to four days if desired. (The skin will turn dark in several hours, but the edible portion will remain unchanged.)

Fresh cranberries: While cranberries keep longer than most berries, they do need to be stored in the refrigerator. Leave them in the container in which you bought them and just before cooking, rinse them in cold water, discarding any bruised fruit.

Coconuts in the shell: These are best stored unwrapped in the vegetable crisper drawer of the refrigerator. Under these conditions, they can be held for one to two months.

A taste of lemon: Try this unusual idea with a lemon. Pare off slivers of rind with a potato peeler, then immerse in brandy or some other spirit. Seal with a lid to avoid evaporation. After a month or so the spirit takes on a fragrant lemony taste and is excellent for flavouring sweet dishes.

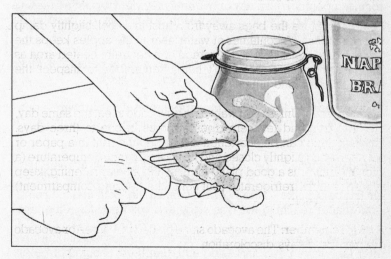

Lemon revival: Since lemons, like other citrus fruit, are composed largely of water, they tend to dry out when kept for a while. Immersing them in hot water for half an hour helps to restore their freshness.

Lemons in a box: You need never be without lemons. To keep them fresh, put them in a lidded plastic container (wipe the lid from time to time to remove any moisture), or in a polythene bag, individually wrapped in clingfilm or kitchen foil. Store them in the lowest section of the refrigerator for up to two weeks.

When a melon is too firm: If the melon you buy is firm but meets the size, weight and colour required, let it stand in a warm room for several hours (or days), away from sunlight, preferably in a moist atmosphere, until the aroma and softness at the stem and blossom end appear.

A ripe melon: Keep whole ripe and ready-to-eat melons in a polythene bag or other foods will take on their aroma. Melons will keep perfectly for a few days in a cool larder or even in the garage if not in direct sunlight.

Buy pears under-ripe: Pears when ripe and ready to eat bruise easily and do not keep well, so buy to ripen at home. Keep them at room temperature for a day or two until they yield to gentle pressure at the stem end just as a ripe peach does. They do need to be checked each day.

Store alone: The strong smell of quinces quickly penetrates other food, so keep them separately in a dry, cool spot.

The best advice: Enjoy fresh pineapple soon after purchase – don't store. When stored a pineapple may change colour and soften but it does not continue to ripen.

Refrigerate when ripe: Ripen guavas and kiwifruit at room temperature. Guavas should give slightly to gentle pressure. Kiwifruit should be soft like a ripe pear for best eating. Both may be refrigerated after reaching the ripe stage and will keep for some time.

Handle with care: Unlike some other fruit, grapes will not improve after they have been harvested and, therefore, should not be expected to ripen once off the vine. Grapes are highly perishable, so handle with care. They should be kept in the coolest part of the refrigerator until required. Use them quickly, whilst at their peak of freshness.

78

On the scent: If plums or apricots seem a little underripe, leave at room temperature for a day or so, the scent of the fruit will soon tell you when they're ready.

Ready berries and currants: Blackberries, black and redcurrants are best used within 24 hours of purchase. Do not wash until required. Store in the refrigerator, uncovered, after removing any damaged or mouldy fruits. If wet, use at once.

Cool oranges: Do not chill oranges when storing. Keep them in the cool for a week or so.

Handle with care: Figs are very fragile and should be stored at room temperature for no more than 24 hours.

Keeping a date: Dates can be stored in the refrigerator for several days. Bring to room temperature before serving to obtain the true flavour.

Wanted and unwanted gooseberries: Always remove any blemished or soft gooseberries quickly. Eat dessert gooseberries on the day bought, but cooking varieties will store for two to three days uncovered, in the refrigerator.

Looking after lychees: Store lychees at room temperature and eat within four days of purchase.

Peaches, nectarines and sharon fruit: Eat ripe fruit on the day of purchase. Leave unripe ones to ripen at room temperature.

Soft fruit: Raspberries, strawberries and loganberries are best eaten within 24 hours of purchase. Do not wash or hull the fruit until required.

Stick together: Store rhubarb in the refrigerator or a cool place for up to three days. Never eat the leaves – they are poisonous.

Flat out: Soft fruit should be spread out on a flat dish, so that the pieces do not touch each other. It deteriorates quickly and just one mouldy fruit can affect a whole plate in a matter of hours. Store it in a cool place, or failing that, the refrigerator.

▓STORING VEGETABLES

Under paper wraps: Asparagus is one of the most perishable vegetables, so cook it as quickly as possible after purchase. Meanwhile keep it in a cool place with the cut ends wrapped in a damp paper towel, kept wet.

Artichoke revival: Artichokes, like asparagus, are not good keepers. They should be cooked on the day of purchase. If they look a little off-colour, cut off some of the stalk and plunge them into cold water for an hour or two.

With and without vinegar: Keep cooked beetroot in a covered dish in the refrigerator or a cool larder. Eat it within a few days. If you cover with vinegar it will keep a day or two longer. Freshly dug – be very careful not to damage the skin in any way – they are best kept in a cool, dark, dry, well-ventilated store.

Remove the wrap: Take carrots out of any plastic bag or covering on return from a shopping trip, as this would make them deteriorate more quickly. Keep carrots in a cool dark, airy place. Those that are unwashed keep better than the washed variety.

Shop ahead for Brussels sprouts: When you want to buy sprouts a few days in advance, it's very important to check that they look fresh and green. Wash them in cold water, then trim them ready for cooking. Put them in a polythene bag or plastic box and refrigerate.

Celery revival: It's better not to prepare celery in advance, simply leave it as purchased in an open plastic bag in the salad drawer of the refrigerator for up to three days. If celery looks limp, cut the base and stand it in iced water for at least half an hour.

Keep away from the light: Chicory must be kept in the dark, the shorter the time the better. Signs of green on the heads indicates that the spears have been exposed to light for too long.

Leave the jacket on: Today many cucumbers are bought wrapped in a plastic 'skin'. Leave the skin on, peeling it back as the cucumber is sliced. Protect the cut end with a piece of kitchen foil or cling film. Store in the refrigerator salad drawer or better still in a cool larder.

Garlic for keeps: If your garage or store area is cool enough, garlic can last nine to ten months from harvest time. Kept indefinitely, cloves either sprout or deteriorate in texture and colour, then they dry out completely or become mouldy. Those who grow their own should be careful not to crack the neck of the bulb when pulling it, as this will tend to make the cloves spoil sooner. Ease the bulbs out of the soil with a fork or spade and leave in the sun until all the skin becomes papery. Store thoroughly-dried garlic in a cool, dry, well-ventilated place out of direct light. Tie or stack bulbs loosely or braid the stems when they become dry enough to be limp, but are not brittle.

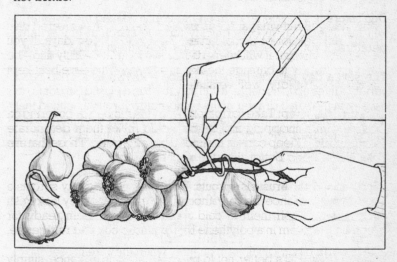

Leave in a pack: Provided they are bought really fresh, mushrooms can be kept for at least three days in the refrigerator or in a cool larder. If they are in a supermarket pack leave them as they are. If they're in a paper bag, put this into a plastic bag, or turn them into a sealed kitchen container.

Fresh-dried herbs: A microwave oven is useful for drying herbs. Put bunches of freshly-picked herbs in the oven on a piece of paper towel. They need to be stirred frequently – use your fingers – so that they dry evenly and also do not become too brittle. Stir every 20 seconds during the first minute, then every 5-10 seconds until dried. Microwave 50 g (2 oz) finely chopped parsley on Maximum (Full) power for 5 minutes. Trim rosemary and basil leaves from their stalks and microwave 25 g (1 oz) leaves for 2-2½ minutes on Maximum (Full). After drying they can be chopped or crushed with your fingers. Store in dark glass bottles or opaque containers and seal to prevent loss of quality.

Strung up: For those without a microwave fresh herbs can be dried by tying them in bunches and hanging them upside down in a cool, dry place. However, they do not retain such a good colour as those dried in the microwave.

Don't store it: The sooner corn-on-the-cob is cooked the sweeter it will be. The sugar in corn quickly turns to starch at higher temperature. If you do need to store cobs, keep them cold and moist.

The seven day lettuce: Iceberg lettuce – known as a crisp head variety – lives up to its name. It will stay fresh in a plastic bag for up to a week in the salad drawer of the refrigerator. If you've noticed that the core-ends of the lettuce turn brown it is simply oxidation taking place – nature's attempt to reseal the 'wound' made at time of harvest or trimming.

It is worth buying shallots in quantity when they are in season. They can be stored for a month or two. Either spread them out on a tray or a box lid or string them like onions. Keep them in a cool, dry place.

Onions in a stocking: Bulb onions store well in old stockings or tights. Separate one onion from the next with a twist-tie. Hang the 'string' in a cool, dry place. Use quickly if they show signs of sprouting or softness.

Cool onions: Spring onions are best stored, after trimming, in a polythene bag in the refrigerator.

The fresher the better: Like other salad greens, watercress is best eaten fresh. It can be kept in the refrigerator for a day or two. Wash gently in cold water, drain well and dry on a paper towel. Place in a closed polythene bag, pressing out a little air, or in a jar or other glass container with a tight-fitting lid and store in the coldest part of the refrigerator.

The green light: The 'greening' on the surface of potatoes is the result of the development of chlorophyl in potatoes that have been exposed to either sunlight or artificial light. If this happens, peel the green area away completely before cooking. If the potato is very green, then discard it.

Store in the dark: Potatoes are best stored in a cool, dry, dark area. Do not keep them in polythene bags which keeps them too moist, transfer them to paper bags or a vegetable rack.

By the sackful: If you buy a sack of main crop potatoes, make sure they are dry with no signs of sprouting. Empty the sack and put on one side any that show signs of deterioration; use these first. Return the rest to the sack. If possible keep the sack off the floor and in similar conditions as above. Never try to store new potatoes, buy them as you need them.

Best without tops: Because of the better keeping quality of radishes without tops, more and more are packed this way. Store them in the refrigerator in the salad drawer. A tiny leaf or two attached to a radish makes for a pretty garnish, but strip off the rest, if the radishes are bunched before storing.

Ripe to unripe: Tomatoes that are red all over should be stored in a cool place and used quickly. It's often better to select tomatoes at different stages of ripeness and ripen them off in a warm spot. Tomatoes produce their own internal ethylene, which increases slightly during the mature – green stage. They proceed to ripen naturally after this. Place unripe or half ripe tomatoes in a paper bag or a drawer. They will ripen more if you include a ripe apple or put a red tomato amongst the green. Only refrigerate tomatoes if you suddenly find you have left them to ripen rather too long. However, remove the tomatoes to room temperature in time for them to warm up before you serve them – they will have far more flavour.

Sprouting beans: Kept more than a day beansprouts take on a 'musty' taste. Sprout mung beans at home to ensure real freshness. Soak the seeds overnight, drain and spread them out on a plate. Add a sprinkling of water, then put the plate in a polythene bag. Leave in a dark place for three days to sprout.

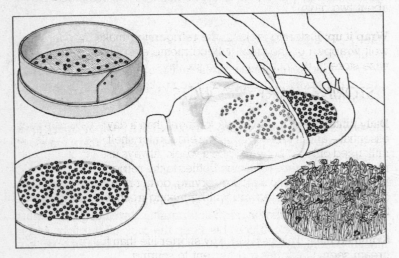

Let them mature: Marrows and pumpkins for winter storage should be left on the plant until just before the frosts. Take care with harvesting: cut before lifting. Store in a net, so that the air circulates and the 'skin' dries.

A cool week: Store aubergines in the cool or the bottom of the refrigerator for up to a week.

Bean store: Keep green beans somewhere cool and use within two to three days.

Cabbage cache: Store in the cool allowing two to three days for the green cabbages but the red and white varieties keep much longer, often well over a week.

Chinese leaves: These will keep well for a week or so in a cool place or in a polythene bag in the refrigerator. Don't shred or take apart until ready to use.

Keeping cauliflowers and courgettes: Store these vegetables for two to three days in a cool place.

Speedy spinach: Discard discoloured leaves from spinach or greens, then wash thoroughly and store in the refrigerator for only about two days.

Wrap it up: If storing leeks in the refrigerator, make sure they are well wrapped or the smell will permeate everything else. Otherwise store in the cool for five to six days.

▓STORING DAIRY PRODUCTS

Daily pinta: To keep fresh milk for more than a day a refrigerator is essential – and if there is enough refrigerator shelf space available milk need only be bought twice a week. Always use in rotation and replace caps before returning bottles to the refrigerator. After milk has been poured into a jug for serving, do not return it to the carton or bottle for storage, as you will be mixing fresh with not-so-fresh. Store covered in the jug.

Skimmed milk: This has a slightly shorter life than full cream milk – cream seems to act as a deterrent to souring.

Away from strong smells: All dairy products should be kept well covered and away from strong-smelling foods, which will affect the flavour.

Yogurt: Whether bought or home-made, yogurt should be kept well covered. Keep it in a cool place for up to two days after purchase or eat by 'sell by' or 'best before' date. Eat home-made yogurt within three to four days of making.

Bowed lids: Sometimes commercial fruit yogurts have a bowed top, which is caused by either incorrect storage or the fact that the yogurt is near to the end of its expiry or 'sell by' date. The yeast in the fruit syrup produces gas (CO_2) which makes the lid bow. This is not harmful but the yogurt should be eaten fairly quickly.

Care with cream: As cream perishes quickly, put it in to the refrigerator as soon as possible. In warm weather keep the time between the shop's chill cabinet and your refrigerator to the minimum by making cream the last purchase and keeping it as cool as possible during transit. If bought from a refrigerator cabinet and kept refrigerated, use within three days of 'sell by' date. The 'sell by', 'eat by' date may be affected if at any stage the temperature of the cream has been raised. Eat on day of purchase if you cannot put cream in the refrigerator.

Winter and summer life: Even in the refrigerator cream has a longer life in winter than in summer.

Long life: When a good shelf life is required, long-keeping, sterilized and UHT creams are useful, though their flavour is not quite like that of fresh cream.

Eggs in store: Eggs can be kept in a cool larder but will last longer in a refrigerator. Make sure they are not resting against the ice cube or freezer area, as they should not be frozen.

Pointed end down: Eggs should be kept standing with the pointed end down, so that the air cell remains floating at the broad end. This delays deterioration.

Wash not: Do not wash eggs as this can destroy some of their natural protective coating – if necessary lightly rub off any dirt. As egg shells are porous, do not place close to strong-smelling food.

Room temperature: Always bring eggs to room temperature before using – about one hour. Cold eggs can curdle a cake mix and will crack if being boiled. A quick tip: immerse a cold egg in warm water for a short time before cooking in the shell, to prevent cracking.

Separated: Yolks and whites can be refrigerated for a few days. Keep the yolks from developing a skin by covering with water; cover whites lightly to prevent evaporation.

Emergency milk: Dried milk is a good standby to keep in store. Date stamp the tin yourself when you buy it. Always reclose the tin firmly after use and keep in the cool and dry. Moisture can affect the quality of the milk.

STORING MEAT AND FISH

At home: Once meat is brought home – and keep the time from shop to home as short as possible, especially in hot weather – it should be taken out of any wrapping, including the supermarket tray. Place it on a clean plate or dish loosely covered in a large polythene bag with the end left open for air to circulate, then put in the coldest part of the refrigerator. The surface of the meat will darken but this does not matter.

Eat quickly: Buy pork no more than 2 or 3 days before you want to eat it and store it loosely covered in a refrigerator, *never* in a larder.

On the rack: If a small rack is available, it's a good idea to stand whole pieces of meat or joints on this over a plate to catch the juices and prevent the meat standing in them.

Extra care needed: The more meat is cut up, the more likely it is to become contaminated. Mince and cut-up casserole meat is best cooked within a day before it deteriorates. All meat should be used as soon as possible.

Same day for offal: Offal should be laid out on kitchen foil or in a bowl bunched together, so that the air can reach it without the juices trickling out. Cover lightly but never with greaseproof paper which will stick to any meat. Try to cook offal on the day that you buy it.

Allow half an hour: Always take meat from the refrigerator at least half an hour before cooking, to bring it up to room temperature. This will relax the meat and, as most recipes assume meat is at room temperature, will make cooking times more accurate.

Fresh birds: Poultry, like all meat, is perishable and must be stored carefully. When chicken or turkey is bought fresh, not frozen, remove the butcher's wrapping and put the bird on a plate or tray. Remove the giblets and deal with them at once; make a little stock for gravy or a sauce to go with the bird. Cover the bird loosely with kitchen foil or slip into a polythene bag with the end left open. A little circulation of air is important. Store in the coolest part of the refrigerator under the frozen food compartment. Treated this way you can buy and store a bird three to four days ahead of cooking.

Chilled birds: Before storing a fresh chilled bird, remove the giblets and deal with at once. The bird itself can be left in the polythene bag in which it was purchased but open up the end to allow air to circulate around. Store as above.

Cook the pieces: Chicken and turkey pieces which have not been frozen must be refrigerated and cooked as soon as possible.

Usually frozen: Ducklings are mostly bought frozen. Prepacked fresh, chilled ducklings usually have directions on the pack which should be carefully adhered to. If not, it is advisable to cook as soon as possible after purchase; refrigerate in the meantime as for fresh chicken.

Game that's hung: If you've a bird that has been hung long enough but isn't going to be eaten immediately, you can store it in the refrigerator for a day or two. Pluck and draw the bird first. Remember that the warmer and more humid the weather, the more quickly game birds become high – check the meat every day!

Fresh for breakfast: Bacon will keep in the refrigerator for a week. Vacuum packs have a longer life but should be used within seven days of the sell-by date. Store bacon in weekly amounts. Wrap closely in kitchen foil or cling film – freezer quality if available – excluding as much air as possible. This applies to joints not in a bag or vacuum pack and rashers bought loose. Do not use greaseproof paper which is porous, sticks to the surface and lets the bacon dry out, causing saltiness on the surface.

Extended storage: Vacuum packing extends the keeping quality of bacon and is usually marked with a 'sell by' or 'use by' date. Once opened treat vacuum-packed bacon as fresh.

Whole ham or gammon: Such a joint is an infrequent purchase, so it's worthwhile knowing that a fresh joint will keep for up to 10 days in a refrigerator before cooking, provided you wrap it closely in kitchen foil to exclude as much air as possible. A vacuum-sealed joint will keep for up to 21 days but follow the directions given on the packaging. Once the joint is cooked, keep it covered and refrigerated – don't leave it in a warm room – you can safely carry on slicing it for about seven days.

Fish facts: Even 24 hours' storage will leave fish with less flavour and rather flabby, unless it is vacuum-packed, in which case it will last longer. Should fish have to be stored for a day or two, put it in a lidded container in the coldest part of the refrigerator with a few ice cubes alongside the fish. Renew the ice cubes as they melt, pouring away the liquid. If the fish must be stored longer, freeze it straight away. Don't store shellfish except frozen (see also page 263).

Smoked salmon: Keep a side of smoked salmon moistened lightly with oil to stop it drying out. This applies whether the salmon has been taken out of a vacuum pack or bought from the fishmonger. Wrap closely in cling film or kitchen foil and store in the refrigerator: the maximum is one week. Slices of smoked salmon should always be interleaved with cling film or cellophane.

▦ STORING DELICATESSEN GOODS

Safe for salami: Hang uncut salami in a cool, well-ventilated place free from draughts – it is best kept out of the refrigerator. The temperature should be in the region of 15°C (60°F). If your kitchen is too warm for salami storage, put it in the bottom of the refrigerator.

Another slice: Although delicatessen meats, such as salami, may not go mouldy, they can develop rancidity, especially after slicing.

When sliced, closely wrap in cling film and always store in the refrigerator. Eat as soon as possible, at least within a couple of days. For best eating quality, take from the refrigerator a little time before it is needed. Treat air-dried ham, such as Parma or Westphalian, in a similar way but serve slightly chilled not cold – warm slices of these hams tend to sweat.

Bierwurst and frankfurters: Sausage, such as Bierwurst, must be refrigerated and eaten within a day or two of purchase. The 'sell-by' date is useful on vacuum packs which should also be kept in the fridge. Frankfurters require the same treatment; for a longer life buy these in a can or bottle. Once opened treat as fresh.

Perfect pâté: Buy pâté in small quantities and use it up quickly. Note that pâtés which contain onion tend to go sour quickly. Keep pâté well wrapped in the fridge, so that it does not absorb from or transmit flavours to surrounding foods.

Keeping cheese moist: The more moisture a cheese has, the shorter its life. Our own hard cheeses, such as Cheddar or Leicester, with a low moisture content, are some of the best keepers. Holding in the moisture is of prime importance whichever cheese you wish to store. It's a good idea to seal the pores of the cheese – run the blade of a rounded knife over the cut surface to smooth it. Wrap each type of cheese separately in kitchen foil or cling film – some people consider the latter does not give the cheese quite as long a life. Even better overwrap in a polythene bag or put in a polythene box.

A question of temperature: An unheated larder or cellar at a constant cool temperature provides the best conditions for cheese storage, however few modern homes have either of these. The next best place is the warmest area of the refrigerator – the salad crisper or vegetable area. Repeated temperature changes are death to cheese. Take out only what is wanted and buy little and often.

A whole round: There are few cheeses more appealing on a party table than a whole Brie in peak condition. And nothing is more difficult to store when there are leftovers. The best way to deal with any free-flowing cheeses once cut is to wrap them closely in kitchen foil, leave at cool room temperature and eat very soon – within 24 hours at most.

Store it whole: All whole, soft-ripening cheeses, such as Brie and Camembert, can be refrigerated whole for a limited time. Ripening will still continue but the process is slowed down. Even a closely wrapped or box wedge can be treated this way. Once cut, however, act quickly as above. It is really best to buy only as needed.

Half a Stilton: The best way to keep half a Stilton cheese (or a whole cheese once it has been started) is to cover it with a moist cloth dipped in water or in brine and store it at 7-10°C (45-50°F) – the temperature of a cool larder. It could be kept in a brick/stone garage provided it is protected from fumes. Keep the cloth moist. The cheese should remain in good condition for about two weeks.

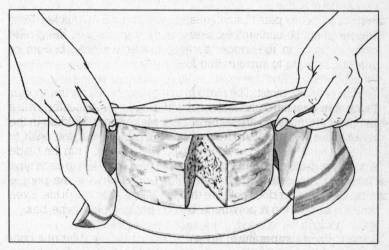

Keeps for a month: Stilton should keep in the refrigerator for up to a month provided it is wrapped closely in kitchen foil to prevent drying out. The same applies to cut wedges. Once opened, pre-packed portions and jars of Stilton don't keep well – they should be stored in the refrigerator.

Greek cheese: Feta should be white, moist and slightly crumbly. Store in its brine or whey mixture.

When in Rome. . .: Keep Mozzarella in a light brine if it is paper-wrapped and refrigerate if it comes wrapped in plastic.

91

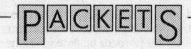

▨ WHAT WILL KEEP WELL AND HOW

Flour power: Store all flours in their bags in a cool, dry, airy place. If, however, they have to be kept in a steamy kitchen, put the bag into a covered container.

New for old: Never mix new flour with old. Always take the opportunity to wash and thoroughly dry the container when a new bag of flour is put in.

Longer plain: Plain flour keeps longer than self-raising, which will keep for two to three months. Wholemeal and brown flours can turn rancid due to the fat present in the grain, so buy in amounts that will be used up quickly. Use organically grown flour within one month.

Yeast at its best: To keep fresh yeast at its best, store in a screw top jar, plastic-lidded container or a polythene bag. It will keep for about four days in a cold place, about seven days in the refrigerator.

Active yet dried: Dried yeast is convenient to use as it can be kept for several months in a tightly-lidded tin in a cool place. As the yeast is used, transfer the remainder to a smaller container so that air space is kept to the minimum. To test for activity, place a little of the yeast in warm water and if it does not dissolve and froth when left in a warm place for 10 minutes, then it is advisable to discard the yeast to avoid disappointing results.

Dried pasta: This needs to be kept in an airtight pack in a cool, dry place. Once opened, re-seal using sticky (adhesive) tape. Aim to use within a year. Wholewheat, because of the fat in the wheat germ, only keeps for about six months. A supply of slightly under-cooked pasta, drained and immediately cooled under running water, can be stored in a covered container for up to three days in the fridge.

Fresh pasta: To prevent fresh pasta from drying out wrap it, then store in the refrigerator for only a day or two.

White and brown rice: Put opened packs of rice into airtight containers to keep the grains dry and clean. Brown rice has oil in the bran so it should only be kept for up to six months on the shelf or a little longer in the refrigerator. Cooked rice in covered containers keeps for one to two days. Grains do become firmer but are restored when reheated in liquid.

Cordon Bleu

TIPS

Pulses and beans are staple ingredients of a high fibre, healthy diet. Butter and haricot beans, brown and red beans, lentils and split peas should not be more than one year old. Kept longer they become hard and despite lengthy soaking and cooking do not become properly tender.

Fresh is best: Since no preservative is used in organically-grown, dried grains, they should be used quite quickly. Storage must be cool and completely dry. Any moisture could cause sprouting. If transferred to a jar, use one that 'breathes', such as porous pottery.

Not just porridge: Oats keep well because all enzymes are killed during processing. There are no additives and only a little fat is naturally present in all oats. Dry, cool conditions around cardboard packs are fine. If there is any risk of steam, seal opened packets inside polythene or other containers. A good way to use up a surplus of oats is to process them to a powder and add to stews, casseroles, soups and sauces to thicken.

Crackle and flavour: Provided the storage is cool and dry, go by the 'best by' date on packets of breakfast cereals. If the cereals are not to be eaten quickly, seal opened cartons in a polythene bag or tip them into an airtight container. An open kitchen shelf is not ideal if there is steam about. If bulk buying, make sure good storage is available; a cardboard box in a damp garage can make nonsense of a manufacturer's date stamp. Poor conditions soon make cereals soften and the flavour deteriorates. A muesli mix that needs eating up is a good ingredient for cakes and flapjacks.

Packet suet: Date stamp a packet of shredded suet yourself when you buy it. If stored in too warm a spot, the suet shreds can stick together, and although they can be separated and used the flavour may be affected. A packet will, however, keep for up to six months in a refrigerator.

Butcher's suet: Make sure any meat particles and skin are discarded before finely chopping or grating fresh butcher's suet. Fresh suet should always be chopped or grated finely and cooked well, otherwise it is indigestible. While chopping, dredge lightly with flour to keep the suet separated. Pack in a sealed container and use within two months. Keep it stored in a cool, dry place.

Teatime: Teas are easily contaminated by strong smells, such as soap powders and spices. Store leaves and bags in an airtight 'caddy' in a cool, dry place not out in the open in a steamy, warm kitchen. Leaves keep longer than bags, which have a much finer tea in them.

Rare leaves: The more delicate and expensive teas, such as un-fermented green tea from China, Taiwan and Japan – gunpowder, so-called because of the metallic colour of the green leaves, chun mee and saw mee – are best kept cooler in the refrigerator. Cover tightly to prevent dehydration.

Fresh coffee: Whole coffee beans keep their freshness for the longest time. They will keep for up to two weeks in good condition. Even then the key to good coffee is to buy a small quantity at a time and grind the beans yourself as you need them. However, vacuum-packed coffee is a good alternative. Whichever coffee you choose, it should be stored in an airtight container after opening, and kept in a cool place, preferably a refrigerator or even a freezer. High temperatures, air and moisture are bad for coffee and can affect the flavour.

Free-flowing sugar: Cool and dry are the best conditions for sugar. Brown sugars are more prone to 'caking' because of their non-sugar (molasses) content, so keep their containers tightly sealed against moisture. The darker the sugar, the more easily this could occur. If it does get solid, keep the sugar overnight in a bowl covered with a damp cloth.

Add some flavour: Flavoured sugar is lovely in all kinds of cooking; add whole spices, such as a cinnamon stick, bruised ginger or cloves to an airtight canister of sugar, see also page 174 for how to make vanilla sugar.

Avoid lumps: Icing sugar is best kept in its packet. Once opened seal well and sieve before using, as a precaution against lumps.

A white coat: Keep dried fruit in airtight packs or containers in a cool, dry place. Moisture can cause sugar to emerge as a white coating on dried vine fruits frequently accompanied by a fermented smell. However the fruit can still go into mixtures like cakes adding a wine flavour. Do not use cork-topped storage jars, as these can absorb the oil used to protect the fruit and may attract mites.

Candied peel: Keep candied or mixed chopped peel away from light or it will bleach out and keep it closely covered to prevent drying out.

Cordon Bleu
TIPS

For keen cake makers, it is useful to keep your cupboard stocked with the following ingredients: angelica, almonds, almond essence, arrowroot, baking powder, candied peel, cornflour, custard powder, dried fruits (currants, raisins, sultanas), dried milk, evaporated milk, flour (plain), gelatine, glacé cherries, sugar, vanilla essence and vanilla pods. Store in a dry, cool and dark cupboard and keep dry goods in airtight containers.

Packet fruit: Pre-soaked packet fruit, such as prunes, should be refrigerated when opened and eaten quickly. Glacé cherries keep well in covered cartons but turn the carton upside down occasionally to let the syrup run through and keep all the cherries moist.

Butter and margarine: Check wrapping for the date stamp and keep completely covered in the wrapper in the refrigerator. Exposed butter can darken by the drying out of the surface and all fats readily absorb other strong flavours. Salted fats keep longer than unsalted except in the freezer when the reverse applies.

Low-calorie fat spreads: These should be kept chilled but should not touch the refrigerator sides because moisture can be attracted which will shorten the keeping time.

No mixing: Never mix leftover fat with fresh and avoid leaving particles like toast crumbs in the fat, as these can contaminate it. Butter and margarine which you are going to use up within a week can be kept soft in a cool cupboard provided they are well covered.

Don't keep the jelly: Make sure that dripping is thoroughly clarified and clear of all sediment, which can go off quickly even in a refrigerator. Scrape off the delicious natural jelly that settles at the base of a bowl of dripping and use straightaway in gravies, sauces and soups. Melt down the dripping and return to the bowl, so that the space left after removal of the jelly is filled. Cover dripping to prevent moisture forming on the surface.

Set and runny: Honey is a natural pure product that does not need a 'best by' date; it keeps indefinitely in a seal-topped jar in a cool place. Clear honey will stand warmer storage. If it does set, warm the open jar in hot water until the honey runs again.

Honeycomb: Honey on the comb should be eaten within three months. Keep in an airtight container in a cool place but not refrigerated. If kept too long, the honey granulates and the wax comb capping absorbs the honey making it darker and spoiling the appearance.

Avoid the mould: Bought jams, jellies and marmalades keep for a month or so once opened. Cling film put on the surface helps prevent mould but the storage must be cool, dry and airy.

Mould can be removed: Take at least 1 cm (½ inch) from the surface, use the rest of the jam quickly and improve storage conditions for another time.

Watery jelly: Jelly may go watery as its structure changes but this is not detrimental, apart from to the appearance. Use it up quickly in marinades, sauces, stews or casseroles. It's also useful in glazes.

Knives out: Keep fatty knives out of preserves because fermenting can result. Cover preserves in serving dishes and do not return to the original jar.

More vulnerable: Low sugar jams are more vulnerable to deterioration, so keep them in the refrigerator and consume quickly.

Keep the crunch: Nuts like it dark, dry and cool. Warmth and dampness turns their natural fat rancid and can shrivel them even in the shell. The hardest nuts, almonds and Brazils, keep fresh the longest; cashews soften the most quickly.

Tough nuts to crack: To crack nuts more easily put them in the freezer for a day and shell them as soon as you take them out.

Airtight container: Keep shelled, open pack nuts in an airtight container. Only put out the amount that is likely to be eaten, as it is better not to return leftovers to the original pack. Keep these separately, in another airtight container, for the next time.

Too good to waste: Both bought and home-made chutneys and pickles keep well in unopened jars with a vinegar-proof cover, see page 299. Check labels to see if preservatives are added; if not, extreme light can cause darkening which is not harmful but is unsightly. Piccalilli is a good example. Once the jar is opened, the contents will keep longer by being refrigerated.

Avoid waste: Always scrape down chutney from inside the sides of the jar to keep all the product moist and avoid waste. If not kept airtight even when opened, the chutney liquid will evaporate and will be more concentrated and firm textured. The vinegar will continue to preserve it satisfactorily. Use tail-ends of chutney and pickles in marinades, sauces, casseroles, and savoury butters.

Ketchup and sauce: Never fail to wipe the tops of bottles clean after use and screw tops on securely. Store away from wines and beer from which yeast spores could cause ketchup to ferment. Keep in the dark. If metal tops get stuck, hold under hot water briefly to expand and loosen them.

Away from steam: Dried herbs store reasonably well kept cool, dry and in the dark. Racks look attractive but are best located inside a cupboard – the back of a door is a good position. Do not measure from the container over a steaming pot, the moisture can spoil the remaining herbs. Stoppers or lids must be kept firmly in place. It's best to buy in amounts you know you will use quickly.

Fresh herbs: Hang fresh herbs on the stem upside down in an airy, dry place.

Volatile oils: Whole spices, such as nutmeg, should be kept intact and grated as required to retain the flavoursome volatile oils. Ready-ground, good quality spices, however, will keep fresh for longish periods under the right conditions which will keep the flavour in, and moisture and adverse smells out. Glass with an airtight top makes the best non-porous container with a large label to stop light getting in. Polythene and cardboard can take in unwanted flavours and leak out moisture. Some strong spices react with metal containers. Keep out of bright sunlight, it can cause bleaching. Store as for herbs.

Lemon stops mould: Keep olives covered with light brine in the jar or sachet when opened. A slice of lemon on the surface can help to stop mould forming. But mould can be washed away without harming the olives. It's wise not to return olives to their storage jar – keep separately, use quickly. Use loose, bought olives within a day or two, storing them in the refrigerator closely wrapped.

Add gloss: A little oil run through drained olives restores a gloss.

Watch those stuffings: Pimento stuffing generally has a preservative, some other stuffings like anchovy shorten storing time.

Not chilled but cool: Chocolate requires a dry, cool storage shelf. Leave in its foil wrapper rather than re-wrapping in cling film which can impart a flavour, as will any strong smelling product nearby.

Revival: Softened chocolate can be revived in the refrigerator just before eating but if left there too long damp spots will appear.

A white bloom: Too high a temperature may create a white 'bloom' on the chocolate, which is the result of fat separation, but this will not affect its performance in recipes.

Grated and melted: Leftover grated chocolate should be stored in a covered glass dish. Melted chocolate that has hardened again will be on the brittle side but can be melted again to add to sauces, cakes, desserts and other mixtures.

Sealed-in flavour: Cocoa and drinking chocolate are best left in their unsoldered tins with tight-fitting lids. Always use clean spoons for measuring from the tin and keep away from steam.

Well spread: Chocolate spread keeps well in the carton; there is no need for refrigeration which hardens the spread unnecessarily. If this spread should harden, warm very gently over a low heat in a small saucepan. The sugar syrup content is restored by warmth to a soft smoothness.

Jelly cubes: Keep well-sealed packets of jelly in a dry, coolish place. When the packet is opened and the jelly tablet exposed, there is a risk of mould appearing, also the jelly can dehydrate and become over-stiff with age. If using only part of the tablet, don't forget the remainder – try it as a hot drink.

Gelatine: Never store either powdered or leaf gelatine in a damp spot. And beware of painted wood cupboards as a storage place: some of today's paints taint gelatine.

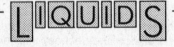

▦ WINE AND SPIRITS

Wine in store: Even the most modest wine is best not drunk the same day that you purchased it; give it time to settle after the journey from shop to home. Wines like darkness and an equable temperature. They prefer to be stored in a coolish place, 10°-13°C (50°-55°F) with some humidity. But, in fact, it will not be disastrous if the temperature is a little higher provided that it does not fluctuate. Wine doesn't react favourably to ups and downs.

Sensible storage: When choosing a home for your wine, avoid a storage area near central heating pipes, under a non-insulated roof, or where an electric light is on constantly, and keep away from strong-smelling neighbours.

On their sides: All bottles of wine should be stored lying down on their sides, so that the cork is kept moist and swollen and cannot become dry thus letting air in or wine out.

Make do: If nothing more permanent is available, the box the wine comes in, stood on one side, will serve as a store bin.

Do not disturb: Labels uppermost is a must for instant identification of wine. It saves disturbing bottles which are not required.

Upstanding port: In the main, ports (other than vintage) are freshly bottled for immediate drinking and the bottles can be kept standing up. There is no advantage in laying them down as they do not develop in bottle.

With the future in mind: Vintage port, bought to store for future use, must be kept lying flat, with the wine against the cork and the label uppermost. This will ensure the whereabouts of any 'crust' or deposit that may have formed, and will facilitate decanting when necessary. Storage temperature is similar to that of wine.

Decanted sherry: Once the bottle is opened, dry sherry deteriorates more quickly than sweet. It is best not to leave it in a decanter for too long as many decanters do not have air-tight stoppers – three to four weeks is the maximum.

Warm rooms: If the decanter is stored in a very warm room, transfer it to a cool place once it is no longer required. Sherry will last longer in an opened re-sealed bottle, as the cork or screw top is likely to fit better than the decanter stopper. Cloudiness is a sure sign that sherry is not drinkable.

Spirits keep well: Spirits should always be kept upright, because spirit can cause the cork or any stopper or cap to deteriorate. Slow evaporation can take place once a bottle is opened. The same applies to liqueurs.

Cool and bubbly: Bottles of cider which have been opened should be stored in the refrigerator. Cider goes flat less quickly when it is chilled and will be still drinkable for two days. If you're just keeping the 'dregs' for cooking, they will last about two weeks.

Bubbles don't matter! Don't leave a half-empty bottle of cider as it is a waste of space; much better to pour the cider into a smaller bottle. If the bottle cap is missing use a cover of cling film. In cooking it's the flavour one is after not the bubbles.

Wine for the cook: Wine should stay fit for cooking for several days if recorked and kept in a cool place. Better still, pour wine into a smaller clean bottle, so that it comes up to the neck, keeping the air space to a minimum. Make a note on the bottle that it should be used quickly, as wine soon turns to vinegar and then you have a different cooking ingredient!

Cool and light: Lager can be left in the refrigerator, so can light ale which responds to chilling very well. If beer is cloudy when it is poured out this means that it is too cold.

JUICES AND MINERAL WATER

Mineral water: Store upright in a cool place – preferably not too cold. Once opened, depending on the amount of air that has entered the bottle, the carbonated water goes flat very quickly and should be finished as soon as possible. Unopened life expectancy is at least 12 months.

Juice in a carton: Carton fruit juices have a 'sell by' date and most manufacturers advise that the product should be kept in the refrigerator and consumed within two to five days of purchase. This allows some leeway. Left longer, the juice ferments and the build-up of carbon dioxide will cause the unopened carton to bulge noticeably. Once opened, the carton should be kept cool in the refrigerator and, as contact with air accelerates deterioration, the pack should be resealed as well as possible. Alternatively, pour the contents into a clean lidded container.

Other fruit juices: Longlife juice should be treated as other carton juice once opened. Although refrigeration is unnecessary for canned and bottled juices, in order to maintain the vitamin C level they should not be stored above 21°C (70°F).

Well chilled: Tomato juice is best served chilled, so it is a good idea to keep a can in the fridge.

Keep well sealed: Once tonics, bitter lemon and soda water are opened but not finished, screw the caps down tightly and use within a reasonable time.

OILS

At room temperature: Olive oil and other oils do not need to be refrigerated but should be kept away from light. Olive oil thickens when refrigerated and changes colour. If this does happen to any oil, leave at room temperature and it will return to its original colour and density.

Long and short lasting: When opened and recapped, olive oil lasts longer than other vegetable oils. Walnut oil has a very short life before rancidity sets in so unless you use it regularly buy in the smallest amounts.

Three to one: Oil and vinegar dressing (or French dressing) keeps well in a screw-topped jar or bottle. Choose a container with a secure, vinegar-proof lid. Mix in the proportion of one part vinegar to three parts oil with seasoning of mustard, salt and pepper and a pinch of sugar if liked. Shake well to combine thoroughly. Do not add garlic or herbs to the dressing until ready to use as they tend to go flat. There is no need to refrigerate. Shake again when required.

CAKES

Yesterday's cake: With a few exceptions, such as rich and semi-rich fruit cakes, a cake tastes better the day it is made, but if well stored as described below, it will be good the second and even the third day. Frosted or iced cakes stay much fresher than unfrosted ones.

Butter in the mixture: Rich butter cakes baked to moist perfection – orange Madeira, light fruit, dessert chocolate with ground almonds and the like – keep their flavour and moist texture for quite a long time. In fact they are even nicer a week after baking. Wrap these undecorated cakes closely in freezer film or kitchen foil to leave space in the cake tin.

The top tier: The top tier, or any surplus from another tier, of a wedding cake can be wrapped in kitchen foil and stored, but preferably not longer than two months, for mould growth may develop between the almond paste and the cake. If the top tier is to be kept for another red-letter day more than two months away, it should be stripped of the almond paste and icing. The cake only should be rewrapped in greaseproof paper and kitchen foil. Anoint with brandy, and ice again shortly before it is required.

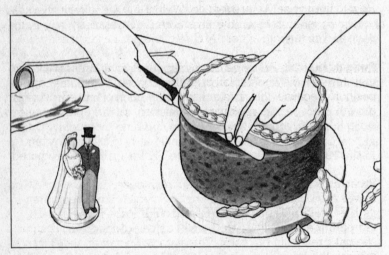

Not quite cold: Some people wrap fruit cakes while they are still very slightly warm which they claim makes them much more moist. Whether you wrap them cool or warm, leave the cake tin lining paper in place, then wrap in unpunctured kitchen foil or a double thickness of freezer film or several layers of greaseproof and a clean tea towel.

Cakes with cream: If a cake has a cream or whipped cream filling or topping, keep it refrigerated until serving time. Cover and store any uneaten portion in the refrigerator until the next day.

Bake today for tomorrow: Teabreads baked in the shape of a loaf are more moist, slice better and improve in flavour if they are wrapped in cling film or kitchen foil, then stored overnight or a few days longer before serving.

Leave to mature: Gingerbread and parkin should never be tasted before storing because the treacle and syrup need time to mature. Wrap closely, put away in a tin, bring out in a few days – maybe a week for parkin – and they should be nice and sticky.

Don't be hasty: Nuts are packed with oil, so cakes with ground nuts in the mixture should be allowed to mellow in an airtight tin.

How to improvize: To prevent damage, place a beautifully finished gâteau or layer cake on the inverted lid of a cake tin or flat cake plate and cover with either the base of the tin or a large deep bowl.

Pudding in store: To keep a Christmas pudding, leave until it is cold, then remove the kitchen foil or pudding cloth. Leave the paper in position because this is sterilized and helps to prevent mould growth. Recover the pudding with kitchen foil or a fresh cloth and store in a cool airy place.

BREADS

Bread at its best: Some breads keep fresh better than others. Crusty loaves are best eaten on the same day as baked. To keep bread at its best: soft, moist and free from mould, store it at normal room temperature in a clean, dry, well-ventilated container, such as a special bread bin or crock. The storage container should not be airtight; the lid of a crock should not fit exactly.

Keep away mould: To discourage mould growth, regularly remove crumbs and wash the container weekly in hot soapy water, then dry thoroughly. A little vinegar in the rinsing water also helps.

Under wraps: Wrapped bread should be kept in its wrapper. A clean polythene bag makes a good cover for uncut loaves. As the bread is used, the wrapper or bag should be folded loosely under the loaf for air to circulate. Either store in the bread bin or on a dry, airy shelf.

Don't refrigerate: A refrigerator is not the best place to keep bread. A loaf kept for one day in the refrigerator is similar in staleness to a three-day old loaf. However, the refrigerator does delay mould growth, so if bread is needed just for toasting this may be the answer. Wrap bread in a polythene bag.

Buttered crumbs: These keep better than fresh breadcrumbs in the refrigerator. Stored in an airtight container, they will last for two months, whereas fresh only last for two to three days. (See page 107 for the method for making breadcrumbs.)

BISCUITS AND PASTRY

The biscuit tin: Although most biscuits or cookies are at their best when freshly baked, they also store happily for a limited time in an airtight tin. Make sure they are completely cold before they are put into the tin.

Best to separate: Keep crisp and soft or moist types of biscuit separately, never together, because crisp biscuits quickly absorb moisture from the soft ones. This also applies to the storage of cakes and cookies.

Restore crispness: Pop undecorated biscuits or cookies that should be crisp but have gone soft, in a low oven for a few minutes to crisp them up.

Make-do tins: If you run short of tins, plastic boxes with snug-fitting lids are good substitutes. Wrap the biscuits closely in kitchen foil or even utilize cleaned, empty coffee tins with reusable lids which do just as well.

Add a sugar cube: Keep biscuits crisp by putting a couple of sugar lumps in the tin with them to absorb moisture, change them once they have become damp. In reverse, keep a wedge of apple with cookies (or gingerbread) that need to be kept moist, change this after four to five days.

Halfway stage: Rubbed-in fat and flour, the first step to making shortcrust pastry, keeps for three months in a refrigerator. Store in a closed polythene bag, or polythene container with an airtight lid, or a screw-topped jar. When the mix is needed remember that in a recipe calling for 100 g (4 oz) flour and 50 g (2 oz) fat you should use 150 g (6 oz) pastry mix. Allow about 4 teaspoons water. Omit the water and add demerara sugar and a few chopped nuts or corn-flakes to the mix to turn it into a crumble topping.

Pastry shells: Baked choux pastry shells are at their best on the day of baking but can be stored in an airtight container or in a polythene bag in the refrigerator for up to two days. Refresh in the oven to bring back crispness.

▓OTHERS

Seasoned flour: Keep a screw-topped or well-sealed jar or con-tainer of seasoned flour made by mixing together mustard powder, paprika, dried herbs and salt with the flour. Test for flavour on the top of the finger. Use this for added flavour when coating liver, sausages, chicken pieces, fish fillets, meat balls, etc.

Home-made mayonnaise: Store in the fridge and eat within a few days. If the mayonnaise should look oily just add a teaspoonful of boiling water and whisk well.

Bread and butter: The speediest way to make buttered crumbs is from a few leftover slices of bread and butter. Crumb these in the blender, turn them out straight into the frying pan or on to an au gratin dish for browning. Bread that starts to curl up is right for old-fashioned raspings (home-made dry crumbs) and better than bought golden crumbs for coating – set the oven at 150°C, 300°F, Gas Mark 2 and bake on a tray until hard and dry, not brown. Process into crumbs and store.

Sweet leftovers: Half-eaten dishes of mousse, jelly or fruit cream are not the most inspiring sight in the fridge. Use them up in a trifle. Break them up and combine with sherry-soaked trifle sponge or macaroons , then cover in a light custard and decorate with grated chocolate. The result looks and tastes like new.

Soufflé ahead: The base mixture for baked soufflés can be prepared several hours, or even a day, ahead and kept refrigerated. Do not fold in the egg whites until baking time. Seal the surface of the mixture with cling film.

More steam: Steamed pudding leftovers, repacked while still warm in a smaller greased basin, reheat well. If it's only a very small portion, parcel it in kitchen foil.

New life for rice: Remove the skin from leftover cold rice pudding and cover with a generous layer of apple purée, then top with a snowy cap of light meringue.

Biscuit saver: Don't buy digestive biscuits for a crumb crust if you've an assortment of broken bits in the barrel. If the crispness has gone, bake the crumb case before chilling.

Boiled to a syrup: Rich, home-made jellied stock can be boiled down to a syrup consistency which, when cold, sets to a firm jelly that will keep for months in the refrigerator. Add the jelly to sauces, casseroles and sautées by the teaspoonful – the flavour is very concentrated.

Keep pork fat: A piece of raw pork fat kept in the refrigerator is handy to rub round a pan before making pancakes. It will keep for about two weeks.

Don't throw away: Save the syrup from canned fruit; it will keep well in the refrigerator for several days. Use it to sweeten fresh fruit such as cooking apples, plums and rhubarb when you want to poach them.

Time to mellow: Most braises, casseroles and stews are better when reheated because the flavours have time to blend together. When reheating do not overcook as this will break down any vegetables present. Fifteen minutes gentle boil is a good guideline.

A smidgeon of leftovers: A couple of cold cooked sausages come into their own – with cold pasta in a speedy curry mayonnaise – as two ample servings for a light snack meal. Flavour the mayonnaise dressing with curry paste, apricot jam and a dash of lemon juice.

Good tempered: Although nicest served straight from the pan, pancakes (crêpes) can be made beforehand and reheated successfully. When quite cold, stack with greaseproof or non-stick paper between each one, then put the stack in a sealed polythene bag. These packs will keep for several days refrigerated. The basic batter without butter can be kept in a covered jug in the refrigerator for up to 24 hours – melted butter should be added just before cooking, as it solidifies on standing.

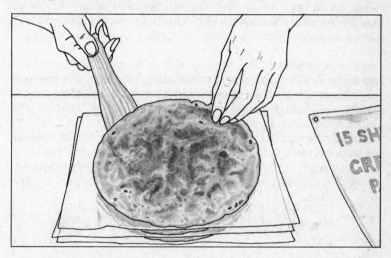

A mellow flavour: Pâtés mellow on keeping and improve in flavour. To extend the keeping life cover with melted pure lard to a depth of 1 cm (½ inch) after the pâté has been weighted down, then cover with kitchen foil tied with string. Leave at least three days in a cool place and up to a week in the refrigerator. Once cut eat on the same day or the next.

A good preservative: Vinegar is a good preservative if you cannot cook meat straight away and have no refrigerator. Make a marinade of oil, vinegar and seasonings, place the meat in this, turn and baste regularly. It will keep in the cool for a day or two, covered.

Salad the second day: Don't waste soggy salad, use it to make piquant Gazpacho, the chilled soup of Spain whose basic ingredients are salad. Other greens blend well too but never add beet-

109

root. Combine the leftover salad with tomato juice, tomato paste and natural yogurt. Give it a few whizzes in a blender and adjust the seasonings.

Come up trumps: When a bird's carcass defeats even the best carver, take a small sharp pointed knife and scrape away every scrap of meat. Combine the chopped scraps with a velvety sauce and use as a vol-au-vent filling. For speed, use a condensed canned soup, mushroom for preference, with sautéed onion, lemon and plenty of chopped parsley added. (And, of course, use the bones to make marvellous soup.)

Re-run vegetables: Don't stick rigidly to recipes, that's the fun of cooking. Add an odd carrot or two or a few peas to a macaroni cheese, or some green beans when a casserole is almost cooked. Pastry shells can be filled with chopped cooked vegetables combined with carefully seasoned sauce. Second day roast spuds can be thinly sliced and shallow-fried until crisp, seasoned well and served with plenty of chopped parsley.

STORED ASSETS

PANTRY PRODUCE

Find a corner: Cans of beans (red kidney, flageolet, butter) and split peas and lentils are worth space in the store cupboard. They are a useful stand-by to stretch soups and casseroles, attractive in salads with a piquant oil and lemon dressing, onion and plenty of parsley, or sieved to make a purée as the base for a dip.

Fashionable spices: Keep a few special spices amongst the faithfuls. Coriander is marvellous in stuffings, soups, casseroles, stewed fruit. Put a few seeds along with pepper in the mill. Cumin, revived from medieval English cookery, is great with minced lamb, beef, pork. Don't leave it out when preparing kebabs. Pine nuts and sesame seeds are useful for scattering over salads.

Life-savers: Canned tuna, prawns, sardines and mackerel are the foundation of many a fast meal. Try concentrated cream of mushroom soup mixed with canned tuna and topped with a little grated cheese and crushed crisps – slip in diced cucumber if you have it – and serve golden and bubbling from the oven. Don't forget to turn cans of sardines from time to time to let the oil run through. The longer they are kept, the better they mature.

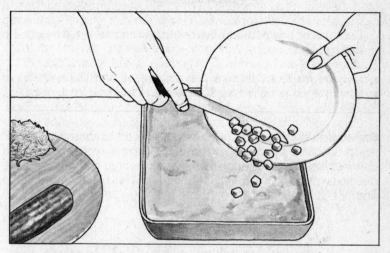

Skin and chop: A recipe often starts with the instruction 'skin and chop the tomato'. Don't waste precious time; buy cans of tomato ready chopped. Make sure you also keep canned whole tomatoes and tubes of tomato paste on your shelves.

A touch of the exotic: Canned smoked oysters and Danish lumpfish are ideal for starters. Roll smoked oysters in wafer-thin rashers of streaky bacon and grill on baby skewers. Fill mushroom caps with soured cream and finish with lumpfish for a tasty appetizer.

A quest for flavour: Soy sauce is useful for its piquant saltiness, rich brown colour, and its very individual flavour. Sea salt is an item that should feature in every cupboard. Coffee essence in chilled milk makes a fantastic milk shake. A range of mustards turn dull food into something quite special. Creamed horseradish is a helpful seasoning, superb with spinach and you can't serve trout without it.

111

Unsalted: Look out for vegetables canned without salt – beans, corn kernels and carrots – they have plenty of texture to make a vegetable mayonnaise.

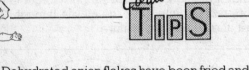

Dehydrated onion flakes have been fried and browned before drying. This means they give good flavour and colour to casseroles and gravies. They are a useful storecupboard standby for those times when you either don't have fresh onions or do not have the time to peel and cook fresh ones.

Something different: Cans of golden berries add fragrance to a fruit salad. Canned figs with a splash of Marsala or canned black cherries flambéed with a tot of brandy and served with cream make delicious impromptu desserts. Canned lychees make a refreshing end to a stir-fried meal.

PROTECTION

▓CARE IN THE KITCHEN

Infestations at bay: Don't store dog and cat cereals, biscuits, etc., in the larder or store cupboard – any infestation that might be present could spread rapidly to other commodities. If this should occur all affected foodstuff must be destroyed, the container washed, sterilized and well dried before re-use.

Keep away visitors: Make sure that all pet food is taken up once the pet has finished its meal, otherwise the dish will encourage flies. This is good training for the pet, too, who will become used to eating the meal in one go.

Raw and cooked meat: Never put unwrapped cooked and raw meat together in the refrigerator, or anywhere else, as this can lead to cross-infection by bacteria.

Reheat with care: To reheat casserole-type dishes, bring to the boil and boil gently for 15 minutes. Thorough reheating is most important. Keeping meat warm for long periods without boiling may encourage the growth of fresh bacteria.

A clean knife: Never use a knife that has cut raw meat or poultry to slice cooked meat without washing the knife first.

Leftovers – take care: Warm food should not be put into the refrigerator as it will raise the temperature of the food that is already there. It should be left, covered with a clean tea towel, in the coolest place in the kitchen. Ideally there should be a free passage of air around it.

No clinging: Cling film, or similar coverings, should not be used on warm food as they can act as an incubator for any germs that may be there. They are excellent for cold food.

A quick cool: Try to cool food down as quickly as possible by placing a bowl, a casserole or saucepan in a little cold water. As the water warms up, change it.

PREPARING

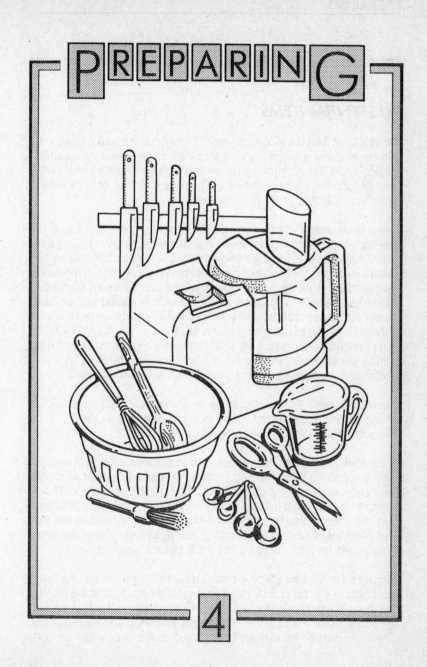

4

▦ESSENTIAL ITEMS

Cook's best friends: Good knives are essential: a small paring knife for vegetables, a large carving knife for meat, and a good strong cooks' knife for chopping and slicing vegetables and raw meats should form the basis of a cook's equipment. A fruit knife, a boning knife and a bread knife are also useful.

Keep them sharp: Carbon steel knives hold a good fine edge and are easy to sharpen but do need regular sharpening and oiling after use. Stainless steel knives need less frequent care but sharpening them takes longer. The very best knives have a section of the blade that extends right along the length of the handle and a thickened piece just before the handle begins which is called the 'bolster'. Slightly cheaper knives may have flat blades and the knife shaft may only extend part of the way through the handle. It is worth investing in a carbon steel large cooks' knife, whereas stainless steel is better for the paring knife, because it is more likely to be used on acidic fruits, such as lemons, which would stain the carbon steel.

Store them well: Knives should be on a magnetic rack or in a knife block. Never leave them loose in a drawer where they can be dangerous and rapidly become blunt.

A cut above: Kitchen scissors are versatile pieces of equipment. As well as opening packets, and cutting greaseproof paper to shape, they can be used to snip herbs, cut rind from bacon quickly and even cut steam vents in pastry or freshly cooked choux balls. Check that any scissors you buy have well-shaped handles so they are safe and comfortable to use even when your hands are wet and greasy. Wash scissors after use and dry well before hanging up.

Measure for measure: For general measuring purposes one large jug holding 600 ml (1 pint) and one smaller holding about half as much are the minimum requirement. For other uses, such as making up concentrated fruit juices, a litre jug is useful. Strong heatproof, glass measuring jugs are the best choice as they are versatile; they can take hot or cold liquids and be put in the fridge or stood in a pan of hot water as necessary. Glass has the added advantage of being easy to read.

Spoon fed: Measuring spoons are necessary because ordinary table and teaspoons vary so much in the amount they hold. Double-ended spoons with metric quantities one end and imperial the other are the best kind. Some have a holder which can be fixed to the wall so they are always close to hand.

For poultry and game: Poultry shears are large sprung scissors that automatically open after use. They are ideal for jointing poultry and game and make the job much easier and quicker.

Sunday best: A roasting tin needs to be large enough to take a Sunday roast or Christmas turkey. Most families find they need two or three tins; one very large and two smaller ones. Some have antisplash trays which hold the meat up out of the tin to allow fat to drip through and be caught under the tray. If you can buy only one tin choose a large one and opt for one with straight sides so that it can double up for large-scale baking. Fruit cakes, soft rolls and chelsea buns can all be baked in a roasting tin. It can also be used as a bain marie by half filling it with water and standing the food to be cooked in the tray. The water bath thus created slows down the cooking of pâtés and egg-based dishes ensuring even cooking.

Frying tonight: Choose a frying pan with a lid, and ensure that it is flexible in use by buying one that is deep enough to hold chops and chicken portions so that complete dishes can be cooked in the pan as well as simply frying bacon and eggs.

Close to hand: General kitchen tools, such as spoons, spatulas and slices, are best kept out on the worktop close to hand. Several different sizes of wooden spoon are essential, together with two or three spatulas. Tongs are useful and some unclip to give two flat sections for lifting foods as well. A ladle with a pouring lip makes serving soups and sauces easier and a metal slotted spoon is useful for lifting meat and vegetables from a pan after browning them.

Pots and pans: Saucepans can be made of a variety of materials and which you choose is a matter of personal preference. Take into

117

account how robust the pan is, how much care the material is likely to need, and how heavy it is. The best nonstick surfaces are now very tough and will certainly save time and effort when it comes to washing up. Cast iron pans are very heavy and usually enamelled because iron rusts unless treated in some way. Enamel can chip if it is not used with care and on thinner metal, such as aluminium, it can craze as well. Look for heavyweight enamel pans to prevent this. As enamel is most likely to chip at the rim some pans have protective metal rims around the top. Stainless steel is hardwearing but really needs a base of aluminium or copper to conduct the heat quickly through the pan.

Gordon Bleu TIPS

The right pot or casserole is essential when pot-roasting. Choose one made of thick iron, enamelled iron or aluminium, which is deep enough to hold a bird or joint of meat without squeezing. The lid must be close fitting.

Pastry wise: A wide pastry brush is quicker to use on large areas of pastry than a round one, and a new, small paintbrush makes a good substitute. Add a little salt to the egg glaze for savoury dishes to give a really golden brown crust. To help puff pastry rise well, sprinkle a little cold water on the tray before baking. The steam produced will give a light fluffy pastry. Most pastry benefits from a rest before use. Allow to stand covered in the fridge after rolling out. One golden rule when making pastry is to keep everything cool. Use iced water for mixing and chill the bowl before use.

Three of a kind: At least three mixing bowls are necessary for making bread, pastry and cakes. Three small bowls for holding ready weighed ingredients or small amounts of sauces and marinades are also useful. Plastic mixing bowls are lightweight, tough and they bounce if dropped! However, they do tend to scratch if a food mixer is used in them and many cannot be washed in a dishwasher. Glass and china are heavier but glass has the added advantage of being transparent and allows you to see if the ingredients are properly combined.

Weighty problems: Accurate weighing in the kitchen is very important. Scales with weights are attractive and robust but do need a fair amount of storage space. Spring scales are more compact. If worktop space is limited, a wall-mounted set of scales will solve the problem. When buying scales check the size and shape of the weighing pan to ensure it will hold enough flour, dried fruit, or sugar for cake making. Anyone who makes jams and preserves is likely to need a larger than average scale pan. Also check the maximum weight the scale can cope with and how easy it is to read.

Whisks: Many people find spiral whisks are the best general purpose whisks, although some cooks prefer the hand-held rotary type. Balloon whisks produce the greatest bulk from foods such as egg whites. A good quality balloon whisk is made up of many fine wire strands. Some cheaper ones have just a few thick strands and are not as efficient. A small whisk is useful for dealing with just a few grams of cream or a single egg white, and a birch twig whisk is good for producing smooth creamy sauces. Birch twigs will not damage enamelled or nonstick surfaces so they can be used inside a saucepan safely.

Home bakes: Keen cake and pastry makers will need a wide range of baking trays and dishes. Baking trays need to be large, flat and thick enough not to buckle in the heat of the oven. Most have raised lips at the edge to prevent foods slipping off but it is worth having at least one tray with a completely flat edge so that fragile foods can be slid from the baking tray on to a cooling rack. Two baking trays about 35 × 25 cm (14 × 10 inches), one 12-hole bun tin, two 18 cm (7 inch) straight-sided sandwich tins and at least one deep cake tin about 20 cm (8 inches) in diameter would be the basics most cooks require for home baking. Loaf tins, square cake tins and a Swiss roll tin could be acquired later.

Cordon Bleu TIPS

If you find you have a round tin but the recipe specifies a square one or if you wish to make a square cake from a round tin recipe the following table gives you the appropriate substitutions:

round tin						
7 inch	8 inch	9 inch	10 inch	11 inch	12 inch	14 inch
square tin						
5 inch	7 inch	8 inch	9 inch	10 inch	11 inch	12 inch

Cool customer: Square cooling racks are generally more useful than round ones because they will take more food. To ensure they are large enough to hold round cakes as well as small buns or biscuits choose racks that are at least 20 cm (8 inches) square. The wire grill pan of a cooker can be used as an extra cooling rack.

CHOOSING AND USING KITCHEN GADGETS

Food processors: These are powerful, versatile kitchen machines. They can chop, mince and purée foods quickly, as well as slicing, shredding and mixing. They are particularly good for preparing vegetables and raw meats, for making pâtés, soups and sauces, and for quick all-in-one cakes, biscuits and pastries. When buying a food processor look for a machine that is easy to handle and simple to operate. A handle or grip on the bowl makes it easier to undo and hold when full of food. Check what accessories are available. A variety of discs for slicing at different thicknesses and shapes are usually offered, and some machines also have juice extractors, pasta makers etc.

On the pulse: A pulse button is a very useful feature on a food processor because it allows the machine to be turned on and off very quickly. This makes controlling the fineness of the food easier and as it is possible to ruin a dish just by running the machine for a few seconds too long, a pulse button is worth looking for. Make a habit of underprocessing foods and then turn on the machine for a few more seconds if necessary.

Batch numbers: Be prepared to process foods in batches if necessary. The size of the processor bowl and the fact that it has a lid limits the amount of food that can be processed at one time. Overloading will result in uneven processing. Machines vary in the amount they can cope with but, as a rough guide, most will mix a three-egg Victoria sandwich cake, or mince about 225 g (8 oz) of meat, or make up to 450 g (1 lb) of bread dough. Beware smaller machines that are really designed only for slicing and shredding and not for making cakes or pastry. Ask to read the instruction booklet in the shop to check the amounts the machine can deal with.

Safety first: The blades and discs on a food processor are very sharp. Never reach into the bowl to lift the blade out of the mixture. Unscrew the bowl to loosen the blade and then spoon the mixture out or hold the blade by the plastic top. Never leave attachments in the washing-up bowl. Stand them next to the sink, where they can be seen, until you are ready to wash them. Rinse under hot running water and use a small brush to make cleaning easier. A bottle brush, or an old toothbrush with a small head, is useful for cleaning the blade and discs. Store the attachments safely out of reach of children. They can be bulky to store but some machines have an integral storage system, and some companies sell storage racks that can be fitted on the wall.

Fast clean: Since processors are fiddly to wash up, arrange the order of the preparation of foods so that the cleanest tasks are completed first. This will cut down the number of times the bowl needs washing. Scrape down the bowl when possible instead of washing it. Keen cooks may well find an extra bowl worthwhile.

New ideas: Many foods that are complicated or time-consuming to make by hand can be made easily in a processor – home-made pasta, sorbets and ice cream, more complex sauces or unusual pastries, for example. A good cookery book will guide you but do take the time to experiment with your processor.

Home economics: Cut costs with your processor; use it to produce purées of soft fruits and overripe avocados when they are in glut and freeze them for future use. Purée left-over meats and make them into pâté-style sandwich fillings by blending with butter and herbs; and make quick soups with whatever vegetables are left in the vegetable rack at the end of the week and a good stock. Grate leftover pieces of cheese and freeze to use in sauces, toppings, or sprinkle on soups. Make breadcrumbs with stale bread and freeze in the same way.

Good snacks: Use the chipping disc to make vegetable sticks for packed lunches or for parties with savoury dips. Make home-made crisps by slicing raw potatoes very thinly, then dry well and deep fry until crisp. Drain and sprinkle with salt before serving.

Meat to mince: Meat needs careful trimming as fatty and gristly bits will still be minced in the processor but will remain hard when cooked. The action of the blade in a processor chops the meat into small pieces rather than mincing it, so the texture is slightly different from traditional minced meat. Cooked meats can be chopped so quickly in the processor that it is easy to reduce it to tiny pieces that lack texture. Leave meats for stuffing pasta or vegetables under-processed so that they retain some 'bite'.

A little lift: Processors are not very good for mixtures that need air introduced to them, such as egg whites or cream. Some cake mixtures need adapting to overcome this. Add one teaspoon of baking powder to a standard three-egg Victoria sandwich mixture to ensure a light sponge. Some machines have whisk attachments but these are not as effective as using a hand-held mixer or whisking by hand.

No go: Wholegrains and coffee beans cannot be ground in an ordinary processor, and potatoes cannot be effectively mashed in one. Some machines can crush ice, but this does tend to blunt the blade so check in the instruction booklet. One or two have special ice crushing discs available as an optional extra.

Soups and sauces: The quickest way to purée a soup in a processor is to drain off most of the liquid, then purée the remaining vegetables and return this to the pan along with the liquid. In this way a soup can often be puréed in one batch instead of several. Avoid overfilling a processor with liquid. If it is too full it will not process well; on some machines overfilling can cause the blade to lift off the spindle while processing and allow the liquid to leak out underneath the bowl.

Christmas special: The processor can be used to make marzipan from fresh whole almonds, giving an excellent flavour. The whole almonds are ground in the processor, then caster sugar, egg and lemon juice are added and the mixture processed until it forms a soft ball. Even royal icing can be made in the machine by mixing the egg white until slightly frothy and then adding the icing sugar a little at a time until it is combined. This gives a lovely glossy icing that pipes easily and is ideal for writing.

Mincemeat and marmalade: Mincemeat is quick and easy to make in a processor too. The dried fruits and chopped apples can be processed in batches and then added to the sherry or brandy, sugar

123

and lemon juice. For a coarser texture mincemeat, process only half the dried fruits and then mix the whole fruits and the chopped fruits together. Peanut butter, rum butter and marmalade and chutneys can all be prepared in the processor, which can save a great deal of chopping, shredding and slicing.

Food mixers: Mixers are primarily designed for making cakes and pastries, whisking egg whites and making bread dough. The large machines with integral bowls can cope with quite large quantities and are best kept out on the worktop, ready for use. Smaller machines, without bowls, can often be wall mounted for storage. Most have a choice of beaters, whisks and dough hooks that fit into them. Check when buying what other accessories are available. Many machines can take slicers, shredders, mincers etc., and it may be worth choosing a model that has a good range of extras so that you can buy them at a later date.

Full scale: For anyone who batch bakes for a large family, or cooks in bulk to fill the freezer or for local church fêtes and the like, a full scale machine is worthwhile since it can save so much time and effort. Most can cope with about 1.5 kg (3 lb) of bread dough or an eight-egg Victoria sandwich mixture, or whisk six egg whites. Smaller machines are useful as general purpose workhorses, taking some of the effort out of everyday cooking. These are likely to be able to make a three-egg cake mixture, whisk two or three egg whites, and some can deal with small quantities of bread dough.

Blenders: These are sometimes called liquidizers and they certainly do blend ingredients for pâtés and dips, and liquidize soups and sauces well. They also grind nuts, make breadcrumbs and are by far the best way to produce light and frothy milk drinks for children. Some have a choice of speeds but it is important to use a blender by eye, watching the food as it is blended and stopping the machine when the texture looks right.

Adding food: A removable section in the lid of the blender is useful as some foods need to be added while the blades are revolving. Breadcrumbs are best made this way, and for mayonnaise it is essential to be able to add the oil in a thin stream while the machine is working. The small section that is removed from the lid is sometimes cup-shaped and marked with liquid measures so that it can be used to hold ingredients before they are added. Check the maximum amounts a blender can cope with in the instruction booklet. The quantities marked on the side of a goblet can be misleading as foods rise up during blending.

Clean machine: The quickest way to clean a blender is to add warm water and just a drop of washing-up liquid to the goblet, put the lid on and blend for a few seconds. This will remove the worst of the remaining food and, after rinsing, may make it clean enough to use again. Once all the food has been blended, dismantle the machine and wash with a small brush. Dry well before putting it away.

Ice cream makers: Good home-made ice cream is a perfect dessert for any meal. When made by hand the mixture needs beating well once partly frozen to ensure the ice cream is light and smooth. An electric, or battery-driven, ice cream machine fits into the freezer and does the beating as the mixture freezes. Ice cream machines can also be used for making sorbets, which is an ideal way of using up overripe fruits. For large families and keen cooks, an ice cream machine can earn its keep by producing a range of desserts to be stored in the freezer ready to use.

Too tall: Some ice cream machines are quite tall and, since many upright freezers have fixed shelves, it is worth checking how much space there is to fit the machine in. Also consider how much ice cream can be made at one time. Some of the smaller ones will not make enough for a hungry family on a hot day. One or two recommend pouring a little water on to the freezer shelf and sitting the machine on this to provide good contact between the machine and the freezer. With open wire shelves in many freezers this is impossible, and a fiddly thing to have to do anyway, so again, check before buying.

Signed and sealed: Since the lead on an electric machine has to come out of the freezer door and be plugged in, it is worth making sure that the seal on the door is strong enough to close over it. Test your freezer by placing the lead from another kitchen machine in the freezer. Put the plug end inside and close the door over it.

Unusual ices: Ice cream is traditionally made with cream but if you want to cut calories and costs try replacing some or all of the cream with yogurt. It gives a sharp taste to the ice cream and by using flavoured yogurts you can vary the tastes easily and cheaply. Sorbets can be made with fresh or tinned fruits so you can try unusual combinations or use out-of-season fruits. Savoury ices can also be made using tomatoes and other vegetables, and these can be served as very unusual starters on a hot day.

Electric carving knives: Experts may decry the use of electric carving knives but many people find them quicker and easier to use than an ordinary carving knife. They are good on hot and cold meats and poultry, and can also be used to slice bread, fruits and vegetables or to cut desserts or gâteaux into slices. For garden parties and traditional tea parties they are a great boon as they will slice large stacks of sandwiches evenly and quickly. Some also have coarser freezer blades to cut up frozen foods. Use these with care as they are very sharp.

A good grip: Look for an electric knife that is comfortable to handle and has good-sized plastic grips on the blades. Use these grips to insert and remove the blades as they are very sharp. A wall storage bracket is well worth using as it keeps the knife close to hand but safely out of reach of children. Plastic covers to fit on the blades while not in use are vital. Never leave the blades in the washing-up bowl. An indicator light that reminds you the knife is plugged in is also useful.

Left right, left right: Any family with both right and left-handed members would be wise to choose a knife with the cord entering at the back of the handle rather than on one side. This makes it much easier for the left-handed to use and is a point worth remembering for most small appliances including handmixers and irons.

Kettles: A kettle must be the most frequently used kitchen appliance. It is a fast and efficient way of heating small quantities of water. Jug kettles are generally made of plastic and they stay cooler to touch than metal ones. The tall jug shape means that the kettle can be boiled with as little as 150 ml (¼ pint) in it, but it may be difficult to fit under the tap if the sink is full of washing-up!

Not so fun fur: In hard water areas the kettle needs defurring regularly, as the scale will slow it down and increase running costs.

A kettle 'crab' or a scale cloth, both available from hardware stores, will help collect the scale and prevent it accumulating on the element. A defurring agent will still be needed occasionally and it should be used with care, according to the instructions.

Pasta makers: Fresh pasta can be made by hand or in a food processor and then rolled and cut by a small hand-operated machine. One or two larger electric machines will perform the mixing and the cutting out. Varying thicknesses of pasta can be made and some machines have extra fitments to make spaghetti, ravioli etc. A little practice is needed to get the pasta dough firm enough to roll out without sticking or cracking but, once the process is perfected, home-made pasta is easy to make and tastes delicious. It can be frozen for two to three months as well. Allow about twice as much fresh pasta per person as dried, since it does not swell to the same extent during cooking.

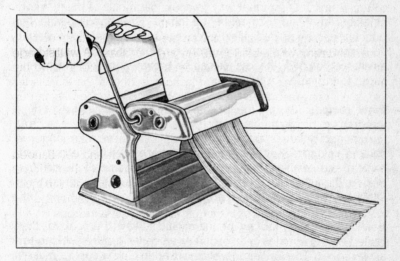

Pressure cookers: For fast cooking, a pressure cooker is hard to beat. It uses the steam produced by water, stock, milk etc, to increase the pressure inside the pan, thus speeding up cooking. A chicken can be poached in 20 minutes, stock made in about 45 minutes and many vegetables cooked in less than 8 minutes. Avoid overfilling a pressure cooker, particularly with foods that rise up during cooking, such as rice. See pages 216 to 219 for further hints.

Which pressure: Low, medium and high pressures are offered on some cookers. Low is useful for softening fruits ready for jam making, medium is needed for bottling fruits, but high level is the most generally used as it gives the greatest time saving. Some models only offer one level, so check that you have the most useful one before buying.

On auto: Automatic pressure cookers will cook at the selected pressure for the chosen time, and then reduce the pressure and ring a bell to remind you to turn the heat off. They are a good choice for anyone who is forgetful, who might leave the food cooking for far too long, and for anyone who is just a little afraid of all that steam muttering away inside the pressure cooker!

Slow cookers: Fuel saving is the greatest advantage of a slow cooker as it uses very little electricity even though it cooks for eight or ten hours. It is an ideal way to cook tough cuts of meat, whole chickens and hams, or make puddings. Even fondues and hot punches can be made in a slow cooker. Since it is safe to leave it to cook unattended it is ideal for anyone out at work all day. Some have a removable pot so that dishes can be browned under the grill and taken to the table for serving.

Right recipes: To get the best results from a slow cooker it is important to brown meats in advance and to cut vegetables, such as carrots and potatoes, into small pieces since these take longer to cook in a slow cooker than meat. Dried herbs and thickening, such as flour and cornflour, should be added at the end of the cooking period; the full cooking time may distort the flavour of the herbs or allow the flour to become stringy.

Bean feast: Dried kidney beans should always be soaked, then boiled for ten minutes in an ordinary saucepan before cooking in a slow cooker. The low temperatures used in a slow cooker make it unsafe to cook kidney beans in them without prior cooking. Tinned beans are fine, since they are treated at high temperatures during the canning process.

No peeking: Avoid the temptation to have a look at the food as it is cooking. This breaks the water seal formed under the lid and allows the temperature to drop, slowing down the cooking considerably.

Transparent lids seem a good idea but they rapidly become misted up in use, so the only answer is to be patient. An indicator light confirms that the cooker is on and working. This is very useful if you are in the habit of putting the cooker on before going out for the day as it warns you if anything is wrong – for instance you may have forgotten to plug in the slow cooker or the fuse may have blown in the plug.

Electric frypans: These look like a large frying pan with a lid. They can roast, bake, casserole, stew or fry foods and are the ideal kitchen gadget for anyone in a bedsit or with limited cooking facilities. Most have a removable electric cable, so that the complete pan can be washed in the sink, and many have nonstick linings. Some come complete with a small baking rack for use when cooking cakes and puddings and they all have accurate thermostatic controls to ensure good results on baked items. Keen party givers may want to choose a model with a lid that can be wedged open so that guests can help themselves to the food while it keeps warm at the table.

Microwave ovens: Possibly the most expensive kitchen gadget available is a microwave oven but it is a very useful addition to the kitchen. A microwave is a complement to a full-sized oven, as it does some things better and quicker (see below) but others, such as browning food, less well. Some more expensive microwave ovens have browning elements or hot air cooking to overcome this. Most families find that a microwave oven that offers a defrost setting and at least a high and low power setting or a variable power control is the most useful type to buy. Turntables rotate the food while cooking to ensure even cooking results, but they do limit the size of the dish that can be used.

The good and the bad: Microwaves are good for cooking vegetables, fish and poultry. They make excellent sauces in a bowl or jug, thus cutting down the washing-up, and they are very useful for many small cooking jobs like melting chocolate, softening butter and so on. They are useful for defrosting foods and reheating plated meals and pre-cooked dishes quickly. They are not very good at tenderizing tough cuts of meat, or at browning foods unless a browning dish or element is used. Most home baking is better done in a conventional oven as well.

Cook's notes: Anyone new to microwave cooking will find it useful to keep a notebook beside the oven and to write down successful recipes with details of the timing and power level used for future reference. Cook by eye at first and stop and check dishes frequently since it is so easy to overcook.

Steamers: Steaming food maintains the delicate flavours and keeps many of the vitamins otherwise lost by boiling. Complete steamers, with a perforated upper pan and a large lower pan, are useful for anyone who frequently steams food but they tend to take up a great deal of space. Insert steamer pans have a perforated base and these can be fitted on top of an ordinary saucepan. When using either type of steamer ensure that it is topped up with boiling water rather than using cold water. The simplest steamer, and by far the most versatile, is the petal steamer. This folds up for storage, but uncurls like a flower to fit inside almost any pan. It can be used to cook vegetables with just a little water underneath and is also strong enough to hold a pudding basin.

Woks: Stir-fried food is very popular and a traditional wok is the ideal vessel for this cooking technique. The sloping slides allow the food to be moved around constantly during cooking and as it is cooked it can be pushed up the side to keep warm and drain. A wok can also be used for small amounts of deep frying and a 'Tempura'

rack can be fitted to the side of the wok to hold the cooked food. Electric woks are available, or ordinary ones can be used on a gas or electric ring. Take care to check how stable the wok is likely to be on a gas stove, but resist the temptation to remove the pan support and just use the metal ring supplied with the wok as this can interfere with the amount of oxygen reaching the gas flame.

▌*EXTENDING THE RANGE*

Pastry board: A marble slab makes an ideal pastry board as it stays cool, even in hot weather. Such slabs are available from kitchen specialist shops. An alternative is to buy a marble top of an old dressing table – sometimes available at a reasonable price in second-hand shops – and ask a local stonemason to cut it into sections and polish them. This way you can create pastry boards to the size you need and the offcuts will make good cheese boards.

Copper bowls: When whisking egg whites the greatest volume can be accommodated in a rounded copper bowl. The round shape and the copper itself all help to increase the bulk of the egg whites. Choose a good quality balloon whisk to use in the bowl. Keep the bowl purely for whisking egg whites and never use acidic mixtures such as fruit purées or juices in it. Store the bowl hanging up to prevent it being dented.

Fish kettle: A long fish kettle allows whole fish to be cooked in one piece. It usually has to stand on two hotplates or burners to heat it evenly. The inner tray has handles to allow it to be lifted out with the fish in place and stood to cool. Once cold, the fish can be moved on to a serving dish to be decorated with less risk of it breaking.

Double boiler: A double pan with water in the lower pan ensures that custards and sauces cook gently without burning. It can also be used to keep foods warm without spoiling. You can improvize with a heatproof dish over hot water, but a double boiler is more stable and tends to be deeper. Some have a steamer insert that can be used instead of the upper pan.

Asparagus steamer: Asparagus seems to sum up hot June days and it really does need to be steamed for the best results. A tall asparagus steamer holds the delicate heads upright so they cook in the steam and keep their flavour and colour. You can improvise by making a foil hat for a large pan and tying the asparagus in a bundle, and propping it upright in the pan. Put the hat over the top and fix it on to the rim of the pan to keep the steam in. Devoted asparagus eaters will generally find a proper steamer well worth while.

Cake tins: Fancy cake moulds allow keen bakers to produce a range of pretty cakes and breads. Kugelhopf tins, angel cake moulds and brioche moulds are widely available. Most of these unclip or come apart in some way to remove the cake since very light sponges and rich mixtures can be easily damaged, and the more complicated shapes are difficult to line with greaseproof paper. A ring mould is the most versatile cake tin as it can be used for cakes, and puddings, or for making jellies or moulded salads. Unusual shaped tins can sometimes be hired from bakers or party shops, which is useful when a numeral or letter cake shape is needed.

Preserving pan: A good preserving pan has a wide top and sloping sides to allow the jam to come to a rolling boil without spilling over. The wide top also allows evaporation to take place. It needs a good thick base so that the jam does not stick and burn. A pouring lip and a handle that can be propped upright to hold spoons with hooks on are useful. Aluminium is the most commonly used material although a few are made of copper. Avoid using copper for chutneys though as there can be a reaction between the copper and the chutney.

Omelette pan: Good omelettes are a matter of practice, but the right pan will help in the making of a fluffy light omelette and in turning it out whole! Whatever material it is made from, a good pan needs to have curved sides to make it easier to swill the liquid ingredients round to give an even shape. It will also allow the omelette to be folded in the pan ready for turning out. A 20 cm (8 inch) pan is the most useful size, as this will hold a two-egg mixture and cook it evenly. Avoid washing the omelette pan. Wipe it round with a piece of kitchen paper towel, oil after use and issue dire warnings to the rest of the family to prevent them cooking bacon and eggs in it!

Pie moulds: Raised game pies look their best when baked in a special waisted mould. These unclip into sections to allow the pie to be removed once cooked, and to make cleaning easier. Make a rich shortcrust pastry for this type of pie using bread flour and egg yolks or a hot water crust. (The shortcrust pastry will give a clearer pattern from the mould.) It will then be easy to handle and to cut to shape to fit the mould, and it will brown well in the oven. Fill the pie with minced pork meat and a mixture of chicken pieces, rabbit meat, or other game in season. Alternate the layers of minced meats with layers of cooked strips of meat so that, when cut, the layers are revealed. Allow the pie to cool completely before attempting to unclip the mould.

ADVANCE WORK

▓ PLAN AHEAD AND STORE

Puff pastry: This will keep for two or three days if wrapped in cling film and stored in the fridge. Frozen pastry, prepared in advance, is also a very useful freezer standby. Shortcrust pastry is best stored at the rubbed-in stage, in a plastic box in the fridge, see page 106.

Coleslaw: Coleslaw is a useful salad to serve when entertaining as the basic vegetable ingredients can be washed, sliced or grated and mixed together. Put them in a plastic bag and store in the base of the fridge. When needed remove and add French dressing or mayonnaise. It will keep this way for three to four days and is ideal at Christmas and other holidays, as it teams well with cold meats. Vary the basic coleslaw mixture by adding peanuts, raisins, grapes or small segments of satsuma oranges just before serving.

Eggs: Eggs keep well in the fridge raw, but can also be cooked ready for use in dishes. Hard-boiled eggs in their shells will keep for two to three days in the fridge. Once shelled the whites tend to go hard if left uncovered. For stuffed eggs, and similar dishes where the whites are used, cut in half and store in a bowl of water for two hours. When needed, drain well on kitchen paper towels. Cooked yolk also discolours and goes hard and is not easy to store. Mix with other ingredients immediately and store the complete mixture, covered, in the fridge. Leftover cooked egg yolk can be sieved to give a savoury garnish useful for fish dishes. Leftover cooked whites can be finely chopped and used as a garnish. This looks most effective used with parsley for contrast.

Quiches: It is possible to partly prepare quiches some time before they need cooking. Line the flan ring with pastry and leave to rest in the fridge for two or three hours. Pre-cook the quiche filling where appropriate and mix with the milk and egg and seasonings. Store in a large jug in the fridge, overnight if necessary. When needed, the filling can be poured into the pastry case and the quiche cooked in the usual way.

Potatoes: Root vegetables, including potatoes, can be peeled several hours before they are needed provided they are stored in salted water in the fridge. Make sure the vegetables are completely submerged or they will tend to blacken. Chips are said by some people to taste better if they are prepared and soaked in this way as the excess starch is soaked out of them, although the vitamin content is also reduced by this method.

Cakes: Try to cook cakes as soon as possible after mixing or the air will be lost. Raising agents begin to work as soon as they become moist so scones and other mixtures also need prompt cooking. If it is impossible to put them straight into the oven, cover them with a cloth and leave somewhere cool until they can be cooked.

Casseroles: It is a fact that casseroles are often improved by being prepared in advance then reheated when needed. This process tenderizes the meat and allows flavours to intermingle. If you prefer not to pre-cook the meal, do the initial preparation step such as browning the vegetables and meat and place them in the casserole dish; add the cold stock and leave to stand in the fridge until needed. Place in a hot oven for the first 10 minutes, then reduce to the normal cooking temperature.

Long grain rice: Once cooked, long grain rice can be kept in a covered dish in the fridge for one to two days. Exclude as much air as possible; use cling film and choose a deep, rather than wide, dish. Use for salads or as a base for risottos or stir-fried dishes. To serve hot as boiled rice, tip into rapidly boiling water, allow to return to the boil and then cook for one minute before draining and serving immediately.

Bread dough: This can be made up in advance and allowed to prove slowly in the fridge. It will keep overnight and can be shaped and cooked fresh in the morning – ideal for breakfast rolls. A crushed vitamin C tablet added to the bread mixture speeds up the proving and it will only need one proving session instead of the usual two. When making rolls for a dinner party, make as usual, prove, knock back and shape the rolls and leave them on the baking tray in the fridge for up to two hours. They can then be cooked and served when needed.

▮TIME AND MOTION

Speed it up: Since cooking absorbs so much of each day, it is well worth following a few basic techniques for speeding up food preparation. Along with a few little tips on how to do things more quickly, it will leave the cook with more time for interesting aspects of cooking.

Methodical madness: Bring a little order into the kitchen. Arrange to work methodically through a recipe; firstly weigh up all the ingredients and place on plates, in dishes or jugs. Set the oven if needed, then sort out the cooking and serving dishes and prepare them. Once everything is ready, start to make the dish. This will avoid mistakes and prevent you starting a dish only to find a vital ingredient is missing! It also means that you give your full attention to the actual mixing or cooking of the ingredients.

Getting into the habit: Good habits take time to acquire but are well worth the effort. Always complete each task before beginning the next; for instance when making mince pies, roll out the pastry and cut out the right number of tops and bottoms; then clear away the flour and wipe the worktop before fitting the bottoms in the tins. Fill all the pies, then fit all the tops on. Then glaze them all. This sounds pedantic but in practice is far quicker than doing some cutting out of lids and some filling and glazing. Watch a chef at work; this is the way professional cooks work at such speed and never make mistakes and still keep the kitchen reasonably tidy.

Oven heat: Plan cooking sessions so that the oven is at the right temperature for the dishes you want to cook, or so that as you remove dishes the oven can be turned down ready for the next dish to go in. Try to arrange to do the same sort of cooking so you need similar ingredients and equipment.

Well equipped: Make sure you have enough of frequently used equipment. If you always make four dozen mince pies or jam tarts buy some extra bun tins so that you don't spend ages waiting for the tins to be free. The same is true of flan dishes and baking trays and sandwich tins; the extra cost is well worth the time saved.

Larder law: Rotate tins and packets as you put shopping away, with the newer containers at the back and the older ones at the front of the shelf. Mark tins with the date of purchase with a marker pen so you can be sure which ones to use first.

Shopping reminders: As you throw away packets or containers tear off part of the label and keep it pinned to a noticeboard or loose in a wicker basket then, when it comes to writing a shopping list, you will know immediately what you have used during the week.

Layer upon layer: When lining cake tins, cut several layers of greaseproof paper and keep the spares in a drawer so that next time you use the tin the greaseproof paper will be ready cut to size. Do the same when making greaseproof piping bags (see page 142).

Oranges and lemons: To make a lemon or orange easier to squeeze, and get more juice from it, roll it between your hands and warm it before cutting and squeezing.

Cold cut: Liver is very slippery to cut up but if cut while still slightly frozen it is much easier to handle. If using fresh liver, roll in a little flour before cutting to make it easier to hold.

Peeling a large quantity of button onions can be particularly time consuming. To speed up the process plunge them first into boiling water for one to two minutes, then immediately into cold water.

Making shapes: Pastry cutters will give a cleaner cut if they are dipped in cold water before cutting the pastry shapes. When cutting out biscuits, dip the cutters in flour before use to give a clean cut and prevent the biscuits sticking.

Quick cuts: The quickest way to clean a mincer is to pass some bread through it. This will pick up the strands of meat and leave the mincer clean enough to use for other foods. Dismantle and wash it if it is being put away. This also works on a food processor; make breadcrumbs after mincing meat and the bowl will be clean enough to make pastry or chop vegetables.

Reduce washing-up: When using a processor, mixer or blender arrange to make the least messy foods first, to minimize the washing-up. So for a quiche, start by making the pastry, scrape the bowl around with a spatula and then slice the vegetables. Finally mix the eggs and milk. This way the machine can be used several times without washing it up.

Roll up: Shape bread rolls easily and quickly by kneading the small pieces of dough lightly, then dip your finger into a little water and press it on to the work top to make a wet spot. Turn the dough over on to this wet spot and lightly roll the dough round with your hand cupped over it. Lift the roll on to the baking tray and repeat with the next one. This gives an even round shape in seconds.

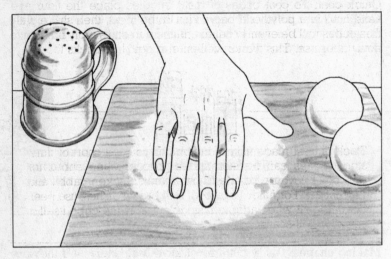

Case proved: Bread dough left to prove, needs covering and traditionally a damp cloth is used. Cling film is just as effective and can be thrown away if the dough rises and touches it. Saves having to wash a cloth!

Fast freeze: For extra quick flaky pastry, freeze the fat until very hard, then grate it out on to the rolled-out pastry, fold and roll out as usual. This is much quicker and cleaner than softening the fat and putting small pieces on to the pastry with a knife. Cover the fat with a piece of foil while holding it to grate. When making both flaky and puff pastry, always remember to turn the pastry the same way; keep the fold to your right. This way all the layers will line up to give really light flaky pastry.

Crumb and coat: Foods often need to be coated with egg and breadcrumbs before frying. Prepare all the ingredients needed and line them up neatly so that the food can be moved from flour to beaten egg to breadcrumbs and on to a board or plate to await cooking. Keeping everything lined up will make the job easier and much faster than having to move food all around the worktop and risk damaging it en route. When using fresh breadcrumbs, egg and breadcrumb the food twice for a really crispy complete coating.

Quick coat: To coat cubes of meat for pies place the flour and seasoning in a polythene bag and add the meat, then shake well. The cubes will be evenly coated and the bag can simply be thrown away after use. This works well on chicken drumsticks too.

Stock is best made from bones but if you are short of time, stock cubes can be substituted. Use chicken cubes for delicately flavoured dishes such as veal, chicken, rabbit and vegetables. For fuller-flavoured, rich brown dishes, use beef. Use less salt when adding a stock cube as the cube itself is already well-seasoned.

▓HOW TO COPE WITHOUT

Improvization: If, halfway through a recipe, you suddenly find you need a piece of equipment you don't have, improvize with what is to hand. It may not be as convenient or give quite such professional results as the real thing, but generally will be good enough to allow you to finish the dish.

Weights: Kitchen weights are useful for pressing pâtés so that they can be sliced easily. Modern spring scales mean that many kitchens do not have weights available, so use tins of food instead. Choose the heaviest and stack them on top of each other to give enough weight to press the pâté.

Thermometer: Good results when deep frying rely on the oil being at the right temperature. Judge this without an oil thermometer by cooking a cube of bread in the hot oil. When the oil is 180°-190°C

(350°-375°F) the bread will brown in 30 seconds. If it takes longer than this the oil is too cool, if the bread browns more quickly the temperature needs reducing.

Steamer: Steaming is a gentle way to cook delicate foods, or to keep foods warm. To create a substitute steamer fit a metal plate over a pan of boiling water. This works well for fish cutlets and small portions of meat and poultry. For steaming puddings, lift the basin out of the water by putting a few washed pebbles underneath it. This is very useful when camping or caravanning.

Pie moulds: Raised pies made with hot water crust pastry are generally moulded around wooden pie moulds, but a straight-sided jam jar will do just as well. Shape the pastry into a fat circle, stand the jam jar on top and then pull the pastry up the sides. Work quickly, while the pastry is warm, as once cold it sets into shape. Leave to cool and then lift out the jam jar. Fill the pie and put a lid on it made from a circle of the pastry.

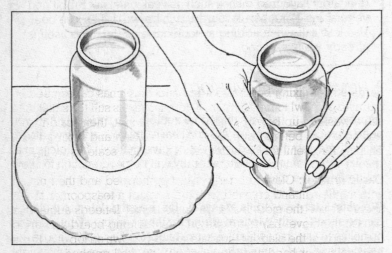

Non-stick silicone paper: This is useful when baking biscuits or meringues that are very fragile and tend to break when removed from the tray. A good alternative is greased greaseproof paper. The fine film of oil on the paper makes it easy to lift off the finished food without breaking or sticking.

Round and rectangular pies: For pies made with rich savoury pastry use a round cake tin with a removable base, as this makes turning the pie out easier, or use a loaf tin for a rectangular pie. Place a strip of folded foil under the pastry so that the ends protrude over the edges of the tin. Once the pie is cooked and cold it can be lifted out whole by the foil strips and cut into slices as needed.

Large-scale mixing bowl: Wedding and Christmas cakes need an extra large bowl to mix them in. If your largest is still too small then use a washing-up bowl. Scrub it well to clean it, then scald it with boiling water before putting the ingredients in and mixing them. This is also useful for breadmaking on a large scale as well.

Garlic crusher: Cloves of garlic can be chopped and then mixed with a little salt and crushed with the back of a teaspoon or table-spoon, or use the side of a large cook's knife. It needs a knack to squash the clove. Lay the clove on the chopping board and bring the flat side of the blade of the knife squarely down on top of it. Press hard with your hand and the clove will be well crushed.

Coffee machine: Fresh coffee can be made using two large jugs and a strainer. Warm the jugs before use. Place the ground coffee and hot water in one. Leave to infuse. Then strain into the other jug through the strainer. For the best results line the strainer with a piece of muslin or a sheet of kitchen paper towel. This technique is useful when catering for large numbers as it is quite quick and you can make a second batch using the same two jugs.

Piping bags: A strong polythene bag makes a useful substitute for a proper piping bag. Choose a thick one if possible and put the food to be piped into one corner of it. Fold the top down so that there is as little air as possible above the food, then snip away a small section from the corner of the bag with scissors. Pipe the food and then throw away the bag.

Small bags: Small icing bags are easy to make with sheets of greaseproof paper. Fold each sheet in half diagonally, slightly off the square, so that the top edge overlaps the underlying edge by about 2.5 cm (1 inch). Cut along the fold and curl the triangles into cones. Turn down the top edge a couple of times to hold it in place and cut the pointed end with scissors to take the icing nozzle.

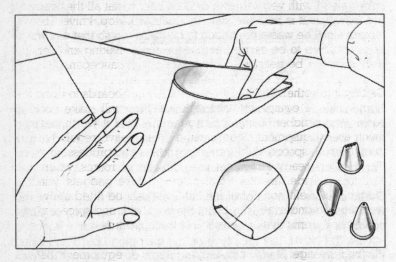

Icing turntable: A turntable brings the cake to be iced up to a convenient level and allows it to be turned easily with one hand. A good substitute is to place the cake on a large flat plate, or a cake board, and stand this on an upturned pudding bowl. It will not rotate as smoothly as a real turntable but it is possible to push the board or plate around carefully as you ice.

▦KITCHEN LAYOUT AND DESIGN

Good planning: A well planned kitchen can be a joy to work in, a badly planned one, a misery. Careful thought is needed when planning a kitchen but even if you cannot move a single cupboard, where you store things and how you use the kitchen is just as important as the original layout. Most of us have kitchens that have grown over the years, rather than been specially planned, but often just re-arranging a few items will make life simpler and cut down on the amount of time spent walking around the room while cooking.

Work triangle: All kitchens revolve around the three basic work areas food storage (larder and fridge); the sink and food preparation area, and the cooker. These three generally form a triangle of one form or another, hence the work 'triangle'. It is worth making sure that all the foods are stored near each other; so keep dry goods in cupboards somewhere near the fridge, tins and bottles in the larder along with vegetables etc. Then check that all the preparation equipment is near the sink and main worktop; knives, bowls, mixers etc. The waste bin needs to be there too so that wet waste does not have to be carried across the room. Baking and serving dishes should be near the cooker, along with saucepans.

Getting it together: Often just re-arranging cupboards to bring the right types of equipment and food together will make cooking easier and quicker. Keen cooks generally find it worth keeping much used equipment close to hand. Many leave regularly used items such as spoons, forks, scales or mixers and processors out on the worktop ready for instant use. Corners of rooms, where the worktop is wide, are the ideal place to store gadgets; window ledges are useful too. Small infill shelves can be fitted above the worktop and under wall cupboards to hold herb and spice jars and other small items that are easily lost in cupboards.

Planned storage: It is worth keeping items of equipment that are rarely used well out of the way on high shelves or backs of cupboards. However make sure that all the items needed for any one sort of cooking are together. Store the preserving pan on top of a wall cupboard but make sure that the funnel, jelly bag and pot covers are all inside so that you don't have to search through all the cupboards to find the extras needed when it comes to making jam.

143

Working walls: Vital storage space in a small kitchen can be provided by walls. Even in a larger room, hanging equipment or gadgets on the walls keeps them close to hand without being in the way. Scales can be wall mounted and many small mixers and blenders have wall storage brackets. Knives can be fitted on to a magnetic knife rack and a piece of pin board will hold a variety of small items on hooks.

Stacking dishes: Dishwasher owners will soon find that it is important to store the plates, crockery and cutlery close to the dishwasher to speed up the daily unloading of the machine. It is loaded gradually as items become dirty, but the unloading tends to be done in one session, so needs to be well organized.

Quick cuppa: Keep tea and coffee-making things on a small tray close to the kettle. It will then be easy to move around, but ready for instant use.

Highlights: For safety and speed make sure the kitchen is well lit. Spotlights look attractive, but can be very hot to work under and collect dust. Angle them to bounce the light off the ceiling or wall if possible to keep the room cool and spread the light. Fluorescent lighting will give good overhead shadowless light and small strip lights under the wall cupboards will illuminate the working area.

Underfoot: Flooring in kitchens takes a great deal of hard wear. Make sure it is smooth and easy to clean and avoid rugs, mats or steps which are time consuming to clean and can be dangerous.

Everything shipshape: Shelves in larders or cupboards rapidly become full and it takes time to search them for small containers and tins. Fit undershelf baskets to hold all the small items and make it easier to sort things out or keep small items, like bottles of colouring and cake decorations, in small plastic baskets on the shelf, then you can lift out the right basket and sort through for the item required.

The home office: A kitchen office helps keep things in order. Just a shelf or small area of a worktop will do. A noticeboard to hold reminders, bills, recipes cut from magazines or given by friends, money-off coupons, plus favourite books and a notepad and pencils is all that is needed. It helps to keep things organized and running smoothly and saves frustrated searches for lost pieces of paper.

Pan stands: Allow a space near the cooker on which to place pans and hot dishes. Keep a small pot stand, or old chopping board, on the worktop or fit a heatproof section to the worktop. Saucepans are best stored near the cooker and extra-wide drawers are available to hold pans. These are very useful to fit under a built-in hob. A simple and cheap alternative is to fit an open shelf above the cooker, wide enough to hold pans.

COOKING

GOLDEN HINTS ON FRYING

Stay put: Never leave the kitchen when food is frying.

No water: If frying oil catches fire, smother it at once with a large lid or metal tray. NEVER pour water on a fat fire.

Dry before fry: Never fry wet food. Potato chips, for instance, should be dried in a cloth before frying.

All together: Use a fine meshed basket to fry croûtons in deep or shallow oil. This ensures an even colour because they are all removed at once.

Little not large: The temperature of fat will be lowered if too much food is put in at one time.

Well drained: Crumple paper towels for draining so that excess fat can drain off thoroughly. Food will be less greasy if drained and thus healthier to eat.

DEEP FAT FRYING

Small batches: Have the pan only a half to two-thirds full of oil and fry the food in small batches.

Prevent splutter: Coat all food (except potatoes) thoroughly for deep frying. This will prevent the escape of juices which causes dangerous spluttering.

Fry twice: Sliced or chipped potatoes need two fries; the first to seal lightly without colouring and the second to colour and crisp them attractively.

Colour match: When frying several batches of the same food it is important the colour should match; try to keep the fat at a constant heat and cook the batches for an equal length of time.

Freezing croûtons: Fried croûtons will freeze well. Warm them from frozen and then serve.

Again and again: Cool oil to lukewarm after frying, then strain it through a piece of double muslin in a bowl strainer and it can be used several times again. A more extravagant way is to use a coffee filter paper.

A crisper finish: When deep frying, hold small fillets of fish at each end and twist before dropping into the oil. This will allow air to circulate on the serving dish and steam can escape so leaving a crisper finish.

Perfect chips: To have crisply cooked chipped potatoes fry in small batches at 180°C (350°F) until soft. Increase the heat of the oil to 195°C (390°F) and fry again putting two or three batches together until crisp. Drain well over the pan, then continue to drain on paper towels and sprinkle lightly with salt.

Less risk: Electric fat baths are safer to use as the temperature is thermostatically controlled, so avoiding the risk of fat fires. Do not allow oil to run down the side on to the dial which will then stick.

▓SHALLOW FRYING

Oil first: When frying with butter, warm a little oil in the pan first, then add the butter, to enable a higher temperature to be used without the butter burning so easily.

Heavy and high: Use a heavy pan if a high temperature is required.

Spoons not knives: Never turn meat or fish with a pointed knife or fork, see page 156.

At the last minute: When turning pieces of food in seasoned flour (flour with a good pinch of salt and pepper) do so *just* before frying or they will stick.

Crisp finish: Add one teaspoon of salad oil to the beaten egg for an egg and breadcrumb coating to give a crisp finish. A teaspoon of milk will also achieve this.

For an even colour: Nick the edges of veal escalopes or gammon rashers so they lie flat in the pan and colour evenly.

Cordon Bleu
TIPS

Clarified butter is excellent for shallow frying as it will brown food evenly but does not burn as easily as ordinary butter since moisture and salt have been removed. To clarify butter, cut into pieces into a saucepan and heat gently until foaming. Remove from the heat, skim well then carefully pour off the clear yellow oil. Leave this to solidify, then discard any remaining liquid or sediment.

Staying crisp: To keep the coating crisp after frying, place the food on a grid in a low oven with the door ajar; and do not cover it once in the serving dish.

Heat penetration: When frying or grilling whole fish, slash once or twice through the thickest part to allow the heat to penetrate.

Preparing liver: Before frying liver, remove the fine outer skin and any ducts or tubes.

A squeeze of lemon: Add a squeeze of lemon juice to mushrooms when frying to bring out the flavour. Fry them quickly and be careful not to overcook.

Lightly smoking: Aubergines will soak up too much oil unless it is shallow and lightly smoking before frying them.

No white line: When frying coated cutlets or noisettes make sure the fat comes half way up the pieces of food to avoid a white line round the middle.

No specks: Always use clean strained oil or fat for frying as crumbs or bits from previous frying sessions will burn and result in unsightly black specks.

Room for manoeuvre: Always leave room for the food to be turned easily in the frying pan.

Brown all over: When shallow frying allow pieces of meat and poultry to seal and brown before turning them over. Only turn once.

Stand first: For light pancakes or crêpes, add a little cold water in place of milk and stand the batter for half an hour or so before making them.

A hot pan: For successful pancakes put a tablespoon of oil or melted butter into the batter and keep the pan very hot all the time.

Thin and even: Tilt the pan round quickly as the batter goes in, to spread it thinly and evenly.

GRILLING

Keep in the juices: Always preheat the grill for about 10 minutes with the grid in place. When the food is placed on the grid it will be sealed quickly and retain its juices.

No sticking: Brush the grid with oil before heating it to prevent food sticking to it.

No salt: Never salt the surface of meat before grilling as salt draws out the juices and meat will not be brown and crisp.

Grilled tomatoes: For tomatoes which have been cut in half, grill skin side first then turn them over and season with salt, pepper and a little sugar. Then grill quickly on the cut side until well coloured.

Even cooking: Seal and brown the food first then lower the grill pan to allow the food to cook through. Lower the pan rather than the heat for even cooking.

Well brushed: Before grilling food brush it with oil or melted butter to protect it and help it to colour.

In the right order: When cooking a mixed grill, begin with the food which takes the longest to cook first.

Kidney lore: To skin kidneys easily, cut them almost in half, then skin and remove the hard white core. Skewer them flat to prevent curling whilst cooking.

Moist kidneys: Grill kidneys skinned side first so they do not look too dry and shrivelled.

Preserving the tail: When grilling whole fish, such as sole or herrings, cover the tail with a piece of foil to prevent it drying and breaking off when serving.

Bare bones: Cover the bare ends of cutlet bones with foil to prevent their burning and looking charred.

Quality pays: Buy really tender pieces of meat for grilling, and firm vegetables such as mushrooms and tomatoes.

Gently does it: Do not prick sausages but cook at a slightly lower temperature than you would normally. Large quantities can be cooked in the oven.

▌BARBECUEING

Large is flexible: A large barbecue is always more useful as it means you can use it for parties or just family meals. If you are only cooking for two, use one end or one side.

Getting it going: Use barbecue firelighters or newspaper to help light the barbecue. Anything else will taint the food.

Safety first: Have a bucket of water at hand to quench the flames if necessary.

See what you're doing: If the barbecue is going to be used in the evening, make sure the area is well lit.

Be prepared: Fresh air makes people hungry – make sure you have plenty of food.

Advance work: Put all the prepared ingredients on to a tray and keep it covered until required for cooking.

Labour-saver: To avoid washing up, buy attractive paper plates, plastic cutlery, paper cups etc.

Non-stick grid: Brush the grid with oil before placing on the food to prevent it from sticking.

Grey heat: Allow at least 30 minutes after lighting before you start to cook on a barbecue. The charcoal should look ash grey with a faint glow, there should never be any flames.

At the right level: Don't place the grid too close to the charcoal, the food burns before it is cooked. Use a foil tray underneath the grid to catch fat and meat juices.

Orderly cooking: Foods that take longest to cook e.g. sausages and some vegetables, should be put on the barbecue first. Fast-cooked foods, such as steaks, can go on last. Allow slightly longer cooking time if the food has just been taken from the refrigerator.

For full flavour: Marinade meat, fish and poultry before grilling on a barbecue to bring out the flavour. Use either salad oil, finely choped onion, lemon juice, garlic and spices or soy sauce with chopped onion and garlic.

Keeping the skin whole: To prevent sausage skins from splitting, put the sausages into cold water, bring to the boil, drain and then cook in the usual way.

Flavour and aroma: Put herbs, such as bay, rosemary, thyme, fennel directly on to the fire while cooking to give an aroma and flavour to barbecued ingredients.

Home-made burgers: Make your own beefburgers using good-quality minced beef, very finely chopped onion, herbs, garlic and seasoning. They would be 2-2.5 cm (¾-1 inch) thick.

Barbecue bake: For delicious barbecued potatoes, scrub them, brush lightly with oil, then roll in salt. Wrap in tin foil and bake in embers for at least 1 hour. To serve, cut a cross in the top of the potato and squeeze to release some steam, then fill. Try butter with lots of fresh herbs or soured cream.

153

Delicious vegetables: Marinaded or plain, aubergines, tomatoes, courgettes and mushrooms wrapped in foil and grilled are full of flavour and moist.

Warmed bread: French bread, brushed with flavoured butter and wrapped in foil, may be heated for 10 minutes on the barbecue.

Tipsy fruit: Bake fruit with a liqueur in foil, for example put orange slices in brandy.

▓ *BOILING*

Rinse first: When boiling milk, first rinse the pan with cold water; this helps to prevent the milk sticking and scorching and it is easier to wash the pan afterwards.

Metal spoon rescue: Put a metal spoon quickly into milk that is about to boil over to break the skin.

Soak it up: After boiling milk, soak the pan in cold water.

The way with vegetables: Green vegetables should be put into boiling salted water and boiled without a lid to give a short cook to keep their colour. Root vegetables should start in cold salted water with a lid on the pan as they need slower cooking and do not discolour.

Bright colour: After boiling and draining, refresh green vegetables with half a cupful of cold water; this checks the cooking process and brightens the colour. Then reheat with melted butter if wished.

Poach pasta: Once pasta has come to the boil, lower the heat and simmer or poach it gently. Do not use a lid.

Separate strands: Add a small spoonful of cooking oil to a pan of pasta to keep the strands separate.

The perfect egg: Eggs should be at room temperature before being hard-boiled. The rounded end of the shell can be pricked with an egg pricker. Plunge the eggs into boiling water then boil gently and time them carefully. Once cooked, cool them quickly in cold water.

Well peeled: If the shells of hard-boiled eggs are difficult to remove, crack them carefully all over with a spoon, then peel off a small piece and hold the egg under running cold water.

Tasty bacon: To make bacon less salty for boiling, soak it in cold water for 12-24 hours. If time is short, put it in a pan of cold water and bring to the boil slowly. Drain, add fresh cold water and any vegetables and commence cooking.

ROASTING

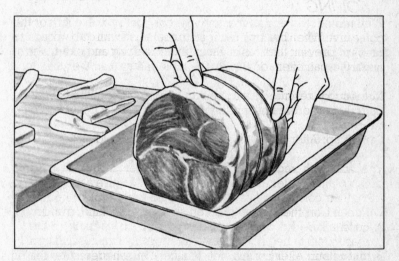

Timing the roast: Before roasting, preheat the oven and check the weight of meat or poultry to determine the time, then add 10 minutes to stand the meat before carving.

Wipe not wash: Do not wash meat before roasting. If necessary wipe it with a damp cloth.

Crisp crackling: Oil and salt sprinkled on to the skin of pork before roasting will give a crisp crackling.

Correct placing: Lay fillet of beef or a duck on a grid in the roasting pan. If no grid is used, stand a joint, such as a round of beef, with two cut sides on its edge to cook rather than flat in the pan.

Pierce a duck: When roasting a duck pierce the skin several times with a skewer to allow excess fat to run out.

The French way: Roast poultry the French way with giblet stock, butter and herbs, to give a moist flesh. This is especially good if the poultry is to be used for a cold dish.

Add onion to gravy: After draining off the surplus dripping from the pan, brown a few slices of onion well before adding flour to thicken the gravy. This helps colour and flavour.

Well turned: Never turn roasting meat or poultry with a fork or the point of a knife. Use two blunt instruments such as tablepoons to prevent piercing and loss of juices, and breaking the golden skin of poultry. It is safer to do this on the table rather than the stove top.

Not too dry: When roasting poultry, cover the breast meat with a butter wrapper for the first 15 minutes to prevent it from becoming too dry.

Cordon Bleu

TIPS

For an evenly browned chicken, roasted to perfection and in good shape for carving, place the bird on its back in the roasting tin to begin with. Baste after twenty minutes and turn on to its side. Once this side is nicely browned, rest on the other side and baste again. Continue cooking until this side browns well, baste and complete the cooking breast side up.

Time is the same: Do not double the time for a long joint, such as beef fillet, as it is of an even thickness throughout.

Avoid toughness: Do not use meat or birds straight from the refrigerator. The meat will take longer to seal and it will be tougher because the juices will run.

Crisp skin: The skin of roasted duck should be nice and crisp. Hang the bird in a draught before cooking for 1-2 hours to achieve this.

Tender duck: To make sure a frozen duck is tender, allow it to defrost for 48 hours in the refrigerator.

Be sure: Make certain all frozen poultry is thoroughly defrosted before cooking otherwise it can be dangerous to eat. Outer parts may appear to be well cooked even though the inside is not.

Flavour for gravy: Meat cooked on the bone has more flavour but if the bones are removed, as when shaping noisettes of lamb, make stock with them for the gravy.

Care with cooking: Do not overcook a best end neck of lamb – judge by thickness rather than weight. Forty to fifty minutes at 200°C, 400°F or Gas Mark 6 is sufficient time.

Baste for best: Baste meat during roasting every 15-20 minutes to keep it succulent and to help with the browning.

Well cooked: Pork should be well cooked and never served even slightly pink. Give it 25 minutes per 450 g (1 lb) and 25 minutes over at 200°C, 400°F or Gas Mark 6.

Moist and juicy: Buy meat for roasting with some fat on it; a moderate amount of fat helps to keep it moist and juicy.

Save time and money: Buy a joint large enough to give a second or third meal. This is more economical on time and money.

Tasty lamb: Roast lamb is delicious with several slivers of garlic inserted into small cuts made in the meat and roasted with a sprig of rosemary in the pan.

Make it tender: Papaya and pineapple juice have a tenderizing effect on raw meat if sprinkled on top and left for a few hours. Alternatively pieces of the fruits can be laid on top of the meat and will serve the same purpose.

Not metal: When using a wine and oil for marinating game, or red meat for braising or roasting, use a deep and narrow container made of glass, earthenware or china but not metal as this taints the flavour of the meat.

▓CASSEROLES AND STEWING

Too salty: If a white stew tastes too salty, add a little more liquid and a lump of butter or 2-3 tablespoons of cream. Two or three large pieces of potato cooked in a brown stew will absorb excess salt.

Easier timing: To cook casseroles in the oven, bring to the boil on top of the stove first then put into a preheated oven. This makes timing easier.

Try ale: Try using half brown ale and half water in place of stock for beef stews. The flavour of the ale is modified by the long slow cooking and mixes with the vegetables and beef juices to form an excellent gravy.

Whole onions: Small pickling or button onions need to be blanched and skinned before adding to a stew. Shave off the root without actually cutting into the onions and they will not break up so easily.

Bigger and better: Try to keep pieces of meat about 5 cm (2 inches) in size. If too small they will be dry and hard.

Quick colour: Before stewing red or dark meats, brown well in 1-2 tablespoons of beef dripping or oil and butter. Colour only a few pieces at a time or heat is lost and they will not colour quickly.

Slowly does it: Allow plenty of time for a stew to cook at a low temperature; cooking it too fast will make it tough.

Prepare blanquettes: For white stews, such as a blanquette of veal or rabbit, soak the meat in cold water with a little salt overnight, then blanch it for a few minutes in fresh water before cooking.

Blanch bacon: If strips of bacon are added, particularly to a white stew, blanch them first for 2-3 minutes. This removes saltpetre used in curing and prevents the pink colour transferring to the white meat. It also reduces the saltiness.

Easy to remove: When using a bouquet garni of fresh herbs in a casserole, tie it to one end of a piece of string, push it well down in the liquid and tie the other end of the string to the handle. The bouquet garni can then easily be removed when the flavour is strong enough.

Saving a stew: If the resulting sauce from a casserole or stew looks thin and greasy, remove the meat and skim and reduce the sauce. If the casserole sauce is well seasoned and reduction is impractical add some butter kneaded with a little flour.

Cordon Bleu

TIPS

There are two types of stew: white and brown. Each has a particular cooking method, which leads to the difference in colour. For a white stew the meat is blanched before cooking to reduce the strong flavours and it is not subsequently browned. It is generally cooked on top of the stove and the liquid is thickened towards the end of cooking. The meat (and vegetables) for a brown stew are browned first then a little flour is added before the stock. It is cooked either on the hob or in the oven.

Improved texture: The texture of a white stew is improved by adding an egg yolk and cream mixture at the end of cooking, but do *not* reboil after this. Use one egg yolk to two tablespoons of cream, mix well and add gradually.

Care with chicken: If joints of chicken are used for a casserole, trim them after cooking. If done before, the flesh shrinks up the remaining bone and hardens.

Use the carcass: When jointing your own bird, lay the leftover carcass on top of the joints in the casserole, then put on the lid. This keeps the pieces down in the sauce and adds flavour. Remove the carcass before serving and add to the leg and wing/bone trimmings with any giblets to make 600 ml (1 pint) or so of stock for later use.

Care with browning: Always allow chicken pieces to brown slowly and well before proceeding with the recipe. Browning a whole chicken may take up to 20 minutes.

Improvization: If you do not have a casserole which can be used on top heat as well as in the oven, brown the ingredients, then make up the rest of the recipe in a frying pan and transfer to the casserole to finish cooking in the oven.

Make a day early: A casserole or stew often benefits from being made the day before and any solidified fat can be removed easily.

Quarter vegetables: Root vegetables for casseroles should be quartered or left in large pieces so they do not disintegrate.

Add vinegar: A few drops of vinegar added to a stew leave no taste but help to tenderize the meat.

Emergency stock: If no stock is available, a tin of consommé diluted is less salty than using stock cubes.

Thick gravy: For an Irish stew, cut up one or two potatoes fairly small and add with the meat. These disintegrate and thicken the gravy.

POACHING

Gently does it: Chickens should be poached, that is gently simmered rather than boiled. Pour in water to come just above the thighs, so the liquid has a concentrated flavour and the breast will cook in the steam. A well-fitting lid is essential.

Chicken check: To check if chicken is cooked, pierce the thick part of the thigh with a trussing needle or a fine skewer. If the juices run clear it is cooked, but if pink in colour it will need more cooking.

Not too much cooking: Do not overcook poached fish as the flesh loses its translucent appearance once cooked. If poaching whole fish you will notice that the eyes turn white when the fish is ready and look slightly raised.

Poaching fish: Use peppercorns rather than ground pepper when seasoning the liquid for poaching; with white fish especially, the appearance can be spoiled with grains of ground pepper. Count the whole peppercorns in and count them out as they sometimes stick under fillets of fish which are being oven poached.

Wine substitute: If white wine is not available for poaching fish or ham, dry cider can be substituted. Lemon juice in water can also be used for fish.

Away with saltiness: When poaching smoked fish use a mixture of milk and water; this will draw out excess saltiness.

Give it backbone: When poaching cutlets or fillets of fish in the oven, cover the fillets with the well-washed backbone if available. If not, use dampened greaseproof paper.

Tender shell fish: Poach any shell fish very gently otherwise they will toughen.

Keep them down: Make sure any flavourings, such as herbs or vegetables, are down in the liquid and not sitting on top of the piece of food being cooked.

Picking brains: To prepare brains for poaching, cup them in one hand and hold under gently running cold water while washing with the other hand and picking off any membrane and dried blood.

Sweet and fruity: Poach pieces of fruit in sugar syrup until tender, then boil briefly so the syrup bubbles up and covers the fruit for a few seconds.

Translucent apples: Poach peeled and quartered dessert apples in sugar syrup. They keep their shape well and can be cooked until they look translucent.

Curves down: If poaching halved round fruit, such as plums or apricots, put them curved side down to cook, then dish them curved side up in a shallow dish.

Long pasta: Do not break long pasta; gather it in one hand and lower it into the simmering water. As it softens, curl it into the pan. Once it is all in stir gently with a fork to make sure none has stuck to the bottom of the pan.

Shells and curves: After draining shell or curved pasta, toss it very gently in the colander to get the water out of the hollows.

161

Hot oil and fresh pepper: After cooking, pasta can be left in the pan just covered with tepid water. When required, drain it well and reheat it with a spoonful or two of hot oil and a little freshly ground black pepper.

Getting ahead: If poaching eggs ahead of time, put them into a shallow dish of cold water once cooked. When needed, replace the cold water with hot water and leave the eggs for a short while to heat through.

Perfectly poached: To poach eggs successfully, put the egg, still in its shell, into hot water just off the boil for 10 seconds. Break it into a small cup and lower carefully into barely simmering water containing a teaspoon of vinegar.

Delicate handling: A potato masher is useful for lifting delicate poached foods and eggs from the liquid and has the advantage that they drain at the same time.

Give them a swirl: When French poaching eggs in deep water, make a whirlpool before lowering in the egg by swirling the water quickly with a spoon. This means the white will swirl round and cling to the yolk for a good shape. Very fresh eggs must be used for this method.

▰STEAMING

Invest in a steamer: If frequently steaming food it is well worth buying a steamer and resisting the temptation to improvize, see also page 130.

Steaming instead of boiling: Many foods which are boiled can be steamed with advantage but it does take longer.

Twice as long: Steaming requires one and a half to twice the time that would be taken to boil food.

Keep boiling: Never allow the water in a steamer to go off the boil.

Replenishing: Watch that the water does not boil away and have near boiling water to hand, which can then be quickly boiled for replenishing.

Keep it gentle: Boil the water for steaming food gently and steadily; too rapid boiling means the water will evaporate quickly and a burned pan may result.

Ready in advance: Always have the steamer ready with the water boiling before the food is put in.

Replace the lid quickly: If the food has to be checked, replace the lid quickly and do not allow condensed steam to drip on to the food.

Direct or covered: Food can be put directly into the steamer (potatoes, for example) or be in a cloth, or in a paper-covered mould or basin.

Good circulation: Do not pack the steamer tightly with food as this prevents the steam circulating.

Season with care: Steamed food is easy to digest but needs careful seasoning.

Steaming fillets or cutlets: A simple form of steaming for fish in fillets or thin cutlets is to put them between two plates which fit over a pan of boiling water.

Grease the basin: Make certain to grease the basin well if making a steamed pudding.

Three at a time: Some steamers have compartments or tiers, so two or three foods can be cooked at once. This is a particularly economical way of cooking.

Cooking in tiers: When a tiered steamer is not available, use a large saucepan with a tight-fitting lid to steam food in a covered bowl. Put two crossed metal skewers under the bowl to prevent it rattling on the bottom of the pan and have the boiling water half way up the bowl. Folded paper can be used under the bowl.

For varying sizes: It is possible to buy a stainless, perforated and collapsible basket for steaming, which is designed to fit into pans of varying sizes. Again a tight lid is essential.

Keep in the nutrients: When steaming vegetables or fruit which are not in a receptacle, be careful not to overcook otherwise valuable nutrients will be lost.

Open and shut case: Shell fish, such as mussels and clams, can be steamed after scrubbing them and checking that none is cracked and that they are all closed. They are cooked when they are well opened. Any that have not opened after cooking must be discarded immediately.

Boiling sausages: Frankfurters and other 'boiling' sausages can be steamed if preferred.

Steam a marrow: Vegetable marrow peeled, cut in good 2.5 cm (1 inch) slices then halved and seeded, steams well and is less watery than when boiled.

Close fit: When making a steamed meat or fruit suet pudding, make sure that the top circle of suet pastry is fitted closely and sealed to the pastry lining the bowl.

Allowing for expansion: Make a pleat in greased greaseproof paper or foil tied over the top of a pudding which is being steamed to allow for expansion.

BAKING CAKES

Prepare for success: Good preparation is half-way to making successful cakes. Set the oven and shelf correctly, then prepare the tin with care and weigh the ingredients accurately, having eggs and fat at room temperature.

White fat: Grease tins with melted white fat because it is better than oil, which may run and seep into the cake, and it contains no residue, as with butter or margarine, which burns easily. Use a brush to grease evenly.

Shelf level: Check oven temperatures for different mixtures; too low and a cake will be soggy and heavy; too high and the crust sets quickly, the cake mixture rises and cracks through the crust. The middle shelf is best for large cakes; put small cakes a little higher.

Whole and light: A piece of fitted greaseproof paper should be placed at the bottom of a cake tin before greasing and then flouring both the base and sides. The cake will then turn out without breaking. A dusting of caster sugar before the flour will result in a crispy sugary crust for very light whisked sponge cakes.

Even dispersement: Sift flour, salt, spices and any raising agent together, to disperse them evenly through a cake mixture.

Where air is needed: Fold in any additions lightly using a metal spoon to cut through the mixture easily. Where air is needed for a light mixture, do not overfold.

Space at the top: Leave about 2 cm (¾ inch) space at the top of the tin to prevent over-flowing on rising.

Avoid rust: After use, wipe tins round carefully, do not scratch the inside surface, and dry before putting away. This is especially important for small moulds which are stacked together to store as they rust easily if damp.

Keep them moist: Do not overcook layer and sponge-type cakes, as they continue to dry out on cooling. Bake to a pale golden brown and they will be moister to eat.

Lighter and lighter: Sponge mixtures made by hand or using a small electric whisk will be lighter if whisked over a pan of steaming water off the heat. Whisk sugar and eggs until your initial can be trailed from the whisk and will 'hold' for a few seconds. The bowl should then be removed from the heat and the mixture whisked until the bowl is cool before adding flour.

No indentation: Sponge cakes, layer and sandwich cakes, should be baked until golden and the cake shrinks in a little from the sides of the tin. When tested with a finger tip, the sponge should spring back, no indentation should remain.

Round-ended knife: Leave cakes to cool for 1-2 minutes before easing round the sides with a round-ended knife to prevent cutting into the cake.

Correct weights: To make a good Victoria sandwich, weigh the eggs in their shells then weigh the butter, caster sugar and self-raising flour, so that each weighs the same as the eggs.

Out with air pockets: Before baking a whisked sponge cake mixure, tap the tin once on the work surface. This settles any air pockets in the bottom of the tin.

For a flat top: When making a creamed cake mixture or a fruit cake, make a slight hollow in the centre before baking. This will then rise evenly in the oven to give a flat top for icing.

Cordon Bleu
TIPS

If a sponge recipe calls for orange flower water but this is not available, grated lemon or orange rind can be substituted. Just the grated rind of half a lemon or small orange is sufficient, otherwise the sponge may be too sticky.

Apricot glaze: Brush a rich fruit cake with warm apricot glaze before covering it with almond paste. This holds down any crumbs and helps the paste to adhere.

Leave overnight: A rich fruit cake need not be baked immediately; the top will be flatter if the mixture is left in the tin overnight in a cool place before cooking.

Softer for soufflés: Whisk egg whites very stiffly for meringues but softer if folding into cake mixtures and soufflés.

Geranium scent: One or two scented geranium leaves put in the bottom of a sponge cake tin gives a lovely flavour to the cake.

Emergency tin: A paper case can be made if a Swiss roll tin is not available. Choose a thick greaseproof or silicone paper. Cut a piece 7.5 cm (3 inches) larger in length and width than the size of cake required, and turn up 4 cm (1½ inches) to form the sides. Fasten each corner with a paper clip or staples and slide on to a baking sheet before filling.

Home-made: Baking powder can be made using 50 g (2 oz) cream of tartar, 50 g (2 oz) finely ground rice and 25 g (1 oz) bicarbonate of soda. Sieve together several times.

Make-your-own self-raising: Two teaspoons of baking powder added to 225 g (8 oz) of plain flour equals self-raising flour.

Grate, don't cut: If the edges of a cake are slightly burnt, grate them with the fine side of a box grater. It gives a neater edge than cutting off the burned pieces.

Close fit: If keeping a cake in a plastic container or biscuit tin which is a close fit, place a strip of foil or doubled greaseproof paper in first with the ends up so the cake can be lifted out easily.

Carry with care: To carry a fragile cake in a container, put the cake on the lid, then cover with the base of the tin or container.

Prevent a gritty texture: If semolina is added to a cake mixture such as Griestorte, leave it to stand 5-10 minutes before completing the recipe; this will prevent a dry and gritty texture.

Crisp shortbread: A mixture of half flour and half rice flour will give a wonderfully crisp shortbread.

Stale crumbs: Stale leftover Madeira or sponge cake crumbs can be frozen and kept for Bakewell or treacle tarts.

Oil the baking tray: Always turn praline (unblanched almonds or hazelnuts cooked in caramel) on to an oiled baking tray or it will be very difficult to chip off.

Keeping powder dry: If praline powder is to be kept for more than a few minutes put it into an airtight jar or tin as it picks up steam and becomes sticky quickly. It can also be stored in a small polythene bag with all the air excluded and tied tightly.

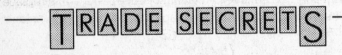

TRADE SECRETS

▧ SAVOURY SENSE

Fluffy long grains: Use a long-grain rice for curries where it needs to be light and fluffy. Time it exactly and refresh it with hot water to prevent sticking.

Garlic contained: Keep a special small board, or use a square of greaseproof paper on the chopping board, to crush garlic with salt under the round end of a palette knife. This way you will avoid spreading a garlic taste to other foods that have to be chopped. This is quicker than a garlic crusher and needs less washing up.

Green peppercorns: If using green peppercorns in a casserole or with fried food, they are best lightly crushed and added about 10 minutes before the end of cooking.

Minimum of flour: When rolling pastry use a minimum of flour and brush off any excess or it will be too dry and harden on baking.

Easy shape: Add a teaspoon of gelatine dissolved in a little water to croquette mixtures before chilling. Shaping will be easier and the gelatine will not be tasted once the croquettes are cooked.

Volatile alcohol: Always warm alcohol to make it volatile before flaming, but do not overheat it.

Special touch: Add a few spoonfuls of Hollandaise sauce to make fish or chicken dishes a little special.

Butter to the rescue: To prevent skin forming on a savoury sauce, press a piece of buttered greaseproof paper, or a butter wrapper, lightly on the surface. If the sauce is to be used shortly a few dots of butter on the surface will have the same effect.

Cling film solution: Cling film can be pressed on to the surface of sauces to prevent a skin forming. If the sauce fills a large bowl, just peel the film back, remove the amount of sauce needed and replace the cling film.

Cordon Bleu
Tips

Leave pancake batter to stand for 30 minutes before using it. This process softens the starch cells so that the pancakes are thin but not tough.

Yolk and cream: Do not try to keep a sauce for long after a yolk and cream liaison has been used; it is better to add it at the last minute.

Slaked arrowroot: When freezing sauces, thicken with slaked arrowroot as they are less likely to separate on thawing.

Plenty of sauce: Make plenty of sauce when freezing casseroles or stews as there never seems to be sufficient when reheating.

Stock to hand: Make your own stock cubes by reducing stock well, then freeze in ice-cube trays, put into bags and into the deep freeze.

Allow for browning: Onions brown quicker than the other vegetables when cooking them for a brown sauce, so cut them a little larger to allow for this.

Salsify: The easiest way to deal with salsify or scorzonera is to scrub it well then boil for about 50 minutes before peeling off the skin. It can be served with butter and lemon juice.

Bitter shoots: If garlic begins to sprout remove the green shoot as it can be bitter.

Remedy for too much salt: If soup is too salty, add rice or small pastry shapes and complete the cooking.

Hot soufflés: Slightly over-season a soufflé mixture for hot soufflés.

Chopped eggs: To chop hard-boiled eggs use a stainless knife or crush them with a fork. They can also be sliced in an egg slicer then turned the other way and sliced again.

Fish pâté: Cold leftover fish can be pounded, or put in a food processor with curd cheese, anchovy essence and seasoning to taste. This can be used as a fish pâté for a fish course or as a filling for sandwiches.

Non-stick meat: Wet your rolling pin or meat batten before using to beat out meat. It will stop the meat from sticking.

A soft roux: When making a flour and butter roux have the butter weight on the heavy side; this will give a soft roux which blends easily into the liquid.

Freezing separates: Never freeze mayonnaise or sauces made from it as it will separate.

Frozen kneaded butter: Freeze or refrigerate kneaded butter (see page 332) in small individual foil containers in a polythene bag. Use frozen or thawed, whisking in as usual.

Holding its shape: Really light raw minced meat mixtures are bound together with breadcrumbs made from bread which is 2-3 days old soaked in milk or water. Squeeze the bread, then beat in with one hand adding a few more spoonfuls of the liquid until the mixture will only just hold shape. The mixing can also be completed in an electric mixer or food processor. This mixture is used for meat balls.

Criss-cross pattern: When roasting a piece of loin or best end neck of lamb, score the fat into a criss-cross lattice pattern to form diamonds about 2.5 cm (1 inch) across. This allows excess fat to drain away during cooking and leaves an attractive pattern.

When to cut sausages: Do not cut sausages apart before frying; curl the string of sausages around the pan and cut when three quarters cooked. This will prevent the meat from spilling out.

Metal for curries: Use metal or plastic spoons to stir curries, as wooden ones will become stained by the spices.

Stitched up: When sewing up meat or poultry, for example in a galantine, use long loose stitches and no knots as the flesh shrinks during cooking and the skin will tear. This also makes it easier to remove the string, pull it steadily and gently in one movement.

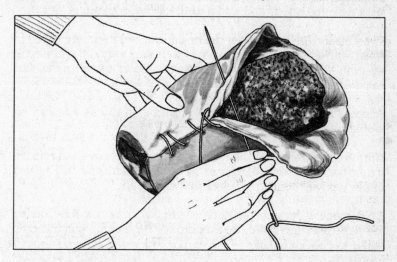

Fine silver skin: When roasting beef fillet, remove the fine silver skin first because the short cooking time is not long enough to soften this skin.

Save time: Roll pastry for sausage rolls in one long strip, fit on the roll of sausage meat, fold the pastry over, seal and then cut into individual sausage rolls. This saves a lot of time.

Fuel saver: Freeze chicken carcasses, adding to them until there are enough to make a large panful of stock; this saves fuel.

The right amount of salt: Too much salt in a bread dough kills the yeast, and too little means the dough will rise too quickly.

Care with yeast: Too much sugar or a cold atmosphere retards the growth of yeast.

SWEET SUCCESS

Topping for a fruit pie: For a glazed crispy top to a fruit pie, five to seven minutes before the baking is finished, brush it with lightly beaten egg white, dust well with caster sugar and return to the oven.

Too much juice: If, when preparing a melon, it is very juicy, sieve the juice from the seeds and add it to dressings or syrups.

Sweetmeats: Any citrus peel can be cut into strips and simmered in water with a pinch of bicarbonate of soda until very soft. Then cook again in a sugar syrup until transparent. Cool, toss in granulated sugar and serve as a sweetmeat.

Scissors for topping and tailing: It is helpful to use scissors for topping and tailing gooseberries.

Not too dark: Use a small heavy pan for making caramel and remove it from the heat before it reaches the required dark colour. The heat of the pan will continue to darken it slowly.

Cold check: If caramel has darkened and is in danger of becoming too dark, and thus bitter, quickly dip the base of the pan into cold water to check cooking.

Caramel dissolved: Leave a crème caramel some hours, or overnight, before turning it out; this will dissolve the caramel so very little will be left in the mould.

No scraping: After making caramel mixtures in a pan or mould, fill the pan with very hot water; never scrape or use a knife as this will scratch the metal.

Water to caramel: Add a saltspoon of water to caramel after making it and before pouring it into the mould for a Caramel Custard; this will help more of the caramel to come away once the caramel is turned out.

Ways with caramel: Pour caramel on to an oiled tray to cool and set, then crack it into small pieces to sprinkle on poached fruit or ice cream. It goes well with oranges and will shine like amber. Broken even finer, it can be used to decorate the sides of a gâteau.

To counteract a wet flan base try the following. You need two baking sheets. Place one in your oven preheated as specified in the recipe and leave it to heat through, then place the second baking sheet containing the flan into the oven on top of the heated one. The effect of this arrangement is to direct additional heat to the base of the flan helping to make it crisp.

Even surface: Brush a very small amount of cold water over the surface of fruit cakes before baking. This will give a smooth and even surface.

Plain topping: Keep a little plain cake mixture aside to spread thinly over the top of a fruit cake before baking; this prevents any fruit poking up and burning.

Custard is lighter: Fill sandwich cakes, or a gâteau, with half cold thick custard and half whipped cream for a lighter filling. Whisk the custard as it cools to keep it smooth.

A better rising: Use soured milk or buttermilk when making oven scones or drop scones to give a better rising.

No moisture: Do not allow any moisture to drop into melted chocolate you are spreading thinly to cut into shapes; it will make it thicken and become tacky.

Gentle heat for chocolate: Use very gentle heat when melting chocolate, either on a plate or in a bowl set over a pan of gently steaming water off the stove. It can also be melted in a microwave oven on the defrost cycle. 100 g (4 oz) will take about 2½ minutes.

Cream of tartar: A pinch of cream of tartar added to the egg whites being whisked for meringues makes them stable.

For sugar syrups: Add a pinch of cream of tartar slaked in water to sugar syrups to help to prevent crystallization.

Do not stir: When making sugar syrups or fondant icing do not stir the sugar while it is dissolving.

Cold water and ice: Add some cold water to the pieces of ice when using them round a metal pan or bowl to chill mixtures.

No guessing: Do not guess at the amount of sugar when making ices: too much sugar prevents a cream or water ice freezing firmly and too little means the ice will be grainy and rough in texture.

Perfect for the freezer: Rounds of meringue, and sponge cakes, sandwiched with whipped double cream freeze perfectly.

Doubling up: Double or treble a good basic creamed cake mixture and make two or three cakes with different additions. Deep-freeze the ones not needed.

Vanilla sugar: Make your own vanilla sugar by putting one or two vanilla pods, cut in pieces as necessary, into a jar of caster sugar. Leave 2-3 weeks. Fill up the jar with sugar when necessary as the flavour lasts well.

Prevent skin: Dust sweet sauces, such as chocolate or custard, with caster sugar to prevent a skin forming. Stir in just before serving.

Alcohol prevents freezing: Too much alcohol in the mixture prevents ices freezing.

Blackcurrant leaf water ice: Washed young blackcurrant leaves make a beautiful infusion in a syrup for a water-ice.

Smooth sorbet: If you do not have an ice-cream churn, 1 teaspoon of melted gelatine added to 1.2 litres (2 pints) of liquid makes freezing easier for a sorbet or ice-cream mixture. You should find that it will be smoother.

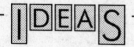

SAVOURY AND SWEET IDEAS

Marmalade for flans: For apple or orange flans sieved marmalade can take the place of, or be added to, apricot glaze.

Raspberry for redcurrant: Sieved raspberry jam can be used instead of redcurrant jelly for everyday use.

Lemon meringue pie: To prevent a lemon meringue pie from becoming weepy, let it cool for several minutes so that a skin forms on the filling before the meringue is put on. Make sure the meringue touches the edges of the pastry.

Puff shapes: To keep the shape of puff pastry or flaky pastry tartlets use a square or round piece of bread in the base. This also soaks up any fat.

Prevent dark lines: Cool boiled eggs quickly in cold water to prevent a dark line round the yolk.

Clear fruit sauces: Use slaked arrowroot to thicken clear fruit sauces and only boil for a few seconds after adding it.

Good fire-lighters: Dry any citrus fruit skins, after serving grapefruit for instance, in the oven. They make very good fire-lighters.

A way with rhubarb: Rhubarb which is poached with a little grated orange rind, sugar and a good spoonful of redcurrant jelly tastes really delicious.

Better shaped éclairs: To give piped éclairs a better shape at the ends, hold a knife above the pipe and pull the pipe up against the edge of the knife.

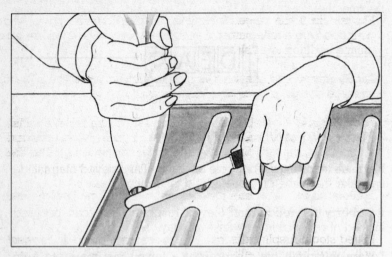

Add some flavour: Reserve a few bacon rinds and any trimmings of mushroom stalks to add to chicken stock for flavour.

Fine solution: If onions are required to be finely chopped, it is easier to grate them into the ingredients or over the pan.

Citrus flavour: Caster sugar can be flavoured with thin dried strips of lemon, orange or tangerine peel.

Juicy lamb: Try roast lamb cooked with 25 g (1 oz) of butter and the juice of half an orange, plus a sprig of rosemary cooked in the roasting tin, see also page 157.

Keeping a good colour: Do not trim the root or leaves of raw beetroot before boiling or it will 'bleed' and be pale in colour.

Fresh horseradish: Keep a root of freshly grated horseradish fresh by moistening well with vinegar and adding a pinch of salt, pepper and dry mustard. Keep in a screw top jar in the refrigerator. Add this to whipped cream to serve with roast beef.

Top with cheese: Grated cheese sprinkled on top of a savoury sauce made with milk stops a skin forming. Use this only where the flavour is acceptable.

Flavour for a fish sauce: Shells from freshly cooked prawns well pounded with a little butter, then sieved, make a flavoursome last minute addition to a fish sauce.

Lamb gravy: Add one teaspoon of redcurrant jelly and a good squeeze of orange juice to a lamb gravy.

For fish stock: The well-washed backbone and cleaned head of fish after filleting will make a good fish stock for fish sauces, aspic and soups. Only simmer it for 20 minutes or the stock will be bitter. The stock freezes well.

Mellow curry: A hot curry sauce will mellow if cooked the day before it is eaten.

Jellied stock: A split calf's foot, pig's trotter or a piece of cow-heel will make beautiful jellied stock, as will scalded and skinned chickens' feet added to the stock pot.

For a first course: Use a ball scoop to shape melon for a first course, then mix together a little ginger syrup plus lemon juice to pour over as a dressing.

Canapés and savouries: Make small choux puffs and fill them with a savoury creamy mixture. These make interesting cocktail savouries or canapés.

Sugar for mint: Use a sprinkling of granulated sugar when chopping mint to prevent it sticking to the knife.

Sherry to preserve: Once peeled green ginger can be kept in a small jar of sherry to preserve it. This method is also suitable for keeping fresh chillies.

A delicious dish: Soft-boiled eggs served on top of a rice salad and coated with mayonnaise make an unusual and delicious dish. The yolk soaks into the rice and makes it creamy and moist to eat.

Boiled instead of poached: Soft-boiled eggs given 4½ minutes can often take the place of poached eggs in a recipe.

Scale removing: When scaling fish use the flat edge of the knife and scrape from tail to head against the way the scales lie.

Getting a grip: To grip slippery fish put a little salt on your fingers.

Well-fed mussels: To plump mussels, buy them a few hours early and keep in cold water with a spoonful of fine oatmeal on which they can feed.

Better taste: Poach white fish in a court bouillon rather than water. The flavour will be improved enormously and a little of the liquid can be used in the sauce for the fish, or kept and used again.

Keep in shape: If freezing a large whole fish that has been gutted, stuff the cavity with freezer paper to help the fish keep its shape.

A personal touch: If using bought sausagemeat for sausage rolls, or as a stuffing, add a personal touch by including finely chopped onion cooked in butter and a pinch of herbs.

Tasty kebabs: Use trimmings of raw lamb, such as pieces remaining after shortening cutlets for kebabs, and marinate in oil and herbs overnight. Skewer with small blanched onions, small whole mushrooms and pieces of green pepper.

Whisky instead of brandy: Try using whisky instead of brandy for a change in some meat or poultry dishes.

Interesting pudding: A few sliced almonds and quartered glacé cherries give added interest to a bread and butter pudding.

Home-made lemon curd: A jar of home-made lemon curd will keep two weeks in the refrigerator. It is useful for filling cakes either alone or mixed lightly into whipped cream. It tastes better than the manufactured item.

Cinnamon chocolate: Stir a cup of hot chocolate with a cinnamon stick for a subtle extra flavour.

Out with specks: To avoid specks of chocolate when melting in a quantity of milk, add it to only a small amount of liquid and warm to a smooth texture before adding the rest of the milk.

Cordon Bleu

TIPS

In summer it is useful to have a quantity of ready-made apricot glaze to hand as a coating for fresh fruit tarts. It keeps well in a covered jar. To make your own you need 1 × 450 g (1 lb) jar of apricot jam, the juice of half a lemon, and 4 tablespoons of water. Put all the ingredients in a saucepan, bring slowly to the boil and simmer for five minutes. Strain the liquid, return to the cleaned pan and boil for five minutes. Cool, then pour into a jam jar and cover.

Caster in a hurry: If you run out of caster sugar, grind some granulated in a blender until fine enough.

Soft cherries: If glacé fruits have hardened in their box, soak them briefly in a little hot water before chopping for use in cakes.

Ice crusher: A food processor can be used to make crushed ice.

Clean baking dish: Wipe the edge of a dish which has been splashed before baking. After baking, a damp cloth and a little salt will remove stubborn marks.

Butter first: Lightly butter the inside of a flameproof dish which is to be used to bake food in the oven. It will be much easier to serve the food and also to wash up the dish.

Useful liqueurs: A few bottles of miniature liqueurs are useful to have in a kitchen for use as handy flavourings.

Prevent mould: If your storage place for jams is slightly damp, run a teaspoon of warmed golden syrup evenly across the top, tilting the jar, before putting on the top covers. This helps to prevent mould.

▓VEGETABLES

Soft pulses: A pinch of bicarbonate of soda added to the cooking water will help to soften pulses. Do not add salt to the cooking water but season after cooking.

Thin-skinned: Save waste by using a vegetable peeler to remove the skins of potatoes and carrots thinly. The skins of turnips and swedes should be peeled thickly with a knife to get below the 'woody line'.

Skinning tomatoes: To skin tomatoes without softening the surface, dip them into fast-boiling water for 8-10 seconds then put immediately into cold water.

Sugar for flavour: Add a pinch of sugar to all tomato dishes, especially when not in season. This improves the flavour, particularly for soups, sauces and salads.

Seeds away: When preparing tomatoes, the seeds can be removed into a nylon strainer. The juice can then be added to the dish or kept and added to a dressing, soup or sauce.

Soft but not broken: If boiled potatoes begin to break up before they are cooked, drain off the water leaving about 4 cm (1½ inches) in the bottom of the pan; cover and cook slowly until soft.

Crusty potatoes: After par-boiling potatoes for roasting, scratch them criss-cross with a fork; then baste with hot fat and roast in a hot oven. This makes them really brown and deliciously crusty to eat.

Floury not sticky: After draining boiled potatoes, return them to the heat for a few seconds to dry; this keeps them floury and not sticky.

Potato purée: When making potato purée or mashed potato the milk and butter to be added should be warmed together, then beaten in over the heat to prevent the purée being grey and sticky.

Baked potatoes: When baking potatoes, choose even sizes and while still damp from scrubbing them rub in a little salt. When baked cut a cross on top and squeeze open to take the butter.

Mushrooms with care: Cultivated mushrooms need not be peeled; just shorten the stalks if they are too long and brush or wipe away any fibre. If slicing, cut through the stalks as well; this prevents the pieces shrinking and losing shape.

French or runner beans: Cook them quickly then toss them in a little melted butter and freshly ground black pepper. If you grow yellow ones as well they look good combined with the green.

Keep mushrooms tender: Fry mushrooms quickly in bacon fat or butter and oil; do not overcook or they will be tough and hard.

Improving the flavour of peppers: To skin red peppers, split them in half, remove the white core and seeds, flatten them with the hand and rub the skin side with oil. Place close to a preheated grill until the skin has blackened. Cool and the skin will rub off easily. This also improves the flavour.

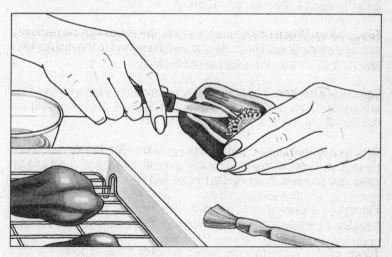

No tears: If peeling onions makes you cry, breathe through your mouth, have the extractor fan on and never rub your eyes with onion on your hand. Peeling them under running cold water also helps.

Clean hands: After preparing garlic or onions, wash your hands in cold water with a little salt; this removes the oil and smell.

Par-boil onions: If peeling more than one or two small onions, put them into cold water then boil for 2-3 minutes. They will then skin easily and are slightly softened ready for their final cooking.

Root last: When peeling onions, remove the root last, trimming it carefully and cutting it flush with the onion, otherwise the onion will fall apart while being sliced or chopped.

Prevent cuts: When chopping or slicing onions large or small, halve them first then place the cut side flat on the board; this way they cannot roll and you are less likely to cut yourself.

Watercress wilt: Watercress wilts very quickly. If the leaves are drying and curling, put it, leaves down, in a bowl of cold water in a cool place for 2-3 hours.

Save the stalks: Good firm watercress stalks can be snipped into a salad or used with a sandwich filling.

Versatile ratatouille: When making ratatouille, make extra as it keeps well for a few days; then serve it with French dressing as a first course, or use it for an omelette filling.

Sugar not salt: Do not salt the water when boiling corn on the cob, but add a pinch of sugar. Really young corn should only need 5-6 minutes boiling.

Nourishing vegetable water: Do not over-salt the water when boiling vegetables, such as leeks, onions, carrots or celery, then save the water for soups and gravies. It has more flavour and nourishment than water.

Scissors for chives: Use scissors to snip chives; they should not be chopped with a knife as they go mushy.

Bayleaf for cauliflower: Add a piece of bayleaf to cauliflower when cooking and boil it gently to prevent it smelling strongly.

Moisture-free and tasty: Fresh spinach, after cooking, should be well drained and pressed between two plates. This will remove most of the excess moisture. The butter for warming it through must be hot and seasoned well with salt, pepper and a few grains of grated nutmeg. A little lemon juice can be added for flavour. A salad spinner, if available, also removes moisture very efficiently.

Buy more: Spinach needs to be washed well as it can be gritty with sand. It shrinks on cooking so buy more than you think you need – 225 g (8 oz) per person.

Crisp celery: Celery for a salad should be well cleaned and then soaked in iced water for up to 2 hours. Dry in a tea-towel before use.

Buttered vegetables: When cooking prepared vegetables in butter alone, that is 'sweating', cover them with buttered paper and a tight lid and put on low heat. This keeps the steam down on the vegetables and softens them.

Subtle garlic: Garlic can be simmered in a little water for 10 minutes then pushed through a strainer to give a less strong flavour.

Rub the bowl: For a subtle flavour of garlic, rub the salad bowl with a cut clove of garlic and squeeze it as you rub.

Right for rice: Wash rice with cold water in a strainer before boiling. To keep it white, add a slice of lemon or a squeeze of juice to the well-salted water and do not overcook it. Rinse thoroughly with hot water after draining in a colander to remove excess starch; leave to drain until dry. Turn into a well buttered dish closely covered with foil to reheat in the oven.

Grains apart: Have plenty of salted water and no lid on the pan when boiling rice by the western method. A small spoonful of oil helps to prevent it clogging.

Stop them floating: To stop globe artichokes from floating while being cooked, place a colander on top of them.

Sweet sorrel: If you can obtain sorrel use it like spinach. The young tender leaves are good in salads.

Care with tins: When opening a heated tin of food, cover all but the cutting area with a cloth in case it spurts and burns you.

No watery pool: Wash all salad leaves carefully then dry them well by patting in a dry tea-towel. This way the dressing will cling to the leaves and not form a watery pool in the bottom of the bowl.

Buttered carrots: Finish sliced cooked carrots with a nut of butter, a little chopped mint and a sprinkle of brown sugar. Small whole carrots are attractive this way.

Good soup: Use fresh green pea pods for soup, together with any older peas and a sliced onion. They make a surprisingly good soup if flavoured with mint and finished with a spoonful of cream.

Mange tout peas: These pods, sometimes called sugar peas, are sweet and delicious. Cook them for a few minutes in fast boiling water and serve hot with melted butter or cold with French dressing and sprinkle over a little chopped mint.

Waste not: Never waste leftover food; a small amount can often be added to a soup, salad or sandwich filling.

Beetroot with beef: Diced or coarsely grated cooked beetroot is delicious heated in a little butter with salt, freshly ground black pepper, a good pinch of sugar and a spoonful of vinegar to taste. Serve it with beef or minced beef rissoles.

Brighten up marrow: Marrow can be dreary if plain boiled, but try it cut in strips with fried onion, paprika, salt and pepper. Add dill seeds and 2-3 spoonfuls of vinegar, then cover and simmer until tender.

Welcome change: Vegetable creams make a welcome change from the more usual methods of cooking and are worth the small amount of trouble involved.

Popular red cabbage: Red cabbage is excellent cooked with a sharp sliced apple and onion; add a little sugar and dill seed and sharpen with vinegar. It is popular if served with rich meats and deserves to be made more often.

Broccoli and asparagus: Scrape the coarse part of the stalks of broccoli and asparagus to remove the fibrous layer before cooking.

Cooking asparagus: Tie asparagus into bundles and cook in an oval casserole if there is no other suitable container. A sprig of mint can be added to the water which may be useful for vegetable soups.

Asparagus plus: To make even more of asparagus either add chopped hard-boiled egg to the melted butter or accompany the buttery asparagus with a hot hard-boiled egg for each person.

Free cabbage leaves: If cabbage leaves are wrapped tightly round the cabbage but are wanted for Dolmas or for lining a basin for stuffed cabbage, dip the whole cabbage, stalk up, in boiling water for a minute and the leaves will peel off easily without tearing.

Cucumber crisp: A piece of charcoal in the water will help to keep cucumber firm and celery crisp.

A head of celery: Keep the bottom of a head of celery, trim it and use to flavour stocks, or grate and add to celery soup.

Preparing aubergines: Sliced aubergines should be lightly sprinkled with salt, left for at least half an hour and patted dry before cooking.

Mashed aubergine: For mashed aubergine, wrap it in oiled greaseproof paper or foil and bake it slowly to give a good flavour.

Extra flavour: Frozen prawns and pieces of lobster will have their flavour improved if they are sprinkled lightly with salt and a little black pepper and lemon juice while being defrosted.

Crisp sauté potatoes: For really crisp sauté potatoes, add cut up freshly boiled and skinned potatoes to hot oil and butter.

Cabbage salad: Shred cabbage for salad as finely as possible, then add some plumped raisins, diced polished red apple and caraway seeds in a yogurt dressing.

▓FRUIT AND NUTS

Fresh strawberries: Rinse strawberries quickly, then drain well before removing the green hull otherwise they can become very soft and unattractive.

Cleaning a grater: Use a small stiff brush to remove grated citrus peel from a grater.

Bitter pith: Always grate citrus peel finely, avoiding the bitter white pith. Use a finely serrated edged knife and a short scraping action.

Cherry pips: Use the tip of a potato peeler to remove the stones from cherries neatly.

Grape pips: To pip green grapes and leave them whole, unravel a paper clip and use the smallest loop to extract the pips. Skin the grapes first.

Peeled apples: Never leave peeled apples in a bowl of cold water, they lose flavour and absorb water. It is better to leave peeling until just before they are needed.

Cores and peels: When cooking apples, reserve the peel and cores, just cover with cold water and simmer with a lid for 20 minutes. Use for poaching any fruit in place of water, or add sugar and reduce to a syrup for glazing.

Brandy peel: Keep finely grated rind of orange or lemon peel in a small screw-top glass jar. If about two-thirds of its volume in caster sugar is added with a little brandy it keeps well and can be used to flavour cakes and puddings.

Wash well: Wash all fruit well before eating raw or cooking it. Apart from spray residue, it has probably been handled several times.

Maximum juice: Put refrigerated lemons into hot water for a few minutes before squeezing as this will help to extract the maximum amount of juice.

Lemon drops: If only a few drops of lemon juice are needed, pierce the lemon with a fine skewer or a thick darning needle to save cutting it.

Cold tea: Soak dried fruit, such as prunes or figs, in cold, strained leftover tea, then cook them in the same liquid. This will help bring out the flavour of the fruit.

To plump and soften: Soak dried fruit for cakes and puddings in a spoonful or two of brandy, rum or sherry to plump and soften it. Failing these, use cold tea or fruit juice.

Better taste: A Seville orange has more character and flavour than a sweet orange and if possible, should be used for flavouring a savoury dish or sauce.

Frozen orange: Seville oranges have only a short season, but freeze well if wrapped individually in foil.

Sugar and peel syrup: If using sugar syrup for a fruit salad, flavour it with a thin strip or two of lemon or orange peel; it should be a thickish syrup as the fruit juices will dilute it.

Ginger syrup: Make good use of the syrup left from a jar of stem ginger: add a spoonful or two when poaching or stewing apples, pears or rhubarb. A little can be added to a fruit jelly or put on top of halved grapefruit and then grilled.

Bananas last: If bananas are sliced about 1 cm (½ inch) thick they are less likely to discolour in fruit salads; leave them until last and prepare as late as possible.

Quince for flavour: If you can get them, a few slices of quince added to an apple pie give a delicious flavour; and try whole quinces baked like apples.

Boiling chestnuts: To skin chestnuts easily, score them with a sharp knife on the rounded side and boil them for 1-2 minutes a small handful at a time. Take one or two out and remove both skins at once, leaving the remaining chestnuts in the water to keep hot.

Lemon for bilberries: When cooking bilberries (blueberries) or making a pie with them, a good squeeze of lemon juice develops their flavour.

Passion fruit salad: Cut the top from passion fruit as you would with a boiled egg and scoop out the pulp with a teaspoon. One or two are sufficient to flavour fruit salad, or add to whipped cream.

Quick to ripen: A ripe banana put into a bag with under-ripe fruit, such as avocados, peaches or plums, will make them ripen more quickly.

Baking apples: Always pierce the skin or make a shallow cut right round the circumference when baking apples whole otherwise the steam pressure from within will break through and spoil the shape.

To skin a peach: Peaches can be skinned by dropping each one into boiling water for 10-15 seconds then putting into cold water.

Colourful mousse: Be sure to use the greatest part of the avocado nearest the skin when making a mousse or avocado dip as this will improve the colour.

Rind for apricots: Add a few strips of thin lemon or orange rind when poaching or stewing prunes, apples or apricots.

Succulent sauce: For a strawberry, raspberry or peach sauce, liquidize and sieve the fruit through a nylon strainer, then sweeten and thicken with sieved icing sugar and add a squeeze of lemon juice to sharpen the flavour.

Lemon to the rescue: Prevent pale fruits discolouring by brushing them with lemon juice as soon as they are cut or peeled.

Off with their stalks: To remove black or redcurrants quickly from their stalks, run the stalk through the prongs of a fork.

Ripe enough to peel: If peaches seem ripe enough to peel without blanching, rub them with the back of a knife to loosen the skin before peeling.

Brittle almonds: If almonds are dry and brittle, soak them in boiling water for 5-10 minutes before grinding or shredding.

To grate almonds: A small cheese mill or coffee grinder will grate almonds efficiently.

Roasted hazelnuts: To roast and grind hazelnuts, put them on a baking tray in a moderate oven until they are toasted and the skins split. Rub them in a coarse cloth and be sure they are cool before grinding.

Apples and pears: Use a potato peeler round and round to peel apples, and from base to top to peel pears.

Central core: Stamp out the central core from a slice of pineapple with a small plain pastry cutter.

Halving plums: To halve plums, apricots and peaches neatly, follow the natural indented line, cut right round and twist the halves in opposite directions.

Remove after cooking: Stones from 'clingstone' varieties of plums and peaches are difficult to get out, so remove them after cooking.

Peeling a lychee: Pinch the skin of fresh lychees until it cracks. This makes them easier to peel.

Loss of fragrance: Do not prepare mangoes until ready to use as the flesh loses its fragrance quickly.

Vitamin C: Virtually all fruits contain vitamin C but the highest concentration is found in guava and kiwi fruits.

How to cut a mango: Cut a mango into two slices horizontally against the stone, remove and cut each fleshy piece into cubes, then remove from the skin.

Cover a melon: Cut a ripe melon in half, remove the seeds with the handle of a tablespoon and cut into portions. Never put melon into a refrigerator unless well covered as the smell quickly pervades other food.

Poisonous leaves: Never use rhubarb leaves as they are poisonous.

Rhubarb for chutney: Use the coarse stems of rhubarb to make chutney.

Red juices: Leftover red juices from bottled fruit can be used for fruit sauces or added to a red fruit compote.

PASTRY

Keep cool: The best conditions for making pastry are when the kitchen is cool.

Light and airy: Only rub the fat into the flour with a light backwards and forwards movement of the fingertips and lift the mixture above the bowl to aerate it and keep it cool.

White is light: For lighter pastry add a proportion of white fat to the butter or margarine. Use lard or one of the white commercial vegetable fats.

Adding a yolk: An egg yolk makes for richer pastry but mix it with a spoonful or two of water when adding, otherwise the yolk will appear as hard yellow specks after baking.

Roll out to relax: Wrap and chill pastry for 10-15 minutes before rolling out to 'relax' it. It will then be easier to roll evenly and it will keep its shape better. Chill briefly again after shaping.

Rising to the occasion: Put any pastry which needs to rise well on to dampened trays, e.g. puff pastry, flaky pastry and choux paste.

Plain for pastry: Use plain flour for pastry making and add a good pinch of salt for flavour.

To add sweetness: For sweet dishes add 1-2 teaspoons of caster sugar to each 225 g (8 oz) flour after the fat has been rubbed in.

Hint for summer: During warm weather, if using a food processor to make shortcrust pastry, cut the fat into 1 cm (½ inch) pieces and chill in the deep freeze for 5 minutes before adding to the flour.

Last of the liquid: Pastry can be wetter than it looks so try to bring it together with one hand then add the last of the liquid if needed.

Blind baking: Tissue paper rather than greaseproof paper or foil will crumple easily and damage the pastry far less when preparing a pastry case for baking blind.

Stones and crusts: Cherry or plum stones boiled then rinsed and dried make a good filling for baking blind. Rice grains are too small and tend to stick. Broken crusts of bread can also be used.

Cool for the jar: Make sure that 'baking blind beans', or fruit stones, are dry and cold before returning them to their jar.

Drying out: After baking a pastry case 'blind' and removing the filling, return to the oven briefly to dry out.

191

Side supports: Whatever is used for baking blind should be packed high at the sides of the flan to support them. The centre only requires a single layer.

Prick the lining: Prick the pastry once or twice with a fork when lining flan rings, tartlet or boat-shaped moulds.

Keeping a good shape: Always pile up the pieces or slices of fruit for a fruit pie in the centre of the dish. It will create a good shape for the pastry on top.

Upper crust: Sugar only between the layers of fruit; if sugar is put on top of the fruit it makes the underside of the top crust soggy.

Inside glazing: When putting fruit into a pastry flan or tartlet cases, glaze the inside of the cooked case beforehand and make sure the fruit is not too wet. Then glaze thoroughly over the fruit. This will seal the pastry and fruit and prevent sogginess.

No stretch: Never stretch pastry as it tends to shrink a little on baking and allowance should always be made for this.

A good finish: Glaze pastry with egg or milk before baking. An attractive finish is made by brushing the pastry with water and then sprinkling with caster sugar. This dries and flakes during baking.

Glazing additions: When using a beaten egg to glaze pastry, add a few drops of water and a pinch of salt.

Simple things first: It is advisable to learn to make the simple pastries, such as shortcrust and rich shortcrust, before tackling the richer pastries. This will help to develop a feeling for pastry-making and enable you to work quickly.

The right heat: Bake pastry at the correct temperature for its type. As a general rule the richer the pastry the higher the temperature.

Success story: It is not necessary to put your hands under running cold water before making pastry. Use only the tips of the fingers, chilled water and, above all, speed in mixing the pastry and the result will be successful.

To line a ring: When lining a flan ring, roll the pastry 2 cm (¾ inch) larger than the ring so that it will slip in without creasing. Then fit neatly into the angle at the base with a small ball of pastry, and bring in the edge a little before trimming.

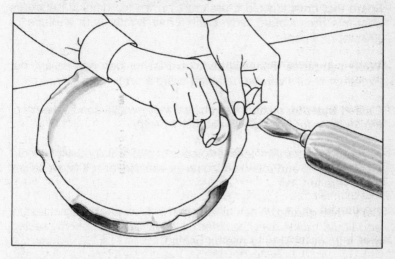

Flan removal: Make sure a flan ring moves freely before removing it and twist as you lift it to avoid breaking the edges.

No turning: Never turn pastry over when rolling it as it will only pick up more flour and become dry. Turn it round as you roll to prevent it sticking and only flour the pin lightly.

Parallel roll: Keep the rolling pin parallel to yourself all the time; if turned at angles across the pastry it will apply uneven pressure.

Cut away: Trim a pie dish or pie plate pastry with the knife turning away from the edge to avoid cutting the pastry short or encouraging it to shrink.

Roll and trim: It is quicker when trimming to roll a rolling pin across the tops of small tins and flan rings.

Roll away: If very thin pastry is to be rolled up lay it first on a floured cloth – as for strudel.

Protect the top: Rather than make a hole in the centre of a fruit pie, lift a small space on the edge of the tin to ensure that any juice running out will not spoil the top of the pastry.

Spare that crust: Should a pie crust brown too quickly before its contents are cooked, cover the crust lightly with a piece of greaseproof paper.

Waxy margarine: Butter is traditional for making puff pastry, but excellent results can be obtained using a firm, waxy margarine.

Chilled water for mixing: Use chilled water with a good squeeze of lemon juice for mixing puff and flaky pastry.

Layered for later: Any leftover pieces of puff or flaky pastry should be layered up and rolled out again for use. Never roll into a ball or the layers are lost.

Care when glazing: When glazing puff or flaky pastry do not let any egg liquid trickle over the sides or the layers will become sealed and will not be able to rise on baking.

In place of flaky pastry: Rough puff pastry can be made in a few minutes and can often take the place of flaky pastry – when making fruit or mince pies, for instance. It is not quite as firm as flaky pastry.

Adding lightness: To lighten suet crust, add fresh white breadcrumbs in place of up to a quarter the weight of self-raising flour.

Steam or bake: Suet crust can be baked as well as steamed and used for baked jam roly-poly or apple pudding made in a pie plate.

Add taste for meat: Season the flour very well for a steamed suet pudding containing meat.

Useful choux: When making choux pastry it is useful to make a large batch. Use part of the paste to make cream puffs, éclairs or profiteroles; add grated cheese to another portion to fry as beignets or cheese aigrettes; add finely diced cheese to the remainder and make a gougère. A small amount can be piped into pea-sized rounds and baked for an accompaniment to soups.

Keep closely covered: Small baked choux can be kept in a closely covered container for a day or two, but do not put in any filling until just before you are ready to serve.

Rising still: If you are wanting to get ahead with your recipe preparation, choux pastry need not be baked immediately, it can be kept for a few hours before baking and will still rise.

No peeping: Never open the oven door until choux pastry has had about three-quarters of its cooking time. If opened too early the pastry will collapse and never rise again.

No guessing: Use plain flour with a pinch of salt for choux pastry and medium eggs. It is essential to weigh accurately and not guess for this pastry.

Crisp and hollow: Bake choux until brown, crisp and hollow to avoid soggy pastry in the middle and a pale soft line round the centre: 30-40 minutes may be needed.

Rising heat: A rising temperature helps when baking choux, that is the heat of the oven is increased during the cooking. Put the choux pastry in the oven at 190°C, 375°F, Gas Mark 5 and after 7-10 minutes, raise the temperature to 200°C, 400°F, Gas Mark 6.

Steam release: After baking, prick individual choux with a trussing needle or skewer to release any steam. If you find that they are still very damp inside, you can return them to the oven for a few minutes to dry out.

Small by hand: Small quantities of choux need to be made by hand but larger amounts by machine.

▓SAUCES

Gravy saver: Should a sauce of gravy start to separate and look oily, skim off a little of the fat, then add more stock or even a little hot water and it will blend together again.

Help for mayonnaise: Use a fresh egg with a good plump yolk (see page 54). The fresher the egg, the easier and quicker it will be to achieve a mayonnaise of the right consistency. It should be an emulsified, fairly solid texture.

The best sauce: The best brown sauces need to be made with a good beef bone stock strengthened with a veal bone.

HERBS AND SPICES

Grow your own: Fresh herbs can make a great difference to the flavour of many dishes, so try growing a few of your own, even if it's just in a flower pot on the kitchen window sill.

Stronger when fresh: Parsley and green fennel are better fresh than dried as they lose strength quickly when dried.

Easy to grow: A pot of fresh basil is easy to grow. Use for pasta, shredded in salads and with tomatoes.

Spring onion tops: If chives are unavailable, the thinnest of the spring onion tops can be used as a substitute.

Pungent herbs: Rosemary is a very pungent herb. When using it to flavour a lamb stew, tie it into muslin and remove before serving because the leaves are hard and spiky to eat. A sprig of rosemary put into the body cavity flavours a French roasted chicken.

Protect from dust: Twiggy herbs such as thyme, bayleaves and rosemary can be dried, then hung in closed polythene bags to protect them from dust.

Mint sauce: A mint sauce should be thick with mint and not too acid with vinegar. A spoonful of boiling water added first to the chopped mint will help the colour, then add the sugar and white wine vinegar or cider vinegar.

French not Russian: When growing tarragon, make sure it is the French and not the larger Russian variety which is a taller and stronger plant, but has less flavour.

Flavour for tomato: Use basil or marjoram to flavour any tomato dish, especially tomato salads, soups and sandwiches.

196

Tarragon for egg and chicken: Tarragon is good with egg and chicken dishes. Cut the leaves coarsely with scissors to add to an egg sauce or scrambled eggs, also to a cream of chicken soup.

Add a bayleaf: Lay a bayleaf on top of meat or game pâtés or terrines before baking and remove on cooling.

Only a pinch: Add a pinch of saffron in an eggcupful of hot water to a rice dish or a fish soup 20 minutes before using. Although very expensive only a pinch or so is usually needed. Buy whole saffron, not powdered.

Tasty seeds: Caraway seeds, usually teamed with seed cake, can be used to flavour red cabbage, soft cheese, breads and biscuits.

Fresh and best: When fresh herbs are at their best in early summer, chop parsley, tarragon and chervil and stir with finely snipped chives into cottage or cream cheese.

Elderflowers with gooseberry: Use elderflowers to flavour gooseberry dishes and rhubarb. Pick them before the flowers are fully open and use two large heads to a pound of the fruit. Remove when the flavour is strong enough.

Savory for beans: Savory flavours broad beans as mint does peas. Use it also in bean soups and salads.

A classic: For the classic herb omelette, use chopped parsley, with tarragon and snipped chives.

The basic bouquet garni: The basic bouquet garni consists of a few crushed parsley stalks, a sprig of thyme and half a bayleaf. To this can be added, according to the recipe, a thin strip of orange peel and perhaps a piece of celery.

Avoid confusion: Be wary of mixing too many herbs in one dish, as this merely confuses flavours. It is also better to add too few rather than too many herbs.

Cooked parsley: Parsley should be chopped or fried before it is added to a dish. Raw sprays are seldom eaten.

The neglected berry: Juniper berries could be used more often and they are not expensive to buy. They can be added to a marinade for game, to a stuffing for game birds or used for many pork dishes such as brawn. They need to be crushed first.

Florentine fennel: When buying Florentine fennel for a salad, keep any little ferny green tops to chop and sprinkle on top, or to use in a fish dish, or to add to a sauce in the same way as parsley.

Pound it yourself: Coriander pounds easily using a pestle and mortar, so buy it whole and pound it yourself as needed.

Coriander for game: Coriander seeds are aromatic, so crush them to release flavour. They go well with lamb dishes and in milky puddings. Use them in a marinade for game. Green coriander leaves, chopped, are excellent on tomato salads.

Delicate dill: Use the dark green feathery leaves of dill with fish, on salads and in pickles. It is more delicate in flavour than fennel. Dill seeds are used in the same way as caraway seeds and many Scandinavian recipes use dill.

Keep them whole: Whole spices keep their flavour much longer than those already ground.

A dried berry: Allspice is not a mixed spice but the name of a dried berry. It can be ground in a peppermill kept especially for it. It is sometimes called Jamaica pepper.

For Eastern sweetmeats: Buy cardamoms whole. They are small pods which are opened to remove the little brown or black seeds. Crush them and use for chicken dishes and milk puddings and Eastern sweetmeats.

Mark with care: Cayenne pepper needs careful marking as it resembles paprika which is mild and sweet by comparison.

Only a little: Use cayenne pepper in small amounts. A little on the point of a knife is often enough, so buy in small packets.

Do not touch: Never touch lips or eyes when using cayenne or removing seeds from chillies.

Toasted for tea: Cinnamon sticks are difficult to grind, so buy cinnamon powdered for adding to cakes, biscuits and puddings, and remember cinnamon toast for tea – it is delicious.

Used for an infusion: Cinnamon sticks are used for infusion when making lemon jelly or syrups for spiced fruits.

Cloves in spice: Powdered cloves retain their flavour better than most. As the taste of cloves is very pronounced they should be used with care.

Cumin for curries: Use ground cumin, or the seeds, with aubergine dishes, to season kebabs and for use in curries.

Keeps better: Curry paste is sometimes preferred to curry powder and keeps better.

Not too hot: Use all spices with discretion and to your taste; curries should never be too hot for the average palate. The mildly spiced dishes can be delicious.

A mixture of spices: Garam Masala in a tin means a mixture of spices used in curries.

In many forms: Ginger comes in many forms – powdered, dried root, fresh, glacé and in syrup. It is used with fruits, in cakes and goes well with dark chocolate or coffee.

Nutmeg for mace: Mace is the web-like outer husk of nutmegs, good with fish and shell-fish, potted meats, fish soups and fish stocks. If mace is not available, substitute a few grains of nutmeg.

▓SWEET COURSES OR DESSERTS

Keeping soufflés cold: If ice is not available for cold soufflés, the ice packs from a picnic basket can be used instead. Keeping the mixture in a metal pan speeds the thickening process as metal conducts the cold quickly.

To the rescue: If a soufflé refuses to set and time is short, turn it into a glass or fruit bowl, decorate it with whipped cream and perhaps chopped nuts or coarsely grated chocolate – whatever is suitable for the flavour.

Three the same: When adding whipped cream and egg whites to a creamy mixture, have all three mixtures as nearly the same texture as possible, otherwise it is not easy to fold them in and the egg white tends to rise to the surface.

Not fresh: Never use fresh pineapple in a mixture with gelatine as it destroys the setting properties. Cooked or tinned pineapple can be used, however.

Mould preparation: To prepare a mould for a fruit juice jelly or a water-based jelly, rinse the mould with cold water. For a creamy mixture using eggs, milk and cream, oil the mould very lightly but thoroughly. Use a brush if the mould has many indentations.

Cool for cream: Chill cream before whipping and in hot weather also chill the bowl and whisk or beaters. Surround the chilled bowl with icy water or cubes of ice high up the sides.

Too solid cream: Double cream is often too solid when whipped; it can be lightened by adding 1-2 tablespoons of iced water to every 300 ml (½ pint).

Mix double and single: For whipping, or a thick pouring cream, mix double and single cream equally. This, when whipped, holds its shape and can be used for filling choux pastries and gâteaux.

Meringue mix: Meringue mixtures are best made from egg whites which are a few days old and at room temperature. One egg white is approximately 25 ml (1 fl oz) and needs 50 g (2 oz) caster sugar.

A few minutes to dry: Shape the meringues and then dredge lightly with caster sugar and leave to stand for a few minutes before baking them slowly. Meringues dry out rather than cook. The dredged sugar gives them a slightly crusty finish.

A rest for meringues: Meringues can be left at room temperature for at least half an hour before baking.

Whisk away: For meringues, whisk whites until really dry. To prevent weeping do not overfold when adding the sugar.

Dry bases: When meringues are dry, remove from the oven and tap or lightly press in the bases, then return for a few minutes to make sure they are really dry. This also makes room for more cream!

Stop that curdle: If a pouring egg custard looks like curdling while making, pour it quickly into a cold bowl and whisk it hard.

YEAST AND DOUGHS

Prevent drying: Before rising a dough, place it in a lightly oiled bowl and turn it over so all the surface is thinly oiled to prevent it drying. Cover the bowl with cling film or a clean cloth.

Polythene bag: Yeast doughs can be kept for some hours or overnight in an oiled polythene bag in the refrigerator. Use a larger bag and tie at the end as there will be expansion of the dough.

Lighter texture: A little white flour used in a wholemeal loaf dough will give a lighter texture.

On the soft side: Keep all yeast doughs on the soft side if they are to be baked in a tin or mould.

Mixed flours: Strong flour makes good bread and stores well but for the sake of economy it can have all-purpose household flour mixed with it.

Add less water when making a dough with wholemeal flour than you would with a finer flour. The wholemeal absorbs slightly less liquid.

Cut down on yeast: The amount of yeast used can be cut down by about a quarter if a dough is kept overnight in a refrigerator.

Do not hurry: Be patient, never hurry the yeast dough through the stages of making.

Warm tins first: Grease loaf tins and warm them a little before filling.

Pizza base: Some yeast dough can be set aside and used for lardy cake or a pizza base.

Brioche dough: Chill a brioche dough so that it is as firm as possible before shaping. Prove the individual brioches slowly and bake quickly.

Croissants and cream: After baking, split croissants through the thickest part, fill with a thick compote of Morello cherries and decorate with whipped cream.

Care with dried yeast: Some dried yeasts need soaking in about 5 times their weight of tepid water for 10 minutes before using. Dried yeast is concentrated, so only use half the amount recommended for fresh yeast in a recipe.

Top with seeds: Rich breads or rolls, those made with eggs, butter and milk, look appetizing if glazed with egg wash plus a pinch of salt, then sprinkled with poppy, sesame or caraway seeds.

▓EGGS AND DAIRY PRODUCTS

Keep in a jar: If grated cheese is left uncovered in the refrigerator it will become drier for sprinkling on top of a dish. Transfer once hard to a small screw-top jar. Shake the jar occasionally.

Strong on flavour: To strengthen the cheese flavour in a Mornay sauce, add a little grated Parmesan cheese and a good pinch of dry mustard to the recipe.

Copper or glass: Egg whites slip around when whisked in a china bowl. For best results use a copper bowl or else a glass one.

Sour milk cheese: If milk sours check it does not taste bitter then add a little salt and drain it well in a muslin bag; season it to taste and use it as you would cottage cheese.

Add to spice cakes: Soured milk can be used to advantage to make batters, scones, gingerbreads and spice cakes.

Hard-boil in advance: If you cook for the family on a daily basis, it is a good idea to keep several hard-boiled eggs in the refrigerator. Mark them H.B. with a pencil so you can identify them. They are useful for salads, garnishes and sandwiches.

Flavour for yogurt: Flavour your own yogurt by buying plain yogurt and adding diced fruit, honey or coffee essence.

Topping for potatoes: Soured cream or plain yogurt with chives makes a good topping for baked potatoes.

Check regularly: Check dairy products in the refrigerator every day for freshness.

Ideal for scones: Buttermilk is the liquid remaining after butter has been made. It makes a cool pleasant drink when mixed with a little iced water. It is also ideal for making scones and soda bread.

Butter for vegetables: Unsalted butter is excellent for a good flavour when cooking, especially if using for butter icing, butter creams and on cooked vegetables.

Whipping cream: If sweetened cream is wanted, lightly whip before adding the sugar, then whip to the required thickness. If a vanilla flavour is required, use vanilla sugar, see page 174.

Crisp surface: When using grated cheese to top 'au gratin' dishes, mix the cheese with a spoonful of browned breadcrumbs to help crisp the surface. The crumbs will also absorb any excess fat that may run from the cheese.

Small eggs: Have a few really small eggs in the refrigerator where they keep well. Often only a small quantity of beaten egg is needed to glaze pastry or scones, to bind a stuffing or add to Pommes Duchesse.

Add an egg: If only small eggs are to hand and you need to thicken or set a mixture, add one more to every three in the recipe.

Yogurt substitute: Yogurt can often be used as a low-calorie substitute for soured cream.

Evaporated milk: A tin of evaporated milk well chilled in the refrigerator for several hours will whip well and can take the place of cream when making milk or cream puddings set with gelatine.

Add whisked white: A small egg white whisked and folded carefully into whipped cream will lighten it and make it go further for fillings. However, it cannot be piped.

Individual junkets: Use fresh milk, unpasteurized if possible, for junket; this is delicious wih raspberries and redcurrants cooked lightly together. Make individual junkets, flavour with coffee and spoon thick, soft cream on top when set. Finish with chopped nuts.

Light omelette: To make light omelettes, add a teaspoon of water to each egg, fork the eggs only enough to barely mix them and make the omelette very quickly.

Add some cream: Many dishes are vastly improved by adding a spoonful or two of cream: a spinach purée, for example, an omelette filling, or young vegetables. A carrot or tomato soup is delicious with cream swirled across the top.

Parmesan for crispness: Grated Parmesan cheese colours and crisps well when used on a dish under the grill.

Off the boil: Never reboil a sauce after adding grated cheese or the cheese becomes stringy; the heat of the sauce off the flame is sufficient to melt it.

Flavour for cheesecakes: When making cheesecakes add lemon juice and a pinch of salt to give flavour.

Orange flavour: To make orange-flavoured whipped cream, rub the surface of a rough-skinned, washed orange with sugar lumps, so that the oil is absorbed into the sugar. Pound them with a few drops of the orange juice to form a thick syrup. Fold this very gently into the lightly whipped cream.

Sauce for the pudding: Soured cream can be thinned with top of the milk or single cream, sweetened lightly and used as a sauce over fruit and baked or steamed fruit puddings.

Prevent thickening: To prevent double cream thickening too quickly when it is being whipped and not absorbing air to lighten it, add a small ice cube to the 150 ml (¼ pint) and whisk by hand.

Well kept eggs: If shelled hard-boiled eggs are not needed for a few hours, keep them in a bowl of cold water in the refrigerator. Dry well if going on to coat them, see also page 175.

Lost flavour: Add mustard to a cheese dish towards the end of cooking as the flavour of mustard is lost on heating.

To make sour milk: To sour milk stir in 1½ tablespoons of lemon juice to 300 ml (½ pint) of milk and stand it in a warm place for an hour or two.

Well whisked: Never leave even a particle of egg yolk in whites if you wish to whisk them. Remove it carefully with half an egg shell. Any yolk is fatty and prevents the whites whisking well.

Using up oddments: Use up any hard oddments of cheese by grating and pounding with 25-50 g (1-2 oz) of butter to the 100 g

(4 oz) of cheese, then flavour with made mustard or a little curry paste or a spoonful of blue cheese. Use as a spread or put on lightly buttered toast and grill it.

Cool for yogurt: Cool a cooked dish slightly before adding yogurt, since overheating may cause a curdled appearance.

Best have butter: Do not economize by substituting other fat for butter where its flavour is important, for example in omelettes and egg yolk and butter sauces and butter cakes.

WINE IN COOKING

Warm before flaming: To flame red wine, sherry and spirits, always warm them first in a small receptacle before igniting carefully with a long taper.

Do not add too much: Measure wine or liqueurs carefully and never add more than the recipe indicates because you think it will taste better, this could leave a dish tasting of little else. Cold dishes, such as pâtés, could taste too acid.

Wine and strawberries: Red wine is good to use when poaching cherries or pears, or sprinkled over fresh strawberries.

Tenderize the meat: Leftover wine that is not considered good enough to drink is ideal to use in a casserole. Its acidity will help to tenderize the meat and the long slow cooking with other flavours rounds off any unpalatable taste.

Best wine: If flaming wine or cooking only briefly, use as good a wine as you can afford. There is no time to improve the flavour of a poor quality wine by long slow cooking.

MISCELLANEOUS

Flavour release: To bring out the flavour of dried herbs, crumble them in your fingers then soak them in a little warm water, white wine or lemon juice. If chopped fresh parsley is also being used chop the dried herbs together with the parsley to release their full flavour.

Handles in: Never have a pan handle sticking out from the stove. Prevent accidents by turning them inwards, but make sure they are not directly over the heat.

Tasty for frying: Bacon fat from frying can be strained into a small covered jar and kept for fried potatoes, frying eggs, sausages or liver. Use it within a week.

Grind at once: Grind whole black peppercorns in a mill over food; its freshness gives an incomparably better flavour than bought ground pepper.

Subtle not dominant: Err on the mean side when using herbs in a cooked dish; the flavour should be subtle and not dominant. This applies especially to dried herbs.

Marinade to stock pot: After braising meat or game add the vegetables from the marinade to the stock pot. The liquid is often added to the sauce.

Get with the giblets: Try to get the giblets with poultry to make the stock for gravy. Do not use the liver for this as it can be bitter. Remove any green or yellow stain, fry the giblets and then slice or chop them and add to the gravy.

Small for strength: Buy ground spices in the smallest containers you can find as they lose strength after a month or so.

Lemon tea: Thin dry strips of orange or lemon peel will flavour tea in a tin or caddy.

Care with Hollandaise: A delicate egg sauce, such as Hollandaise or Béarnaise, can be warmed until tepid in a bain-marie or double boiler. It can also be kept warm by this method. Remember that if it gets too hot it will curdle.

Lightly season first: When making stocks, season very lightly. The seasoning can be adjusted at a later stage, when using the stock as part of a recipe.

Avoid cloudy stock: Never boil stock – let it barely simmer with the lid on otherwise it will be cloudy.

Avoid curdling: When making cream soups with acid vegetables, such as onions and leeks, add scalded milk to avoid curdling. This will also sweat the vegetables.

Rice in salt: Put a few grains of rice in a salt cellar to keep the salt dry and running freely.

Advanced pancakes: Pancakes required for rolling or filling can be made the day before, see page 109. They are firmer and handle more easily than when freshly made.

Quick re-heat: To reheat pancakes, fill them and lay in a buttered dish; brush the top with melted butter and heat through quickly but do not harden the surface.

Fresh horseradish: If making horseradish cream with fresh horseradish, whip the cream until it is only just pourable. As the seasonings and grated horseradish are folded in the cream will thicken more.

Soft margarines: Soft margarines have a higher proportion of oils which remain liquid at room temperature. They are good for all-in-one cake mixes as they cream very quickly.

Hard margarines: Use these for pastries when the fat has to be rubbed or rolled in. Soft margarines won't trap as much air and so the pastry isn't so light.

Soft lard: The super-refined variety is odourless in cooking. It is good for pastry but, having no flavour, needs to be mixed with butter.

Thinner rashers: To make bacon rashers thinner, remove the rind, lay on a board and run the back of a large knife, held almost flat, from one end of the rasher to the other.

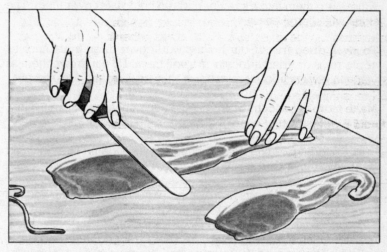

A small brush: Keep a small stiff brush, similar to a nail brush, by the sink to scrub vegetables and help to clean graters and strainers thoroughly.

No starch: Never add starchy material, such as potato or thickened gravy, to a stock pot or it will sour quickly.

Cooking in a jug: Kippers can be cooked by putting them in a jug, pouring on boiling water and leaving them for 5 minutes. Drain and serve with pats of butter.

Stock should match: Do not use pork, lamb or rabbit stock in recipes based on other meats as the flavour will predominate.

Bone meat: To bone meat and poultry use a small, sharp boning knife and follow the line of the bone closely.

Warm pudding: If you need to keep a steamed pudding warm for a short while, cover it with the basin it was cooked in.

Moist cake: A whole apple in the cake tin will help to keep a cake from becoming dry too quickly.

Skinning almonds: To skin almonds boil them for a few seconds in water, turn them into a strainer and run cold water over them. The skins will slip off easily.

To swell dried fruits: Pour boiling water over dried fruits, such as apple rings or dried apricots, to swell them. Do not drown them as you can always add more water if they soak up the first amount.

Make more of mincemeat: To extend mincemeat or if it seems dry, add a tablespoon of coarsely grated or chopped apple.

Bread pudding: Make old-fashioned bread pudding in a buttered small roasting tin and sprinkle the top with sugar for a crusty finish.

Under a cold tap: Always rinse a lemon squeezer and grater under a cold tap shortly after using. This makes it much easier to clean.

Greater volume: Any light mixture using whisked eggs and sugar will whisk better over steaming water. This gives greater volume for cold soufflés, mousses and sponge cakes.

Use again: Cinnamon sticks and vanilla pods can be washed, dried and used again.

Hard jam: If jam in an opened pot has hardened, stir in a spoonful or two of boiling water to make it spreadable and use within a week.

Avoid monotony: To prevent getting in a rut with everyday meals, try a new dish, say once a fortnight or once a month.

Learn the names: It is worth learning the names of cookery equipment, so that recipes can be interpreted easily.

GENERAL HINTS

Bake blind first: When using a ceramic flan dish always bake the pastry blind for 8-10 minutes before filling with the chosen mixture, to give a crisp pastry shell.

Keep wood dry: Wooden-handled knives, rolling pins or chopping boards should never be left in a sink or bowl of washing-up water or they will swell.

Cool before heat: Allow very hot pans to cool a little before putting cold liquids into them.

A tainted flavour: Use a nylon strainer or sieve to sieve acid fruits, especially if fresh soft fruits. Metal, unless stainless steel, will give a tainted flavour.

Air the board: Find a good solid chopping board and after use scrub it and stand it on end to air.

Good contact: For efficient chopping use a medium to large knife and make sure the blade is not worn. It must be in contact with the board along the whole of its blade.

Sharpen before use: Keep a carborundum and a sharpening steel in a kitchen dresser as knives should always be sharpened before use.

Easier than translating: If you frequently cook with American or Canadian recipes, it is worth trying to obtain an American measuring cup and spoons.

No washing: Keep an omelette pan just for omelettes and, if suitable, for pancakes. Do not wash the pan, just wipe with a damp cloth.

Guesswork: A sugar thermometer is needed if making confectionery and fondant or fudge icings; guessing can be inaccurate and result in failure.

Another opinion: Before buying an expensive piece of equipment it is wise to get a professional opinion from an organization, such as the Consumers' Association.

Waste not: Rubber or plastic spatulas get the last of the mixture from bowls and pans and there is a small narrow version for jars.

Mill for grinding: A pepper mill is needed to grind whole black peppercorns for freshness. Allspice and white peppercorns should also be ground in a mill.

Avoid splashes: A conical strainer ensures that gravy or sauce is directed down into the sauce boat whereas the liquids splash if a bowl strainer is used.

Use a dredger: Dredgers make work easier; a flour dredger and a finer one for caster and icing sugars.

Fine string: Really fine string is needed in a kitchen for sewing meat or poultry into shape after boning or stuffing. Coarse natural thread will do if fine string is not available, but do not pull it tightly or it will tear the meat or skin.

Wipe at once: If food spills on to a hot stove top when cooking, wipe it up as soon as possible otherwise the heat of the stove cooks it and it will be twice as hard to remove.

Simple removal: Flan rings used on a firm baking tray are easier to use than sandwich tins for flans, and removal is simpler.

Prevent chipping: When washing up delicate china lay a clean tea towel on the draining board to prevent chipping.

Important item: A strong tin opener is a must for a well-equipped kitchen. The blade should be washed and wiped after using.

In order: It is often useful to rearrange the order of mixing a recipe in order to complete the making in the food processor. For example if making a roughly textured pâté, use the steel blade and drop in the cut-up onion through the feed tube while the motor is running and add the herbs and a clove of garlic, put in the meat cut into pieces starting with the meat which needs to be finely minced. Add the brandy or egg, and finally the seasoning as the last pieces of meat are fed into the processor.

FOOD PROCESSORS

Force it clean: To clean the blade empty the bowl of as much mixture as possible, then switch on again and the centrifugal force will clean the blade.

Sterilize sometimes: Soak the blade in babies' bottle sterilizing solution from time to time and use a bottle brush to clean thoroughly inside.

Fresh storage: When putting the machine away, place the blade on its side in the bowl, turn the lid upside down, then replace the feed tube. This allows air to circulate and helps to keep the bowl fresh smelling.

Not too short: When making pastry, always add the full recommended amount of water or even a little extra, so that the finished pastry is not too short.

Knead it yourself: When adding liquid to a fat and flour mix for pastry, stop the processing when the mixture forms large lumps, before it comes together completely. Turn out on to a pastry board and knead together well.

Chop carefully: When chopping high-moisture foods, such as mushrooms, be careful not to overprocess, as the food will purée quickly. Add the ingredients to the machine carefully through the feeder tube while processing rather than switching on with the food in the bowl. This ensures more even chopping.

Fine breadcrumbs: When making breadcrumbs allow bread to dry out for two or three days. The bread will then produce finer crumbs.

Successful mayonnaise: To make mayonnaise successfully you must use sufficient egg yolks, i.e. 6 yolks to 1¼ litres (2 pints) oil. Spare mayonnaise keeps well in the refrigerator for up to one week.

▓SLOW COOKER

Defrost first: Frozen vegetables should be defrosted and added towards the end of the cooking time.

Warm on the side: Use a slow cooker during a party on a buffet or side table to keep soup, casseroles or mulled wine and such, warm for the guests.

Best not reheated: Food should not be reheated in a slow cooker; it is best brought to the boil, then simmered for 10 minutes before transferring.

Less liquid needed: Less liquid is required in a recipe cooked in a slow cooker because there is far less evaporation.

Boil first: Bring liquids to the boil before using in a slow cooker.

End of cooking time: Milk or cream are usually added towards the end of the cooking time.

Fewer herbs: Because the flavours are concentrated, use less seasoning and fewer herbs than usual when slow cooking.

Ideal for stock: The slow cooking method is ideal for making stock.

Do not leave in: Ingredients should not be left in the slow cooker to cool after they have been cooked.

Trim first: Trim meat of excess fat before cooking in a slow cooker.

Coarse oatmeal pogridge: Porridge made with coarse oatmeal is delicious made in a slow cooker.

Good for puddings: A slow cooker is ideal for cooking steamed puddings and for softening the fruit for marmalade.

▓FREEZER AND REFRIGERATOR

Keep coffee fresh: An opened packet of ground coffee is better turned into an airtight container and kept in the refrigerator.

Frozen stock: Reduced bone stock can be frozen as ice cubes and then stored in a freezer bag; when required, reconstitute with boiling water.

Pretty for parties: Freeze pieces of fruit or maraschino cherries in ice cubes before a party to add to fruit cup or other drinks.

Straight from the freezer: Pizza and quiches can be taken straight from the freezer and reheated in a hot oven.

Square is best shape: Square or loaf-shaped cakes pack together more tightly than round ones and, therefore, take up less room in the freezer.

Store when cheap: When lemons are cheap, squeeze the juice and freeze as ice cubes, then store in a polythene bag; or freeze in small cartons leaving head space.

Roll flat: To freeze pastry, roll into a flat round as it will thaw quicker than if in a ball.

Freeze coffee and tea: Coffee and tea can be bought cheaper in bulk and will retain an excellent flavour if frozen.

Avoid bacteria: Always freeze stuffing and bird separately for larger stuffed poultry; otherwise it may take so long to thaw that bacteria develops.

Cook quickly: Cook completely thawed birds as soon as possible; they lose juices if left too long and will be dry to eat.

Loss of Vitamin C: Exclude as much air as possible when freezing food which contains Vitamin C, as this vitamin is easily lost in the freezing process.

Prevent sticking: Thaw and reheat thick soups in a double boiler to prevent sticking and burning.

Better shape: If small cakes and scones are open frozen before packaging together, they are less likely to crumble and break, and keep their shape better.

Freeze homogenized: Only homogenized milk freezes really successfully; thaw when needed and use it quickly.

Very rubbery: Never freeze hard-boiled eggs or dishes containing them as the whites end up very rubbery.

Frozen meringues: Bake meringues until really crisp then break into large pieces and fold carefully into whipped double cream flavoured with chocolate or coffee, orange or a liqueur. Pack into a suitable container and freeze. Unmould and leave in the refrigerator for ½ hour or so before serving with a fruit sauce.

Stop separation: It is a good idea to thicken sauces at the end of cooking with arrowroot if to be frozen. There is less likelihood of separation on thawing.

Wrap it up: Wrap hard cheese closely in foil or cling film to exclude air and keep in the bottom of the refrigerator. Remember to use it up within the date code.

Economize with space: To freeze liquids such as stock or soup, fit a polythene bag into a square container, freeze and lift out. This is then a good shape for economy of space in the freezer.

Protect from hardening: If keeping jelly or aspic in a bowl in the refrigerator, run cold water carefully over the surface and it will protect it for a day or two from hardening on the surface.

Raw choux: Freeze shaped raw choux paste on to a sheet of non-stick silicone paper, store on the lid of a rigid container with the container itself uppermost, then slide on to a baking sheet to bake them and allow 7-8 minutes extra time in the oven.

PRESSURE COOKER

Save time: Always read the instructions first, not all models are the same and this can save time and failed recipes.

Liquid level: A pressure cooker should never be more than two-thirds full when cooking solid foods and no more than half full when cooking liquids or high liquid content dishes.

Check first: Because of the high pressure in the cooker, it is important to have enough liquid, otherwise the food will stick on the bottom and burn. Check the recipe or liquids chart for the correct amount for the ingredients and for the cooking time.

First and last: When a given amount of liquid is used, always put it in the cooker first to make sure that the cooker is never sealed without using liquid. However, when making stock or casseroles, add the liquid last to enable you to check the fluid level.

Thicken at the end: Thickeners should always be added at the end of the cooking time and once added, there should be no further pressure cooking. This avoids sticking and burning.

Surface skimmer: When cooking foods, such as rice or stocks made from bones, that will throw up a fair amount of scum as they come to the boil, bring to the boil without the lid. Skim well, then put on the lid and bring up to pressure as usual.

Save over cooking: Unless a recipe states otherwise, always bring the cooker to high pressure as quickly as possible. This will save any over-cooking.

Brown well: When the colour of the finished dish depends very much on the initial browning of the ingredients by open frying in fat, do this really well to achieve the desired colour, as, unlike oven cooking, once the cooker is sealed there will be no way of increasing the colour by removing the lid and so allowing outside heat to brown the ingredients further.

The need to open: A pressure cooker cannot be opened while it is under pressure. If you need to open the cooker quickly or reduce the pressure, quickly stand the cooker in cold water or run cold water from the tap over the top until the hissing stops and the weights can be removed without a rush of steam escaping. Do not open while it is still hissing.

Check the gasket: Always check the rubber gasket ring to make sure it fits well and is not damaged. Also make sure when cleaning the pressure cooker that the ring is removed so that the lid can also be thoroughly cleaned.

Store carefully: When storing a pressure cooker arrange the lid in such a way as to allow air to circulate freely, so that the inside does not become musty.

Concentrated stock: A pressure cooker is useful for making concentrated stocks.

Many vegetables: More than one vegetable can be cooked at a time. Large vegetables need to be cut in pieces of an even size.

Correct timing: Check the timing given in a pressure cooker recipe carefully and make sure that you follow this accurately.

Quick for pulses: A pressure cooker is useful when cooking pulse foods, such as dried haricot beans and dried peas, as it cuts the cooking time considerably.

Turns to steam: The liquid used in the cooking should be thin so that it turns easily to steam when boiling.

Fuel saver: Pressure cooking is an excellent method for cooking tougher, and therefore cheaper, cuts of meat quickly as it saves fuel; also the vegetables can be cooked with the meat.

Prevent discoloration: When steaming puddings or other food in a container, add 1 tablespoon of either vinegar or lemon juice to the water to prevent discoloration of the pan.

Quicker puddings: Hours are saved if Christmas puddings are cooked in a pressure cooker; and cereal milk puddings can also be made more quickly.

Lighten the mixture: All steamed puddings should have a preliminary steaming before bringing the pan to pressure to give the raising agent time to work and lighten the mixture.

Easy way to a custard: Egg custards can easily be made in a pressure cooker.

Season first and last: Season pressure-cooked food moderately before cooking and correct the seasoning before serving.

Covering a pudding: The top of a pudding cooked in a pressure cooker should have a double thickness of buttered greaseproof paper with a pleat in it, or foil over the top. String should be tied under the rim of the bowl tightly, and a handle of string made across the top and secured on the opposite side.

Adapt for marmalade: If adapting your own marmalade recipe use half the amount of water as there is no evaporation while the peel is softening; then add the rest of the water.

Fast fruit: When bottling fruit a pressure cooker saves a lot of time.

MICROWAVE COOKER

Correct clingfilm: When covering food to be microwaved in clingfilm, ensure that special microwave clingfilm is always used.

Save tears and waste: Keep plated meals of children's favourites in the deep-freeze. If they don't want what the adults are eating, it only takes a few minutes to heat their favourite, saving tears and waste.

Dual way to cook: If you want to save time by part microwaving the Sunday roast beef, but like a crisp brown joint, finish the meat in a conventional oven as you cook the Yorkshire pudding.

Quicker rising: On lengthy yeast doughs, use the microwave to rise and prove doughs. Use 15 second bursts at Maximum (Full) power and rest the dough for 15 minutes and continue until the required rise is reached according to the dough used.

Waves absorbed: Avoid dark coloured dishes and stoneware; they slow the cooking time by absorbing the waves.

For an evenly cooked result: Use round dishes and avoid squared corners; food will not cook evenly in these.

Check the dish: Any metal or metal-trimmed containers should never be used in a microwave. Check the suitability of a dish for use in the microwave by placing it next to a glass jug filled with 300 ml (½ pint) cold water. Set to Maximum (Full) power for 1 minute. If the dish becomes warm then it is not suitable since it is absorbing some of the microwaves and will slow down the cooking by preventing the waves going through to the food.

Prevent bursts: Always pierce commercially prepared 'boil in the bag' products to allow steam to escape and so prevent bursting.

Pierce apples and potatoes: Pierce the skin of whole potatoes or apples to prevent bursting.

Keep in place: If covering with greaseproof paper, to keep food moist, or paper towels, to prevent splattering, keep these in place with wooden skewers or cocktail sticks.

Two are better than one: Cold paper plates are rigid, but don't forget when heated with damp food they become soft and unmanageable. Heat on two paper plates to give firm support for transporting to the table safely.

No wax paper: Waxed paper plates do not like prolonged heating and the wax will melt into the food after 2-3 minutes reheating. They are best not used for cooking.

Avoid scalds: Pierce cling film before removing from dishes or plates to allow built-up steam to escape that might otherwise have given a scald.

Spills absorb energy: Wipe up spills as they occur. If left they will absorb energy intended for the next dish.

Half cover only: Half cover large amounts of liquid, such as soups, to leave room for a spoon to be put in to stir without uncovering, thus not wasting cling film.

Turn the cakes during baking: Turn cakes two or three times during baking to give extra even texture. This applies even if a turntable is in use.

Mix salt carefully: Vegetables require very little added liquid to cook them. Salt should therefore not be sprinkled directly on the vegetables or it will be left high and dry. Mix it with the liquid at the base of the dish or season after cooking.

Home test: All microwave ovens have wave patterns. To check the pattern of your own oven to allow correct spacing and placing of dishes, test this by placing a series of lightly filled glasses or small dishes/bowls evenly and equidistantly over the base of the oven. Give Maximum (Full) power; those that heat first will show hot spots in your particular pattern.

Rough rule for timing: If unsure about timing, allow one quarter of the time taken for conventional cooking. Test the food, then if necessary heat again for small amounts of time until cooked.

Even cooking: Allow the waves to circulate beneath the food especially for larger joints and such by placing over an upturned plate or bowl for even cooking.

Loss of moisture: Moisture is lost during baking. Add a little extra liquid to conventional recipes, for example to a 3-egg Victoria Sandwich add 2 tablespoons of hot water at the last moment.

Salt concentrates: Don't use the usual pinch of salt with flour for baking – the water loss in microwave baking concentrates the salt and makes an unpalatable mouthful.

Avoid steam: Steamy kitchens and lots of space taken up on the hob can be avoided by using the microwave to 'steam' puddings. They contain enough moisture to cook through beautifully, covered with cling film with a small slit made in it. For steak and kidney puddings, cook the filling separately first, cool and then enclose in the suet pastry and complete in the microwave.

Warm and cheering: On cold winter evenings mulled wine or cider is delicious and is quickly made in the microwave.

Small is a pleasure: Jams, chutneys and preserves require large bowls to bubble up in, but excellent results, although in small amounts, make this type of work a joy in a fraction of the usual time.

Fresh for a good shape: Eggs can be poached in buttered tea cups or ramekins. Eggs can also be French poached in a bowl of boiling salted water. The fresher the egg, the better the shape because the white will hold tightly round the yolk as it falls into the water.

Way with eggs: It is not possible to hard-boil eggs in the microwave because they would burst from the steam pressure built up within the shell. French poach instead, as above. These will not be suitable as a garnish of neat slices, but can be chopped for sandwiches, or the white finely chopped and the yolk sieved to sprinkle on as a garnish on dressed crab or salads coated with mayonnaise.

Juicy result: Use the defrost setting to casserole and stew. It will take a little longer but will give a more tender juicy result.

Crisp with oil or butter: Make a crisp coating for thin slices of fish or escalopes by putting a little oil or butter at the base of the dish and turning the food over half way through cooking.

Flan topping: As a crisp finish for flans, try a savoury biscuit crumb mixed with a little melted butter to bind and some grated cheese.

Good filling: Scrambled eggs mixed with a little cream or top of the milk and shredded tomatoes or smoked fish make a good filling for a crumb crust flan, and can be served hot or cold.

Cut down on liquid: The short cooking time for soups allows little evaporation, so if using your favourite conventional recipe, cut down on the liquid used.

Add it hot: If using more than 600 ml (1 pint) of liquid for a soup, add it hot because it takes too long to heat in a microwave to be economical on fuel.

Looks improved: To enhance savoury foods when cooked, sprinkle with breadcrumbs and melted butter and grill until browned.

Way with cheese: Grated cheese melts in the microwave, but overcooks quickly and becomes tough in a sauce. To produce a brown topping, it is better to sprinkle the cheese over the surface and grill it conventionally.

Method for sauce: Hollandaise sauce requires only a third of the vinegar of a conventional recipe and can be warmed with added flavour; for example a few leaves of tarragon, a slice of onion, before mixing with the yolks and melted butter, and heated for 15 seconds, stirred and heated again until just thickened. Do not forget to have a bowl of very cold water ready in which to place the container of sauce the moment it is ready, or it will carry on cooking and curdle very quickly.

Reheated sauces: Frozen Hollandaise or Béarnaise sauce can be thawed and reheated in a matter of moments.

For leftover vegetables: Leftover green vegetables, such as peas, spinach and cauliflower, can be sieved, liquidized or food processed, then added to a white sauce made in the microwave and reheated to serve as soups.

Fresh taste: Pancakes made previously can be reheated a few at a time. They can be filled or plain, served hot and sprinkled with lemon juice and sugar at the table. They will taste as good as the moment they were originally fried. While you eat them, put a few more in to heat for second helpings.

Add some colour: Microwave meat can look a little pale so learn to use colourful garnishes that can be warmed or cooked at the last moment as the meat has its standing time. For example button mushrooms, red or green peppers finely sliced, peeled, seeded and shredded tomatoes, sliced oranges, or apple rings brushed with melted butter.

Hot rolls: Thaw rolls directly from the freezer in a cane basket, covered with a piece of paper towel, and take straight to the table warm and fresh to serve with the first course.

Gluey coating: Line moulds with cling film or non-stick silicone paper. A light greasing may be required, but never flour a cake container. It comes out as a gluey coating.

Ring mould: A tumbler in a round glass dish or microwave baking dish will give a ring mould or tube tin shape.

As a rough guide: If doubling a recipe allow third to half extra cooking time: if halving a recipe allow two-thirds cooking time.

For herb bread: For herb or garlic bread, where French bread is sliced two-thirds way through and these slices spread with flavoured butter, cover the end crust with small pieces of aluminium foil to prevent drying, provided that your manufacturer's instruction booklet confirms that it is alright to use the foil this way.

Better top crust: Bread and rolls should be brushed with melted butter or oil for a better top crust and poppy or sesame seeds sprinkled on top. Wholemeal doughs are usually sprinkled with nibbed wheat.

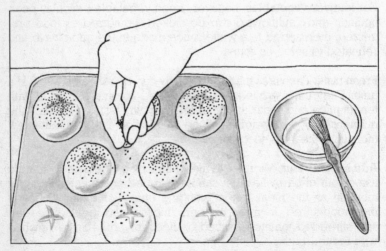

Under-baked: Always remove a cake when slightly under-baked and leaving moist soft crumbs on the finger tip when lightly touched. It will carry on cooking as it stands.

Add icing: Large scone rounds which are cut in wedge shapes and still joined, benefit in appearance if you pour a light icing over them.

Better set and shine: Icings can be warmed lightly in the microwave before use and, if used warm, give a better set and shine. Do not allow to get hot; or the icing loses its shine and becomes fudgy.

Pale finish: Microwave baking leaves a pale finish unless chocolate or heavy spices are used. Be prepared to ice, glaze, use cherries, chopped, browned nuts etc., to decorate.

Soften angelica: If large strips of angelica or candied peel are sugary and dry, place them in a bowl, lightly cover with water and bring just to the boil in the microwave. Drain and dry. They will now be softer and easier to use.

AMERICAN COOKERY

Fat for pastries: 'Shortening' given in American recipes means the fat used in baking cakes and pastries.

Scones are biscuits: Small cakes are called 'cup cakes' and scones are 'hot biscuits'.

Cookies for tea: Cookies come in two basic types, thin and crisp, or softer and about 2 cm (¾ inch) thick and these latter can be served as small cakes for tea-time.

Black treacle: The best substitute for molasses is black treacle adding a tablespoon of hot water to each 100 g (4 oz).

Vanilla: In America, vanilla *extract* is used for flavouring; if substituting vanilla essence only use a quarter as much.

Use less sugar: American cake recipes usually call for a fairly large proportion of sugar; this can be safely cut down a little.

Bitter chocolate: Unsweetened chocolate may be hard to find; use a bitter plain dark chocolate and cut down the sugar in the recipe slightly.

Sweet salads: American salads are sweeter than is usual here, but go well with cold meats and chicken. They often include fruit and nuts. These are improved by marinating in the dressing some time before serving. Pile the mixture on to the undressed lettuce or salad leaves at the last minute.

A meal in themselves: The American chowders are thick with ingredients and can make a meal in themselves if served with hot crusty bread.

Use walnuts: If pecan nuts are difficult to find, use walnuts instead.

A squeeze of lemon: Blueberries are also known here as bilberries or whortleberries; they need a squeeze of lemon juice to bring out their delicate flavour.

Popular breads: Fruit and nut breads made using baking powder instead of yeast are very popular sliced and buttered. They are quickly made and freeze well.

Level measurements: American measurements for cups and spoons (see page 363) are taken level. Fill the cup loosely, then level off with a knife.

Patty tins: Layer cake pans are similar to sandwich tins but a little deeper; any leftover mixture can be baked in patty tins.

A pint is not a pint: The American pint is 16 fluid ounces compared with the Imperial pint of 20 fl oz. Remember this when using American packet mixes and allow *slightly* over 450 ml (¾ of a British pint) for 1 American pint.

First course: Jellied salads are often served as a first course, using a sharpened fruit juice, such as pineapple or cranberry, with gelatine. Chopped fruit is added and the jelly allowed to set, then it is cut in slices and served on a bed of green salad leaves with a plain dressing spooned over.

CHINESE COOKERY

Cut up to avoid carving: All the food used in a Chinese dish should be cut into a convenient size in the kitchen either before or after cooking to avoid carving at the table.

Chopstick eating: Cut all ingredients as even in size as possible and to a size convenient for eating with chopsticks.

Well-washed rice: Wash rice well to rid it of excess starch. When you wish to have fluffy rice allow 1½ times as much water by volume as rice and twice as much water as rice for a dish requiring softer and moister rice.

Sherry or brandy: If Chinese wine is not available, sherry or brandy may be used instead.

Delightfully scented: Chinese tea, often delightfully scented, is served clear, never sweetened or with milk. It is drunk before and after meals.

Essential item: A steamer is essential for Chinese cooking.

Fresh ginger is a common ingredient in Chinese and Indian dishes. It can be preserved by a form of pickling. Remove the skin then cut it into pieces and place in a clean jar. Pour in white distilled vinegar to cover the ginger pieces and prevent a mould forming, then fit the lid. The pieces can then be sliced or ground as and when they are needed.

Soak in tepid water: Dried Chinese mushrooms need soaking in tepid water for 20 minutes before using. Discard the stalks.

Oil for vegetables: Sesame oil is frequently used when cooking vegetables. Only a few drops are needed to obtain a delicate, subtle flavouring.

Fry quickly: When fried, food is cooked quickly, 4-5 tablespoons only at a time in preheated oil, often peanut or bean oil.

Preparing takes the longer: Expect the careful preparation of Chinese food to take longer than the cooking time.

Deep pan: If you do not have the authentic Chinese pan, the wok, a deep frying pan can be used.

Cooking in layers: When using a Chinese steamer, cook the food in layers. For example put scrubbed small potatoes at the base, trout seasoned and stuffed with fresh herbs in the second layer and finally, sliced courgettes and seasoning in the top layer.

Bones for stock: Stock is frequently made with chicken, or pork and chicken bones, and simmered for 4-5 hours. It is an essential ingredient of many Chinese soups.

Glossy thickener: Cornflour, frequently used in Chinese sauces, needs mixing with a little water before using to thicken the sauce and make it glossy.

GERMAN COOKERY

Fridatten: Leftover pancakes rolled up and sliced finely make a good addition to clear soups as 'noodles' and are known as Fridatten.

For a schnitzel: If veal is unavailable for schnitzels, cut thin diagonal slices of pork fillet or a thin slice of a pork steak and bat out to flatten, then proceed as usual to flour, egg and crumb and fry.

Cucumber salad: A side salad of cucumber coarsely grated or finely sliced and tossed in a sweet and sour dressing of vinegar, water, sugar, salt and black pepper goes well with schnitzels.

Water for sauerkraut: Taste a little sauerkraut before cooking; if it is very acid loosen it with a fork and rinse it well under cold water. Water is better for cooking it than wine or stock as it is already acid. Add a quartered onion and one clove when cooking it.

Sauce for dumplings: A horseradish sauce made on a velouté base with lots of freshly grated horseradish added, is served with roast beef and a boiled dumpling. The dumpling is sliced and the horseradish sauce served on it.

Serving oxtail: Oxtail soup is popular in Germany. However, it sometimes can be a little too fatty and should be skimmed from time to time while cooking. Serve with either hot toasted rolls or, as a rather unusual combination which the Germans serve, with macaroons.

Wonderful alternative: Veal makes a wonderful alternative to beef in a goulash.

Good pudding: For a good pudding or an accompaniment to coffee, pat a sweet yeast dough out thinly and place in a greased and floured Swiss roll tin. Lightly cover with halved plums or apricots, then sprinkle with a 'crumble' topping and bake.

▧INDIAN COOKERY

Substitute fat: Clarified butter or ghee (see page 150) is the best fat to use for cooking, but vegetable fats make an acceptable substitute.

Wrap in a cloth: All types of Indian unleavened breads should be served piping hot and as soon as possible after making. If they have to be kept for any time, wrap in a cloth and keep in a pan or tin with a tight lid.

Juice from garlic: To get the juice from garlic or green ginger, pound in a mortar after peeling, adding two or three teaspoons of cold water while pounding and squeeze in a piece of muslin.

Tempting drinks: Wine is not served with curried dishes. Serve slightly sweetened tea, hot or iced with a slice of lemon or lime. Fruit drinks made with melon or mango purée mixed with iced water are refreshing, as is also lightly salted yogurt with chopped mint and iced water to thin it.

Coconut variation: Coconut milk can be made either by adding four tablespoons of hot water to 25 g (1 oz) of coconut cream to dissolve it, or, alternatively by stirring 150 ml (¼ pint) very hot water into 65 g

(2½ oz) desiccated coconut, infusing for 35 minutes and squeezing through muslin.

Fresh spices: Curry spices should ideally be ground fresh using a special curry stone but a coffee grinder can be used instead.

Mustard oil: The oil used for cooking is mainly mustard oil which does not burn as easily as butter. Have the oil really hot before adding the food.

Salt for curry: Do not forget to use salt as seasoning when making curry or spiced dishes.

No lard: Lard is not used for Indian dishes.

Shallow pan: Use a shallow pan for the slow cooking of spiced dishes to thicken the sauce and develop flavours.

Do not brown in a hurry: Slice onions as evenly as possible for frying, so that they colour slowly to a good even brown, and do not hurry this process.

Allow plenty of rice: For rice to accompany curries, use a long grain such as Patna or Basmati as the grains are less likely to clog together. Allow plenty of rice with curry.

Indian food is not served in rigid courses. As a guide you might start with a rice dish, such as a pilau, followed by meat or vegetable dishes with unleavened bread. Side dishes of salads, sambals or cooling raitas are served at the same time. The meal could finish with a sweet dish or a bowl of fresh fruit.

Better to buy: Indian sweetmeats are delicious but not easy to make, so are better bought in Indian shops.

Tamarind substitute: Where tamarind is not available for a dish, an equal mixture of redcurrant jelly and lime or lemon juice will make a reasonable substitute.

Use chilli with care: A curry dish should not be fiery but delicately spiced or hot according to recipe and taste. Use chilli powder cautiously in curries or it can overpower the other fragrant spice flavours.

Garlic powder: Instead of fresh garlic, garlic powder can be used, if wished.

Reheat curry; Leftover curry can be reheated easily; it may need a little more liquid if it seems dry.

Shallow for fish: For spiced fish, rub fillets or cutlets of fish with equal amounts of turmeric, salt and chilli powder before shallow frying in oil or butter.

Puréed mangoes: Indian mangoes can be bought fresh or tinned. They are a superb fruit to eat raw, or, if puréed first, they make water ices and fruit fools.

Cardamom and rose water: After a curried meal, serve fresh fruit or one of the Indian milk puddings made with semolina or ground rice and milk. Flavour with crushed cardamom seeds and rose water and serve chilled.

Fish instead of meat: Many excellent fish or all vegetable curries can be made to avoid using meat.

Side dishes: Several side dishes add authentic variety and interest when serving curry and most of them are easily prepared, for example, rice, dahl, raitas, simple salads using chopped tomatoes, chopped onion and coriander leaves, sharpened with lemon juice, a pinch of salt and sugar.

A special tang: Bharthas are relishes made with spiced mashed vegetables such as cooked potatoes, aubergines or tomatoes adding chopped chillies and lime juice. They have a tang different from the usual chutneys and pickles.

Plain or spiced: Poppadoms, made with lentil flour and plain or spiced can be bought ready to grill or fry. Shallow fry them quickly until they are barely coloured, turn them once, drain them well and serve straightaway.

Chutney choice: Fresh chutneys are refreshing with curries but make only as much as you need as they cannot be bottled and kept.

Cutting remarks: When making curries all vegetables should be cut to the same size. This ensures that they cook evenly as well as enhancing the presentation. Meat in curries should be cut in to bite-sized pieces.

Dry-roasting: Many spices are dry-roasted first to bring out their full flavour. To do this, gently preheat a non-stick or heavy-based frying pan, then add the spices. Keep the heat very gentle and stir the spices for a few seconds.

Thin it: If the sauce for a curry or dahl has become too thick, thin it down with a little boiling water.

SERVING

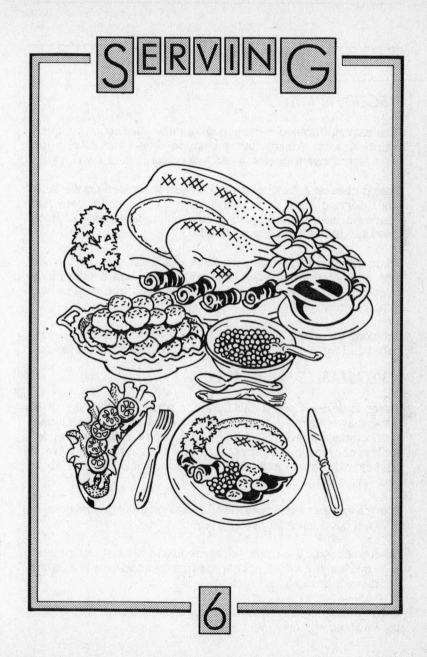

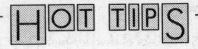

▨ *SOUP*

Pass it round: Instead of putting cream into a hot soup, try lightly whipping some cream, adding snipped chives and serving this separately for your guests to add a spoonful to their own bowl.

Grated cheese: A bowl of grated cheese is needed on the table when serving pasta or a mixed vegetable soup. Gruyère and Parmesan mixed are a good choice but a hard piece of good Cheddar grated can be substituted.

To go with soup: To accompany soup, toast a slice of bread on one side, spread the untoasted side with butter and a little made mustard, sprinkle with dry grated cheese and grill until brown. Remove crusts and cut into small fingers.

Croûtons for soups: Dice a potato or a Jerusalem artichoke into cubes and fry in oil and butter to make croûtons for cream soups.

▨ *VEGETABLES*

Easier to serve: Cook a cauliflower in sprigs, leaving any small green leaves attached, until the stalks are just soft. Put into a lightly buttered bowl with all stalks facing to the centre. Press firmly under a circle of greaseproof paper. Turn out on to the serving dish and pour over browned butter or a suitable sauce. It looks like a whole cauliflower but is easier to serve.

Spinach and nutmeg: A sprinkling of a few grains of ground nutmeg makes a good finish for spinach purée.

Golden almonds: Use chopped or shredded almonds fried in butter to a golden brown as a tasty garnish to scatter over cooked cauliflower, broccoli and sprouts.

Carrots need sugar and mint: Finish cooked carrots with a little brown sugar and mint.

MEAT AND FISH

Savoury butter: Serve pats of savoury butter with grilled meat to compensate for the fact that no salt is used in the cooking.

A spot of colour: A neat 'bouquet' of carefully selected watercress adds freshness and colour to a dish of grilled food, see page 246.

Looks best: When serving fried food place the side which was fried first uppermost as it usually has the best appearance.

For a contrast: Serve a savoury sauce or butter with fried foods to provide a contrast of texture and flavour. For example, anchovy butter with fried fish or Maître d'Hotel butter with cutlets.

Perfect foils: The classic accompaniments were chosen to go well with the particular meat, for example apple sauce offsets the richness of pork or duck.

The right gravy: The gravy for beef and game should be thin or very lightly thickened. The gravy for mutton, veal and lamb can be a little thicker, and that for pork a little thicker still.

Dilute the gravy: The gravy in a meat pudding will be concentrated so have a jug of boiling water on the table to dilute it when serving, pouring a few spoonfuls into the pudding basin after the first cut.

Served from the bowl: Steamed suet puddings are turned out, but steamed meat puddings are served from the bowl with a napkin folded round.

Crisp brown apple: Fry unpeeled, but cored, 2 cm (¾ inch) circles of crisp dessert apple in shallow, hot oil and use to garnish grilled pork. Dust them first with caster sugar so that they brown well.

With rich meats: Spiced fruits such as peaches, pineapple and oranges are good for serving with rich meats such as pork or ham.

Croûte for game: Sit a cooked fillet steak or a small roasted game bird on a croûte of fried bread or toast to protect it from the heat of the plate and to keep it moist.

Cucumber and mint: Chunks or barrels of peeled cucumber sweated in butter are good served with lamb and fish dishes. A few spring onions can be cooked with them. Finish with a sprinkle of chopped mint.

Easy carving: Allow roasted meat and birds to stand for about 10 minutes in a warm place before carving; slicing will then be easier and less juices will be lost.

Carving know-how: Carving meat and jointing birds is much easier if you know something of their anatomy, such as where the bones and joints are, see pages 63, 65 and 67.

Limes as an alternative: Quartered limes can be served instead of lemon wedges with papaya, melon and fried fish dishes. Whether using lemon or lime, keep them a practical size for serving.

PUDDINGS

Hot gingerbread: Serve gingerbread mixtures hot with sweetened apple sauce as a pudding.

Sauce for the pudding: Make bought custard powder as usual and mix in the same quantity of plain yogurt or soured cream. Serve as a sauce for steamed puddings or stewed fruit.

GENERAL TIPS

Tasty bread: Cut bread very, very thinly, remove crusts, spread generously with garlic, anchovy flavoured butter then roll up tightly like a cigar shape. Cook in a hot oven until crisp and well browned. Serve hot with first courses.

Keep it hot: Pour boiling water into a vacuum flask to heat it before pouring in the liquid. This will keep it as hot as possible.

Hot for a picnic: Hot potatoes can easily be taken on a picnic in a wide-necked flask with a good bunch of mint on top of the potatoes.

Finish for pasta: A simple and good finish for pasta is to toss it in melted butter or warm olive oil, sprinkle with black pepper from a mill, then top it with good, well-flavoured grated cheese mixed with a spoonful of fresh chopped basil or marjoram. This makes a delicious and economical first course.

Raita for curries: Add diced cooked potato, mint, cucumber or aubergines to plain yogurt to make different varieties of Raita and serve as a cooling accompaniment to curries.

Warm sauce: Keep a quantity of Hollandaise sauce warm in a wide-necked vacuum flask which has been rinsed out with very hot water or warmed first.

To separate the grains and improve its appearance, use a fork to fluff up rice before serving. Do not try to do this with a spoon which will only crush the rice as it cuts through.

HOSTESS TROLLEY

Heat in advance: Trolleys generally need to be preheated before they are used for keeping food hot. Check with your manufacturer's instruction book.

Do not cover: Never cover roast or chipped potatoes or any food you want to keep crisp.

Loose over vegetables: Cover green vegetables loosely with buttered paper or a butter wrapper or foil, not a tightly fitting lid.

Under greaseproof: If serving puréed or boiled potatoes, place a piece of greaseproof paper over the potatoes before covering with the lid.

Keeping crackling crisp: To keep duck skin and pork crackling crisp, carve the meat, moisten it with a little gravy, place the skin or pieces of crackling on top but do not cover.

Care not to overcook: Do not overcook the food as heat is maintained and will spoil the food.

Way with rolls: Bread rolls can be warmed from cold in the hostess trolley.

Avoid egg dishes: Egg dishes do not keep warm well.

Set meringues: If the trolley is thermostatically controlled, it may be used either to cook meringues or to set the meringue on top of a pudding.

Avoid soggy pastry: Pastry should not be covered or it may become damp and soggy.

Pink if wished: Undercook beef and lamb, so that you can serve it pink if you wish.

Straight from the trolley: Mulled wine can be kept hot and served from the trolley.

Fresh garnishes: Do not garnish dishes before they are placed in the trolley. Garnishes should be placed on the dish just before serving so that they look fresh, see also pages 244 to 249.

Help themselves: Croûtes should not be put into the soup – dust them lightly with salt and keep them warm separately. Allow guests to help themselves.

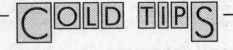

COLD TIPS

▥ CHEESE

Straw mats: There is a convention that says cheese should be served on straw or cane mats, so that it can breathe from below as well as above. If you do this, bear in mind that it is difficult to cut on a straw mat and that it will harbour crumbs and become unhygienic if not cleaned very thoroughly. A wooden cheese board is a more satisfactory surface; plastic ones blunt the sharpness of knives. Avoid covering cheese with a glass or china bell which will make it sweat.

Rinds: Some cheese rinds are edible, others not. Make sure that people have sharp enough knives to remove rind if they do not wish to eat it.

Scooping out: Tradition has it that Stilton should be scooped out from the centre, which should then be moistened with port to prevent it from drying out. A more satisfactory method of portioning it, and one that the Stilton makers recommend, is to cut slices in circles from the top. Cut as you would a piece of cake about 2.5 cm (1 inch) deep and take slices all round the cheese until the top circle has been removed. Repeat down the cheese in layers and it should not dry out *or* require port poured on it.

Put it away: Remove cheese from the table as soon as the cheese course is completed and store it away wrapped. This is particularly important at the end of a dinner party, since cheese, if left on the table, will absorb cigarette smoke and other flavours and also become warm and sweaty.

▓PUDDINGS

Fill in advance: Well-baked meringue shells or cases should be filled at least 2-3 hours before being served. This makes them much easier to slice before serving. They can be left overnight in a refrigerator.

Orange shells: Washed halved orange or tangerine shells can be used as a case in which to serve the same flavoured mousse or jelly. A jelly can be decorated with rosettes of whipped cream and a thin angelica stick.

Gordon Bleu
TIPS

To serve a fresh pineapple use a serrated knife and slice off the bottom. Place it on its side on a chopping board, hold firmly, take a sharp, stainless steel knife and cut out the 'eyes' in vertical lines. To do this make two cuts, one on either side of the eyes, at 45°. The eyes should then come out in strips. Now cut off the top and slice the flesh. Remove the woody core from each slice with a grapefruit knife.

Tip for strawberries: When serving strawberries with meringues, a gâteau or ice cream, slice them thickly or quarter them, then pour over 2 tablespoons of melted redcurrant jelly mixed with a little grated orange rind and the juice of half an orange.

Contrast textures: Serve a large thin, preferably home-made, biscuit with creamy puddings such as fruit fools and ice-creams for a contrast in texture.

▓CAKES

Patterned top: Cut even strips of paper and lay on top of a sandwich cake, spaced apart, then dust fairly heavily with icing sugar. Remove the paper carefully to leave a pattern.

242

Quick effect: If there is no time to ice a sandwich cake or a sponge, dredge the top fairly thickly with icing sugar to give it a finished look; this can be done through a paper doily for a lacy effect.

Easy icing: To ice small cakes easily, put each cake on the end of a palette knife and hold it over the bowl of icing while coating with a large spoon. Transfer the cake to a rack using the point of a skewer.

Icing a large cake: To ice a large cake with glacé or fondant icing, set it on a rack over a large dish or tray and pour the icing over the top from a low height.

Add a little shine: A small teaspoon of flavourless salad oil added to chocolate glacé icing helps to make it shine.

Easy filling: To split a sponge cake easily for filling, use a long serrated bread knife and saw evenly. Carefully slide a plate under the top piece of cake nearest to you to help to lift the top without breaking it. Fill as wished, then use the plate to help you to reposition the top.

Bakers' hint: Professional bakers often use a strong taut thread to cut through the centre of cakes quickly and neatly.

GENERAL

Well chilled melon: Segments of melon are much nicer to eat if they are well chilled beforehand.

Fresh start: Iced soup or a chilled consommé makes a refreshing start to a meal on a hot day.

Pepper not sugar: Try strawberries dusted with a *little* freshly ground black pepper which develops their flavour.

New style butter: Use flavoured butter when making sandwiches, for example mustard, anchovy essence, chopped herbs. Choose one which complements the flavour of the main filling.

More seasoning: If serving chilled food it will need more seasoning than if served hot.

Remove membranes: When serving grapefruit halves do not just loosen the segments but remove the membrane between them and lift each segment slightly as well. This allows the person eating the grapefruit to get each segment out easily.

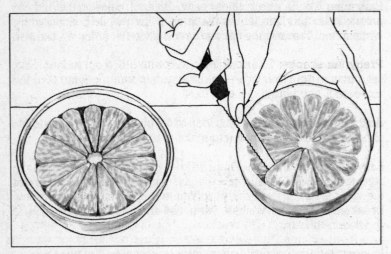

Add succulence: Boiled or poached meat, such as ham and chicken, that is to be served cold should be left to cool in the liquid. It will be succulent to eat.

Easy slicing: To help to slice brown bread and butter thinly put it in the freezer for an hour until it is firm. Butter to the edges before slicing with a sharp serrated bread knife.

GARNISH AND DECORATION

Good enough to eat: A garnish should always be edible, fresh-looking and neatly arranged.

Useful surround: Aspic is a useful glaze and finish for savoury food. It should be well flavoured. It can be brushed on, chopped or cut into shapes to surround food.

Crisp addition: Crisp bacon slices or bacon rolls grilled are good to garnish a dish of chicken.

Pretty not practical: Butterflies and twists made from thin circles of lemon or orange look pretty but are not very practical as they are too thin to squeeze the juice.

Lemon for fish: Quarters of lemon or eighths from a large lemon are a classic accompaniment and garnish for fried fish. Remove the white line of core so the juice is directed downwards on to the food.

Pretty fan shapes: Gherkins look decorative if cut into fans. Slice lengthways from the wide end three or four times leaving the stalk end intact, then spread them open.

Button mushroom caps: The caps of firm button mushrooms can be fluted and 'turned' before lightly cooking to garnish steaks.

Cordon Bleu Tips

Olives for garnish can be stoned without loss of shape. Black ones are simple, just slit one side and ease out the stone, then press together again. Green ones, because the flesh is not so soft, are more difficult. Use a small, sharp knife and make a small cut across the top of the olive without cutting right through. Next keep the blade of the knife against the stone and remove the flesh from the stone working in a spiral. Remove the flesh from the bottom, then take out the stone and reshape the olive.

Useful garnish: A box of small cress is a useful garnish on a salad or neatly arranged in a bunch on cold dishes. Cut it carefully with scissors holding the cress bunched in the fingers of the other hand to keep it together.

Fried parsley: Parsley garnishes also add extra flavour to a dish and should be eaten. It is best chopped fairly coarsely or finely according to the dish. When deep frying food turn off the heat for a few minutes after the main cooking has finished and lower dry sprays of parsley on a string into it briefly, then cut off the coarse stalks before using.

Perfect parsley: Shake parsley to remove any grit then chop finely on a board discarding any bits of stalk. Put it in the corner of a cloth, wash, then squeeze dry so it will sprinkle perfectly.

Green decoration: Watercress, now easily available most of the year, needs to be picked over for hairy stalks and any broken or yellow leaves. Bunch in one hand, so that the stalks can be cut fairly short and set this 'bouquet of watercress' stalks down at one side of the dish. Run several bouquets together if the dish is large.

Attractive garnish: The pale clustered leaves from the inside of a head of celery make an attractive garnish to cold savoury dishes if watercress is not available.

Open radishes: The red skin of radishes can be cut round in petal shapes and the radish left to open in iced water.

For cold meat: Celery can be shaved into thin slices and left to curl in iced water. Celery and spring onion can be cut into 'tassels' and used to garnish platters of cold meat or salad dishes.

Tomatoes in sixths: Tomatoes can be cut in sixths from top to stalk end but not right to the base, so that they look partly opened. Use firm perfect tomatoes for this.

Restoring a shine: If halved or quartered tomatoes are used as a garnish, brush them with a little oil to restore the shine.

Tomato rose: Remove skin with about 3 mm (⅛ inch) of flesh from a firm tomato cutting round in a long strip with a small serrated knife. Turn the strip so the skin is on the inside and curl round tightly to form a small 'rose'.

Orange garnish: Thin peel of an orange cut round and round can be curled into a spiral and used for a garnish.

Keep them small: Soup garnishes should be really small or they are difficult to manage on the spoon.

Fried bacon: Crisp small pieces of fried bacon can be sprinkled on top of pea, lentil or bean soups.

Texture contrast: Croûtons cut into 5 mm (¼ inch) cubes go well with all creamy soups giving a contrast of texture.

Soured cream for bortsch: A spoonful of soured cream looks good on a bortsch or beetroot soup and the combination of flavours also improves the taste.

Remove excess sugar: If using angelica, remove excess sugar by putting it into hot water for 1-2 minutes; wipe it dry and cut into even-sized diamonds or small sticks.

Leftover angelica: Keep any odd pieces of angelica from shaping and use in any fruit cake recipe.

Sticky cherries: If glacé cherries are very sticky with syrup, rinse in warm water and dry well before using for decoration. Do not cut them too small.

A good finish: If piping cream or butter icing on a cake, keep the pattern simple. Even-sized rosettes, judging the spacing beforehand, give a good finish round the edge.

Dry it well: If any decoration looks moist, dry it well before setting on whipped cream or icing.

Lemon needle shreds: Fine needle shreds of lemon or orange rind, blanched for one or two minutes and well dried make an effective decoration where the flavour and colour are suitable.

Walnut halves: Decorate a chocolate iced cake with walnut halves dusted fairly heavily with sifted icing sugar. Do this separately and lift them carefully into place, using the point of a knife, when the icing is not quite set.

Contrasting decoration: Whole browned hazelnuts, toasted in the oven and skinned, make a contrasting decoration for coffee icing.

Desiccated coconut: Toasted coconut can be used to decorate small iced cakes. Spread desiccated coconut on a shallow tray and put in a moderate oven for about 15 minutes until golden brown.

Colour evenly: To colour coconut put a few drops of food colouring into a screw top jar with a little water, put in the coconut and shake the jar to colour evenly.

Personal touch: For children make small iced cakes and pipe the child's name on top. They are especially good for a party.

Brandy snaps for decoration: Form small brandy snaps while still very warm into cone shapes; cool, fill with whipped cream and use to decorate desserts.

Piping chocolate: Add one or two drops of water or glycerine to melted chocolate to use it for piping. If it becomes too thick add a little flavourless salad oil.

Chocolate decorations: Gently melted chocolate can be spread on silicone or waxed paper and left to set. Cut out shapes and use for decoration on cakes or puddings.

Cool touch: Chill chocolate before grating and if it has to be handled for decoration pick it up on a palette knife.

Smooth shave: When shaving chocolate, warm it very slightly along the edge to be shaved then use a swivel peeler to take thin strips from along its length.

Feathering: Feather icing while it is still moist by running spaced lines of piped smooth redcurrant jelly or chocolate across the top; then draw the point of a knife or skewer well apart through the lines, and go back between the design drawing the knife in the other direction. Work quickly or the icing sets. A smooth whipped cream topping can also be feathered in the same way.

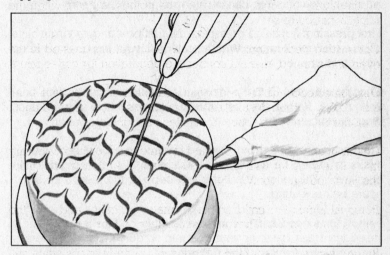

SALADS AND DRESSING

Prevent leaves wilting: Toss a leafy salad in oil and seasoning first, then add the vinegar. This stops the leaves wilting too quickly.

Colour it green: When peeling cucumber use a vegetable peeler down the length leaving some stripes of green peel for colour. Alternatively, scrape down the length of the skin with a fork, then slice it or cut into batons, or sticks, for variation in a green salad.

No bitterness: It is an advantage to sprinkle salt *lightly* on to prepared cucumber and leave it for half an hour on a tilted plate, then drain it and pat dry. This removes bitterness.

Vinegar last: Use a firm hard cabbage shredded very finely for cabbage salads. Dress it first with oil and seasoning, toss thoroughly until every shred is coated and only then add the vinegar.

Leek salad: Cooked young leeks thickly sliced make a tasty and unusual salad ingredient.

Vinegar plus: Make your own herb vinegar by steeping a few sprigs of the chosen herb in a bottle of white wine vinegar. Remove after several days or when the flavour is strong enough. Two or three halved cloves of garlic can be steeped in the same way.

First pressing: For salad dressings, the first pressing, or virgin olive oil, is excellent. It is pale and delicate in flavour but does not keep well once opened.

Chunky chicory: Chicory for salads should be white with pale yellow tips. Rather than separate the leaves, cut it in fairly thick diagonal slices.

Brown sugar and beetroot: Cooked beetroot can be sliced, cut into sticks or cubed for salad. Add a teaspoon of brown sugar to the dressing with a good grind of black pepper, then leave for some hours before eating.

Lemon for a good finish: Tomato salad can be finished with finely shredded fresh basil, or with fine thin shreds of blanched lemon peel and lemon juice in the dressing.

Rice is nice: Rice salads make a change and are good with chicken or seafood. Add colour to the rice with diced cooked or raw vegetables and season well.

Keep it simple: A few simple ingredients are often better for a salad than mixing a large assortment of vegetables.

No wilting: Do not put salad ingredients on a dish of hot food; nothing wilts quicker than lettuce on a hot plate.

A plate for the salad: If serving a green salad to accompany a hot meal, such as with roast game, lay a small bowl or side plate at each place for the salad.

Dress while warm: To dress potatoes for potato salad, turn them in a well flavoured French dressing while still warm.

Time saver: Keep a supply of French dressing in a screw-top container in a cool place. It is easy to shake up and emulsify and it keeps well.

Light dressing: Use a good light oil for dressings and mix olive oil with it. If, after making, the dressing tastes oily, try a pinch more salt before adding more vinegar or lemon juice. The salt will prevent it becoming too acid.

Curdle-free: Do not keep mayonnaise in the coldest part of the refrigerator as it may curdle.

Warmth is essential: Home-made mayonnaise is less likely to curdle during making if the oil and yolks are at room temperature. If the weather is very cold, warm the bowl.

Loose olives: Buy black or green olives loose as you need them; they are cheaper this way.

Care for anchovies: To draw the saltiness from anchovies, halve them lengthways and lay them flat on a plate. Barely cover them with milk and leave for 10 minutes or so. Drain, dry and use. Longer soaking will soften them so they can be crushed with a fork or pounded for flavouring.

Sugar syrup: Keep a covered jar of stock sugar syrup in the refrigerator, especially during the summer. It is handy for iced coffee, fruit salads and compotes. It also gives a shine to glacé icing.

Cordon Bleu
TIPS

To make a stock syrup you will need 450 g (1 lb) of lump or granulated sugar and 300 ml (½ pint) water. Put the sugar and water in a saucepan, bring to the boil and boil steadily to 105°C/220°F or when a little of the cooled syrup feels smooth when rubbed between thumb and forefinger but still clings to the skin. Leave the syrup to cool, then pour into a clean, dry, screw-topped jar.

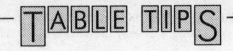

TABLE TIPS

▓MISCELLANEOUS HINTS

Easy to keep warm: Potatoes which are thinly sliced and baked in stock or milk are easy to keep warm; for a more attractive presentation, wipe the edge of the dish if the liquid has splashed on and coated into hard brown patches.

Warm rolls: To warm bread rolls put them in a dampened paper bag and place in a hot oven for five minutes.

Well-polished: Polish any stainless steel or glass dishes that you intend to use.

No gravy: Never dish gravy or sauce over fried foods as it will spoil the crisp coating or finish.

Do not swamp: Only dish liquid half way up the meat for a casserole, serve any extra in a sauce boat otherwise the food will look swamped in sauce.

Keep them cool: Chill serving dishes, plates and bowls thoroughly at least one hour before serving any chilled or iced food, and in the hot weather chill bowls for salads and jugs for cold drinks.

Well travelled: Use the ice-pack bags for picnic food which needs to be served cool or cold and make sure you choose food which will travel well.

A question of size: It is important to choose the right sized dish for the food being served; if too small, food will spill over as the first portion is being taken out and if too large it is out of proportion, making quantities look mean.

On a flat dish: Set a soufflé dish or small pots of chocolate mousse on a flat dish or plate to make them look more attractive and to provide a resting place for the spoon.

Tuck it in: Tuck damp greaseproof paper over moist food to keep it warm or hot.

Make them hot: Serve hot food on a warmed dish and heat the plates. This can be done in a warm oven, on a rack above the stove, or over a pan of boiling water.

Either very hot or very cold: Cold soup is unpleasant to eat; serve chilled soups well iced and hot soups very hot.

Taste first: Always taste food and correct the seasoning if necessary before serving.

FREEZING

7

▓FRESHNESS

Freshness really counts: Freezing is one of the safest and easiest methods of preserving food but the most important point to remember is that anything you are going to freeze must be super fresh, of prime quality and in perfect condition. It is a waste of time to freeze stale or inferior products.

Pick-your-own: Vegetables are best just picked from the garden or from a pick-your-own farm or bought from a recognized supplier, who really does sell very fresh produce.

Meat matters: Raw meat and meat products should come straight from a reputable butcher, supermarket or farm shop and preferably from someone who knows the meat is to be frozen.

Know your game: Game must come from a source where you know the date of shooting and length of hanging.

Chicken and turkeys: Poultry must also come from a reliable source where the birds are properly hung and prepared, whether whole or in portions.

Store to store: Supermarket fresh poultry may also be home frozen, provided it is taken straight home and frozen immediately without warming up at all and provided the sell-by has not been passed.

Fish out of water: Fish should come straight from the water; fishmongers often stock fish which has already been frozen, so always ask if unsure.

Really fresh fruit: Fruit again should come straight from the garden or orchard.

Storage: Each different type of food requires individual preparation and will store at its best for only a recommended length of time. The food is safe to eat for a time after this but it is likely to begin to deteriorate by losing colour, texture and flavour. Bought cooked frozen products should not be stored indefinitely for you are never quite sure how long they have been in the cabinet before purchase. Two months, generally speaking, is a safe storage time for bought cooked frozen products.

▦LIVING WITH A FREEZER

The process of freezing: The basic principle of freezing is to preserve the food as near as possible to its natural or original state with the minimum loss of texture, colour, flavour and freshness. Once frozen the food is stored at 18°C/0°F or lower, when chemical changes in food are practically halted and the micro-organisms become virtually inactive. Once the food thaws it will continue its deterioration from the point at which it was frozen and the process may be accelerated. Freezing will not improve the quality of food, which is why only prime quality produce or products should be subjected to freezing.

Freezers are available in a wide range of sizes. To help you calculate what capacity you will need, you should be able to store 9 kg of food per 30 litres (20 lb per cubic foot) or slightly more if it is in commercial packs. You are not likely to need less than 120 litres (4 cubic feet) unless you live in a town and just want the freezer to store small quantities of commercially frozen food.

Where to put it: Site the freezer in a dry, well-ventilated place, where it can be easily reached and inspected. Make sure that the air ducts and ventilation on the machine are not blocked up by furniture or other appliances and that the lights which indicate the freezer is working, on the outside of the cabinet, are easily visible. This is especially important if the freezer is going to be kept in the garage or an outhouse.

New freezer owners: If you are a new freezer owner it is essential to read all the instructions in the manufacturer's handbook thoroughly before even switching the cabinet on. Instructions are given for washing out prior to use; how long to allow before adding food; how much food to freeze at one time and, of course, how to use the fast freeze compartment.

Extra protection: If it is to be kept outside in a garage or outhouse, the freezer will need extra protection. Stand it on bricks or wooden blocks to raise it from the floor and polish the exterior regularly with a good silicone polish to help guard against rust.

Everyday check: It is essential that you check that the lights are working and that the freezer plug is firmly pushed into the wall socket every day.

Safety from children: If there are children around who might play with the switch and accidentally turn it off, it is an idea to tape over the plug, switch and socket with coloured tape.

Insurance: When you buy a freezer take out an insurance for the machine and contents – it is well worthwhile in case of accidents or breakdowns. Most freezers can be insured until they are ten years old either on a household policy or special freezer policy.

Open the box: It is advisable to open the door or lid as little as possible, since immediately it is opened, the warm air rushes in and begins to raise the temperature in the cabinet, which in turn can begin to thaw the food. The fuller the freezer the less this is likely to happen. Some freezers have special safety door locks which once closed will not open again for some minutes to give time for the cold air to recirculate.

Prolonged power cuts: Cuts of over twelve hours are often announced by the Electricity Board in advance. In this case it is a good idea to line up somewhere to move your frozen foods to, or to obtain some dry ice which will help keep the food frozen (mind your fingers for it can cause bad burns). Often a butcher or shop with a lot of freezer space will help out temporarily or sometimes the Electricity Board itself will have suggestions about where to store the food, especially if the cut is caused by them.

Short power cuts: Whatever you do **don't** be tempted to open the freezer during a short power cut. The fuller the cabinet, the longer the food will stay frozen. If only a small amount of food is inside, then it will warm up that much quicker. With a fairly full freezer, there is no need to worry for up to nine to twelve hours. Some people suggest piling rugs on top of the cabinet, this may help but is not essential. Keep the room as cool and well-ventilated as possible.

Fast freezing: Always remember to switch the fast freeze switch on in plenty of time before adding a large amount of new produce. Make sure that the fast freeze compartment or area is empty and remember to **switch off** again after the recommended length of time. I write a note to remind myself. You don't need to use the fast freeze switch if you are just putting one or two items in the freezer, unless they are very large.

FRUIT AND VEGETABLES

To blanch or not to blanch: Vegetables should be prepared and blanched before storage, if they are to be frozen for longer than six weeks, as this will help to prevent oxidation (see page 261). However, they could be prepared, packed and frozen without blanching if you are going to eat them in under four to six weeks, though the colour, texture and flavour will begin to deteriorate after about two weeks. After six weeks they are best discarded. Unblanched vegetables are only an emergency method: not to be recommended.

Cauliflower: Add the juice of a lemon to the blanching water to help keep the florets white during freezing.

Flabby vegetables: Certain varieties of vegetables have a higher water content than others, which makes them less suitable for freezing, e.g. tomatoes, lettuce, watercress, cucumber. Try to use only those varieties which are recommended for freezing (usually stated on the packet of seeds or ask the nurseryman or green-grocer) and take care to drain all vegetables very thoroughly after blanching. Always 'fast-freeze'. (See above.)

Microwave: A microwave can be used to blanch vegetables. Follow directions for the individual type of microwave. No water is needed with the vegetables and they are simply cooled under cold running water and drained while the next batch is being cooked.

Avocados: Although avocados do not freeze well in their natural state, when cheap and plentiful they can be used in a soup or a mousse and will then freeze successfully.

Free-flow vegetables: Lay the blanched and dried vegetables on trays lined with foil or freezer paper and open freeze until solid. You will then find that they can be poured into large polythene bags or containers for storage and will remain free-flowing. Remove and use as required but always reseal the container after use.

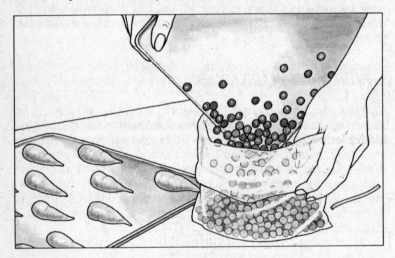

Mixed vegetables: A good time-saver is to freeze small packs of diced or sliced mixed vegetables to use for soups, stews and casseroles.

Soft option: If fruit is on the soft side or picked when wet, it is better to purée it before freezing. Simply sieve and sweeten (if liked) or heat gently, sweeten to taste and sieve or purée in a food processor or liquidizer.

Jam fruits: If time is short, fruits, such as plums, damsons and rhubarb can be prepared and stored in the freezer for up to a month prior to use for jam. This means you can do your jam-making at a convenient time, rather than when you have a glut of fruit.

Remove the stones: Where possible you should remove the stones from fruit, otherwise a strong almond flavour may permeate the fruit after two to three months storage.

The exception to the rule: Plums for jam should be frozen with stones left in to help the flavour and pectin content but do not leave them for more than about six weeks.

Marmalade oranges: If there is no time to make marmalade when the Seville orange season arrives this fruit can be frozen whole or halved for up to a year. The odd Seville orange is also excellent for adding to orange sauce to serve with duck.

Quick fruit salads: Freeze mixtures of suitable fruits in a syrup. All that is required to make a fruit salad is to thaw out and add a few fresh fruits.

Darkening fruits: Prevent discoloration and darkening of fruits by adding lemon juice to fruit purées and those which are lower in vitamin C. Fruits which tend to discolour, e.g. apples, pears, apricots, plums, should be eaten as soon as thawed or while a few ice crystals still remain.

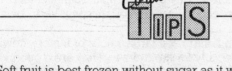

Gordon Bleu
TIPS

Soft fruit is best frozen without sugar as it will keep its texture better that way, however, most other fruits are frozen either with dry sugar or with a sugar syrup. The dry sugar will have the effect of drawing the juice from the fruit to form a syrup. Both forms of sugar also protect the fruit against oxidation.

Oxidation: This may occur in meats and fish with a high fat content or in unblanched vegetables. Oxygen penetrates the tissues causing the fat to oxidize and turn rancid. Always remove as much excess fat from meat and poultry as possible before freezing, for example from inside the cavity of poultry, or from the outside of chops.

▰MEAT AND FISH

Tender and good: For good flavour and tenderness, make sure all meat is well hung before freezing – the exception being pork. Fresh meat may be tough. Well-hung meat should look brown not bright red. If in doubt, ask your butcher about the length of hanging.

Prepacked meat: Ask the butcher to cut the carcass into the type of joint you want and to the size you require.

Whole and half carcasses: It is cheaper to buy meat by the whole or half carcass or, in the case of beef, by the quarter. Discuss your requirements with the butcher or supermarket, for example, how you want it butchered and the size of joints which will be most convenient for your particular needs. The butcher usually prepacks the meat for you and will do it as you want, provided you have given him details at the time of ordering.

Salted meats: Bacon, ham and other salted meats should be stored for only the minimum amount of time: no longer than six to eight weeks. The saltiness tends to give a rancid flavour or sometimes a fishy or musty flavour if kept too long. The milder cures will keep better, but it is advisable to buy only in small quantities and use quickly. The vacuum-packed rashers and joints will keep best.

Bargain packs: Some butchers sell large packs of mince, stewing steak, chops, etc., especially for the freezer. They are a good idea but need to be packed into smaller amounts to suit your family needs before they are put into the freezer.

Chops apart: When freezing chops always separate one from another with freezer foil, tissue or paper for easy removal.

Care with cooked meats: As soon as meat is cooked it should be cooled rapidly and chilled. Either wrap the whole joint securely or chop it as you intend to use it. Store for up to two months, although ham and bacon are better used within four to six weeks.

Keep the crackling: As crackling is not spoilt by freezing leave the rind on pork joints and chops.

Separate the giblets: The storage life of giblets is shorter than the bird so do not pack them into the cavity of poultry or game. Wrap them in polythene bags and freeze separately instead. Chicken livers can be frozen all together in tubs for making pâté. Poultry and game will thaw quicker without the density of giblets in the cavity.

The rules for game: Birds should be hung and prepared before freezing. Waterfowl are best frozen after only one to two days of hanging. Rabbit should be frozen fresh; hare after hanging for two to three days. Venison should be hung for about a week according to weather conditions and personal taste. Cook all game as soon as possible after thawing.

Unplucked game: In an emergency, game in the feather can be wrapped in polythene and frozen as it is, however care must be taken not to contaminate the rest of the freezer. The frozen bird should be removed as soon as possible and, after defrosting, plucked, drawn and cooked quickly.

Bad shot: Game that has been badly shot is not really suitable for freezing unless the shot parts are removed or it is cooked first. The putrified flesh will deteriorate quickly even in the freezer.

Venison in store: Although the recommended storage time for venison is one year, venison joints have been found to improve with freezer storage – probably because the meat is virtually fat free – and are quite excellent after two to three years storage. Do not cook from frozen.

Protecting fish: To prevent fish from dehydrating make sure it is extremely well wrapped before it is put in the freezer.

Gut first: Gut and clean fish before freezing. Most fish should have heads removed – the exceptions are trout, salmon, etc. – and even they can have heads removed if freezer space is limited.

Freeze it whole: The best way to freeze a large fish is to leave it whole and unwrapped; then dip it in ice cold water to form a glaze, repeating several times. When an even coating of ice is achieved wrap the fish carefully in foil and return to the freezer.

▮DAIRY PRODUCTS

Hard cheese: When hard cheese has been stored for longer than about two months it tends to crumble. An alternative is to grate it and store in polythene bags or small containers. The cheese will last for much longer and can be used in cooked dishes.

Stilton and blue cheese: Both Stilton and blue cheese will freeze well, so if a half cheese is given as a present, then part of it can be frozen for later use. However, do wrap in foil or double cling film and overwrap with foil or a polythene bag to contain the smell.

Cream cheese: It is best to blend cream cheese with whipped double cream to make it into a savoury dip before freezing in order to prevent separation. Another solution is to add sugar as a stabilizer if the cheese is to be used for cheesecakes.

Soft cheese: Either wrap first in cling film, then foil or put into a small plastic container. Label clearly and store for up to six to eight weeks maximum.

Butter: Keep an emergency packet of butter in the freezer. It will spread almost immediately on hot toast.

Savoury butters: Make up various flavoured savoury butters and roll in foil or polythene to store until required. A slice or two adds interest to chops, fish, steaks, vegetables and such and takes no time to remove from the freezer.

Yogurt: Only some commercial makes of yogurt freeze well for they contain a stabilizer. Home-made varieties tend to separate and are not appetizing, although perfectly safe to eat.

Icings – to freeze or not: Do not freeze icings, such as fondant, royal, glacé, boiled and American frosting, as they crack and crumble on thawing. Butter creams are excellent for freezing as they have a good proportion of fat which helps to keep them in good condition.

Butter cream: When icing a cake, make extra butter cream and store in small cartons in suitable amounts. It can be left plain and flavouring added when thawed, or frozen ready flavoured.

Cream: Provided cream contains at least 40% butter fat, it can be whipped and frozen (see page 50). It can also be piped into rosettes on non-stick paper, open frozen and then stored in a rigid container. A touch of sugar added to the cream before whipping keeps it more stable and less likely to separate on thawing.

Ice cream: Home-made ice cream freezes well but the synthetic flavourings in bought products may intensify if stored for too long. Use pure or fresh flavourings only, such as vanilla essence rather than vanilla flavouring.

Egg caution: Do not freeze whole eggs in shells, they will explode.

Egg whites: Raw egg whites can be frozen in small containers or ice cube trays. Label clearly stating quantities. Thaw out completely and use as fresh egg whites within two days of thawing. Whisked egg whites cannot be frozen.

Egg yolks: Raw egg yolks will coagulate during freezing unless salt or sugar is added as a stabilizer. For each six egg yolks add half a level teaspoon of salt or caster sugar, beating well. Label clearly stating whether for sweet or savoury use. Thaw completely, then use immediately for soufflés, omelettes, cakes, etc.

COOKED DISHES

Double up: It is a good idea to make double or treble quantities of casseroles at one time for freezing to save time and electricity.

Casseroles and cooked dishes: Before freezing casseroles and other cooked dishes season only lightly and adjust when served in case the seasonings intensify in the freezer and spoil the flavour.

Low fat: When making cooked dishes for the freezer, keep the fat content as low as possible to prevent the possibility of it turning rancid. Remove excess fat from the surface of casseroles, soups, etc., when cold and before freezing.

Cornflour is best: Choose cornflour rather than flour as a thickening agent for sauces, as it does not separate on thawing.

Soups that don't curdle: When large amounts of eggs and cream are added to soups they tend to curdle on thawing. Add them for flavour or thickening on reheating instead.

Condensed soups: To save space in the freezer, do not add all the stock or milk required when making soups; simply freeze the thick purée or soup and add stock or milk when thawed.

Too strong on flavour: Do not freeze soups which are highly flavoured with onion, curry, herbs, etc., for longer than about two weeks, for they tend to take on a musty flavour.

Concentrated stocks: Boil made stock until reduced by half to give a concentrated liquid. This will save freezer space. An equal quantity of water can be added on thawing.

Meringue discs: Make meringue shapes (discs, shells, baskets) as usual and pack in rigid containers for use as required. The shells can be used straight from the freezer for decoration.

266

Bake bread in bulk: When baking bread do so in bulk and freeze the surplus. Yeast products tend to dehydrate easily, so wrap well and carefully, making sure the package is completely airtight.

Fresh yeast: It is not always easy to obtain fresh yeast when required, so buy in bulk – say 450 g (1 lb) and pack in usable quantities of 15-25 g (½-1 oz). Wrap individual amounts tightly in polythene and label. Bundle the small packets into one larger bag to keep them tidy. Fresh yeast will store safely for up to a year.

Bread dough: When baking a batch of bread dough make extra and store suitable quantities in a ball tightly wrapped in polythene. It takes up less space than baked loaves and freezes well. Thaw completely before shaping and continuing as usual.

Home-made bread rolls can be frozen once they have been partially baked. Bake them in a preheated oven at 150°C, 300°F, Gas Mark 2 for 20 minutes, then freeze. Half an hour before serving, allow to thaw for ten minutes, then complete the baking in an oven preheated to 230°C, 450°F, Gas Mark 8.

Crisp pastry base: When making fruit pies add a little cornflour to thicken the fruit juice to help prevent the base pastry going soggy during storage.

Puff and flaky pastries: Always make at least twice as much pastry as you require. It takes no longer to make larger quantities but the extra will freeze well, saving time and effort the next time pastry is needed.

Shortcrust pastry: A supply of made-up shortcrust pastry is a good idea; it only takes a short time to thaw provided it is packed in a usable amount of say 225-450 g (½-1 lb) and is formed into a block which is not too thick.

Pastry flan cases: When time allows, bake some pastry cases for flans. Stack up separated with foil or freezer paper and store in a rigid container. Remove a flan case as required, fill while still frozen if necessary and reheat. It only takes a few minutes to thaw. Both savoury and sweet flans can be frozen.

Raw pastry circles: Ready-cut raw pastry circles can be stacked, separated with discs of foil or freezer paper, and frozen. Each one is then ready to remove, thaw and use to line a tin all in one go.

Sausage rolls at the ready: Sausage rolls can be made as usual but left in a long strip ready to be cut into the required size before cooking. Freeze, wrapped carefully, so that the roll doesn't break and leave to thaw for just a few minutes, when it can easily be cut up and baked.

Cheese nibbles: If you are left with trimmings from cheese pastry or other flavoured pastries, cut them into fancy shapes and bake; then freeze. Use as soup garnishes, cocktail nibbles and canapé bases.

Sliced cakes: Rich cakes, teabread, etc., can be sliced and separated with paper, then reassembled and overwrapped before freezing. This allows the required number of slices to be removed as required, which is ideal for packed lunches.

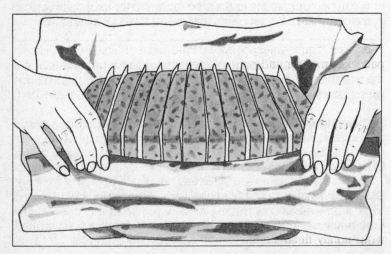

Fruit cakes: These store well if kept completely airtight by wrapping closely in foil. Thaw slowly still in the wrapping, then dose with extra brandy or rum if possible.

EXTRAS

Breadcrumbs: Turn all dried bread into crumbs and pack in polythene bags. The crumbs will stay fresh and separate and can be used for stuffing, garnishes, etc. They can be used either from frozen or thawed out first.

Buttered crumbs for garnishes: To make tasty toppings and garnishes, melt 25 g (1 oz) butter with 1 tablespoon oil in a frying pan and add 100 g (4 oz) fresh breadcrumbs. Fry gently, stirring frequently until evenly browned and golden. Drain on paper towels and when cold, pack in polythene bags. Add sugar if to be used to top a sweet dish.

Raw cake mixture: Any excess uncooked cake mixture, such as a Victoria Sandwich can be frozen in a plastic carton with a tight-fitting lid. When required, thaw completely, add any flavouring and bake at once.

Chocolate decorations: Coarsely grated chocolate, curls, leaves, etc., can be open frozen and stored for two to three months in rigid containers ready for use. They can be removed while still frozen.

Pancakes: If one tablespoon of oil is added to the batter it will keep pancakes moister and prevent them becoming rubbery. Stack the made pancakes between layers of foil, greaseproof or non-stick paper and wrap the whole pile in foil or put into a polythene bag.

Cocktail ice cubes: Freeze sprigs of mint, orange or lemon peel or slices, cocktail cherries or olives in cubes of ice.

Oranges and lemons: Slices of orange and lemon are ideal for drinks and garnishes. Slice and remove any pips, then open freeze. Pack into small containers or polythene bags for storage.

Fruit rinds: Grate the rind, finely or coarsely, from citrus fruits and wrap tightly in small amounts in foil. The rind can also be thinly pared from the fruits with a potato peeler, cut into julienne strips and blanched. Pack as above and use to add to soups, sauces, casseroles, etc., and for garnish or decoration.

Fruit flavours: Often a small amount of fruit juice is needed to flavour something, so freeze any small quantities in ice cube trays, ice cube bags or very small containers.

Lemon and orange curd: Make curd as usual and pot in small plastic containers or cartons. Cover, label and store in the freezer for up to three months; this extends the shelf life of curds.

Fried bread croûtons: For canapés and soup garnishes, cut slices of bread into 5 mm-1 cm (¼-½ inch) slices and then into cubes or into fancy shapes with cutters and fry in shallow or deep fat until golden brown; drain thoroughly and pack as for breadcrumbs. They will freeze well. To thaw and refresh, place them still frozen but uncovered in a fairly hot oven for about five minutes.

Sandwiches and filled rolls: Provided care is taken with the fillings, sandwiches and filled rolls freeze well. Avoid salad ingredients, hard-boiled eggs, mayonnaise and jam. Keep the crusts on for freezing and stack sandwiches of same filling together in usable amounts, then wrap tightly. Do not mix fillings in one package or the flavours will mingle. Thaw out in their wrappers. Wrap rolls individually first in cling film before packing into a polythene bag.

Toast: Keep a sliced loaf of bread in the freezer for emergency toast. The slices will remain separated and can be toasted from frozen by increasing the cooking time on the toaster.

Pâtés: If pâtés are very acid, e.g. those with liver and lots of wine or onions, they should be turned out of the tin they were baked in and wrapped in greaseproof or non-stick paper before wrapping securely in foil to prevent any acids from the pâté eating into the foil during storage.

Sliced pâtés: Freezer tissue can be used to divide slices of pâtés, so they are easy to remove and serve slice by slice at any time.

Mincemeat: If not carefully stored, mincemeat often tends to ferment in jars. An alternative is to make a freezer mincemeat containing a much higher proportion of apple, which stores with no problems and makes an ideal filling for so many things. Consult a freezer cookbook for a suitable recipe.

Jelly: Plain jelly or aspic jelly does not freeze very well as it becomes granular on thawing. Gelatine is fine when added to cream and fruit purées, as in soufflés and mousses or savoury dishes containing jellied sauces, but take care if there is a very high proportion of gelatine in a recipe.

Strong flavours: If strong-flavoured items, such as curries, strong cheese, onions, leeks, smoked fish or high game, are not carefully packed they will spread their flavour to other foods in the freezer. They should be overwrapped to be on the safe side.

Iced coffee: Make up concentrated or very strong black coffee and freeze in ice cube trays or ice cube bags, then store in polythene bags ready for use as a refreshing drink.

Basic sauces: Sauces can be made in bulk using stock or milk or other ingredients, such as tomatoes or mushrooms, when cheap and plentiful. Freeze in usable amounts such as 150-300 ml (¼-½ pint) and complete the sauce when thawed.

Fried foods: Before freezing fried foods, drain thoroughly on paper towels to prevent the items becoming soggy during freezing.

Fresh herbs: Parsley and other herbs can be frozen unblanched separate from their stalks in small polythene bags or containers. Crumble into the dish while still frozen – there is no need to thaw and chop.

Herb cubes: Chop fresh herbs either in single varieties or made into a mixture and pack into ice cube trays, adding a little water to hold in place and freeze. Store the frozen cubes in a polythene bag and use as required by simply adding a cube or part of a cube to the dish during preparation.

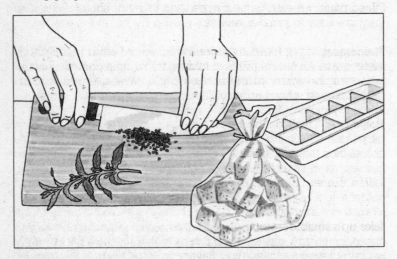

Packed meals: A selection of the following will make excellent packed meals: individually wrapped sandwiches or rolls, slices of cake or small cakes, individual pies – sweet or savoury, pasties, individual mousses or portions of stewed fruit. They can then be removed complete and left to thaw overnight ready for the next day.

Children's meals: After school children often need to eat before the rest of the family. When preparing a dish for the freezer, cook extra and freeze this in individual portions in foil containers ready to thaw and reheat as required.

Special diets: These can be catered for by cooking several amounts of several dishes at one time and freezing separately in individual containers. This is particularly useful for salt-free and fat-free diets.

TYPES OF PACKAGING

Packaging: Use suitable packaging according to the type of food to be frozen, as described below.

Foil: Heavy duty or freezer foil should be used where possible as it is stronger and less likely to tear during packing or storage. It is the easiest to use when moulding around difficult shapes and for padding bones and protrusions.

Polythene: Thick gauge or freezer bags or sheets of heavy-duty polythene should be used for extra protection. Discard after use unless completely cleaned and airtight. Thinner polythene can be used for overwrapping and for storing several small polythene or foil packages of one type of food.

Waxed containers: Liquids can be stored in waxed containers but take up valuable freezer space, so use sparingly. Do not add anything hot to the container or the wax will melt. They are only reusable if well washed and they are the lined variety of container. Otherwise line with a polythene bag before using again.

Polythene and plastic containers: These are excellent for storage as they are virtually indestructible and have airtight lids. They are also easy to stack in the freezer, thus saving space.

Foil containers: Foil dishes, plates and trays are ideal for baking all sorts of items for the freezer. They are easy to seal (keep the foil side of lid in contact with the food) and store, and can be taken from freezer to oven – but not to the microwave.

Plastic cartons: Use empty, well washed yogurt, cream, margarine cartons, etc., which come complete with lids for storage. The small cartons are particularly useful for storing small quantities in the freezer.

Ice cube polythene bags: Available in rolls, these are ideal for ice as well as small quantities of condensed stock, gravy, cream, baby foods, chopped herbs, etc. Simply pull off one or more cubes as required.

Packing around protrusions: Always pad any bones or protrusions with foil, waxed paper or other paper to prevent tears in packaging during storage.

Extra protection: This can be given to awkward-shaped parcels which might tear during storage by overwrapping with a piece of muslin or by wrapping in sheet polythene.

Freezer burn: This is an unsightly patch or patches of brownish or grey-white on the surface of foods, often appearing on meat, poultry and fish. It usually appears because the packaging has been torn causing dehydration, or there is too much air left in the package. It is not harmful but makes the product tissues go spongy and tough. Take care with proper packaging to avoid this.

TYPES OF FOOD

Liquids: Liquids must always have a headspace of 2.5 cm (1 inch) left in the container (of any type) for they expand during freezing and can cause the container to explode. This includes soups, stocks and all liquids.

Baby foods: Small amounts of baby food can be stored in small yogurt or other containers provided they are well cleaned and sterilized (as for baby's bottles) before filling.

Casseroles and stews: These also need a headspace left in the container, but 1 cm (½ inch) is usually sufficient. Try to make sure that the lumps of food are all covered by liquid, as those which tend to be exposed could deteriorate. If necessary put crumpled waxed paper in the container to keep them submerged.

Casserole dishes: Cook your casserole or stew in casserole dishes lined with foil. Cool and freeze still in the casserole: when solid remove the foil parcel from the dish, overwrap and return to the freezer. The casserole dish is then ready for use again and the contents can be returned to the same dish to reheat and serve.

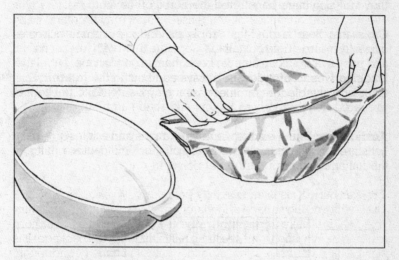

Decorated cakes: If decorated cakes are to stay looking good they must be open frozen first. Once firm, pack into a rigid container standing the cake on a strip of foil or greaseproof paper, so it is easy to lift in and out the container. Label the lid carefully stating 'This Way Up' to prevent accidental damage by turning upsidedown in the freezer. Undo the top of the container before thawing and remove from the container completely if it will be difficult to do so when thawed.

Dinner parties: Plan well in advance so the necessary items can be located in the freezer; or be cooked, prepared and stored in the freezer to ease the cooking load on the day. With care and thought a whole meal can come out of the freezer (unknown to your guests!).

Ice crystals: When these appear in packages of frozen foods they have been caused by moisture in the food cells expanding when frozen and have formed ice which punctures and destroys the surrounding tissues. Fast freezing cuts this down dramatically.

Too much headspace: If the headspace in the container is too large (because of the amount of casserole and unsuitable sized container), ice crystals will form. This can be remedied by putting crumpled waxed paper between the contents and the lid. If the ice crystals have already formed, scrape them off before thawing the food, but they will also have penetrated the fibres of the food.

Croissants: Bear in mind that croissants tend to crush unless frozen carefully in large rigid containers. Separate them with freezer tissue and pack in a rigid container to keep them in good shape. Label the box clearly, so that it doesn't get tossed about in the freezer. This takes up valuable freezer space, so it may be better to freeze the prepared dough, ready to roll out and shape and bake.

Acidic fruits: Fruits, such as lemons, oranges and apples, are best not stored in foil containers as eventually the acid causes pitting in the foil and will spoil the fruit.

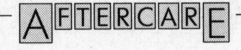

▓WHAT TO DO AND WHEN

Records: Although a bit of a nuisance, it is advisable to keep some sort of a record of the freezer's contents. List date, contents and positon to avoid items remaining at the bottom of the cabinet beyond their freezer life.

Labelling: It is essential to have a log book in which to keep records of food as it is put into the freezer, so that you know what is in the cabinet, when it was frozen and the date it needs to be consumed by. Label the food packets themselves, too. Write clearly and include the type of food, number of servings or amount, as well as the date of freezing.

Thawing: This can take place at room temperature, in a cool place, the refrigerator or in a microwave cooker. It is usually best to thaw out slowly but large items, such as turkeys are best thawed at room temperature rather than in the refrigerator which would take several days.

Room temperature: This should not exceed 18°C/65°F. Thawing food should be kept out of direct sunlight.

Once thawed: Food once thawed should be used as quickly as possible and kept in the refrigerator. It should never be left lying around at room temperature between thawing and cooking.

Emergency thawing: If you need to accelerate the thawing process, this can be done by immersing the sealed food in a bowl of warm water or holding it under a running tap. Make sure the water does not come into contact with the food, however, otherwise it will spoil the flavour and texture.

Safe thaw: Bags of liquid should be thawed standing in a jug or bowl, since they collapse as they thaw.

Thawing and cooking instructions: When using commercially frozen products, follow the thawing and cooking instructions carefully. If it says to thaw first, then it is wise to do so.

Cooked dishes: Never thaw and then refreeze cooked dishes.

Removal of frozen food: If food has to be taken out of the freezer, whilst it is being repaired for example, wrap the frozen packets in thick newspaper and rugs, put in a cold place and it will be fine for up to two hours (or three to four hours in cold weather). For longer storage try to obtain dry ice (use thick, heavy-duty gloves when handling it) and pack into boxes or containers with the food. A cold box with frozen ice blocks will also help to keep the food cold for several hours. (See also pages 258 and 259.)

Well-stocked freezer: Keep the freezer well stocked as it costs just as much to run a nearly empty freezer as a full one.

Amounts to freeze: For best results don't add more than 10% of the capacity of the freezer at one time otherwise it will slow down the freezing process and impair the quality of the frozen food.

Checking the temperature: This is simple if a freezer thermometer is kept in the cabinet.

Defrosting: To reduce the need to defrost, use a plastic scraper to remove excess ice as it forms in the freezer. Complete defrosting is only necessary every 12 months or so, but more frequently if the freezer is not kept fairly full.

Used containers from freezing: These must be washed out very carefully and thoroughly before using again for freezing to make sure any scraps of food or micro-organisms are removed.

Microwaves: These ovens are marvellous for thawing and reheating dishes straight from the freezer but make sure the food is not in any type of foil dish or container or a china container with a metallic edge. Metal prevents the microwaves from penetrating the food sufficiently and will crack and mark the metallic part on china. Remember, too, to cover food with cling film with several holes in it before reheating. Sometimes the food spits and explodes as it heats and this can make an awful mess in the oven, apart from spoiling the food, if it isn't covered.

Cooking meat from frozen: It is wise to use a meat thermometer when doing this to make sure the joint is completely thawed and cooked through in the centre.

Poultry: For safety all poultry *must be completely thawed* (i.e. no ice crystals left in the body cavity) before cooking. Precooked poultry dishes can be reheated from frozen but they must be completely cooked through and boiled. Remove a portion of chicken and make sure that it is piping hot right through.

Game: Game birds, hares, rabbit, etc., must all be thawed out completely before cooking as a safeguard against the possibility of the flesh not being completely cooked through.

Marinade: Chops and joints of meat and poultry can be marinated by putting the frozen or semi-frozen items straight into the

278

marinade. They will thaw and marinate together, thus cutting down on time on both processes.

Casseroles and cooked dishes: These must be thawed and re-cooked, not just reheated, for safety. Take care not to break up the ingredients when stirring casseroles and stews, etc. They can be cooked from frozen either in the oven or in a saucepan but it must be done carefully and slowly. It is better to thaw first, if possible.

Fish: Small whole fish, fillets and steaks can be cooked from frozen but if they need to be coated in egg and breadcrumbs or batter, they should be partially thawed first otherwise the coating will not adhere to the food.

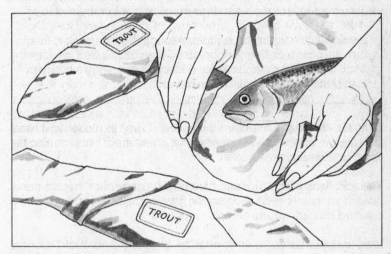

Frozen vegetables: Whether commercially or home-frozen, these are served at their best if cooked from frozen in the minimum amount of fast-boiling water with salt added if liked, according to personal taste.

Thawing tomatoes: If tomatoes have been frozen in their skins, allow to thaw for a few minutes then the skins will slip off easily. This removes the necessity of peeling them before freezing. They will be too soft for salads but excellent for cooking. Tomatoes can also be frozen ready-peeled, whole, sliced, chopped or puréed.

Soft fruits: In some cases, e.g. raspberries, strawberries, logan-berries, currants, soft fruits can be turned frozen into a fruit salad where they will thaw out and chill the other ingredients all in one go.

Soft fruits for decoration: These should not be allowed to thaw completely but should be 'caught' while there are still some ice crystals left in them so they hold their shape.

Cordon Bleu
Tips

To unmould an ice cream dessert made in a bombe mould or cake tin, have ready a large bowl of cold water. Draw the mould or tin two or three times through the water. Dry, then turn out on to a chilled serving dish. Silver or stainless steel are best. If the cold water treatment doesn't work, wrap a hot cloth round the mould for just 30 seconds.

Fruit for stewing: Fruit can be thawed slowly in a saucepan and reheated in one process if stewed fruit is required. This can also be done in the microwave oven.

Pies and flans: Stand pies and flans on a baking sheet that has been heated up in the oven to accelerate thawing of the pastry base, start cooking quickly and prevent sogginess.

Iced cakes: These may appear to become over moist during thawing but when completely thawed they will be fine and return to their normal state – so do not worry.

Dairy products: All dairy products are much better if thawed out slowly in the refrigerator.

Thawed ice cream: This should not be refrozen and indeed it is not safe to try it.

Iced lollies: Allow these to thaw for at least five minutes before giving to children, as the frozen ice could stick to lips or tongue.

Rolls: Wrapped in foil these can be reheated in the oven from frozen in about 10 minutes.

Pitta bread: This will thaw in a microwave in a matter of a minute or so; or in the oven wrapped in foil in about five minutes.

Herb rolls: Halve and spread fresh rolls with herb butter, re-assemble and freeze. They can be thawed out in the oven when required, ready to serve with soup, etc.

Thaw a whole loaf: Place the loaf, unsliced, in a fairly hot oven, tightly wrapped in foil for about 20 minutes and it will be ready to slice and eat.

Suet puddings: Meat or fruit suet puddings can be re-steamed from frozen. The meat pudding will need 3 to 3½ hours and the fruit 2 to 2½ hours.

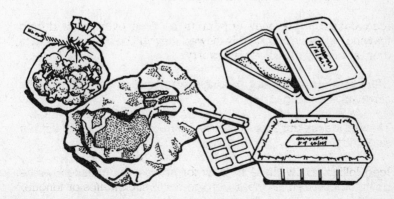

PRESERVING

8

 JAMS

▦STARTING OFF

The structure of jam: Good jam contains the right balance of fruit, containing acid and pectin to form the 'set', and sugar. Water is added to fruits high in natural pectin and acid, thus increasing their yield. Blackcurrants are a good example of such fruit and jam made from them is easily set.

Small is tasty: The smallest quantity of fruit which can economically be made into jam is 1 kg (2 lb).

Start right: Prevention is far better than cure, so start with a reliable recipe and fruit which is just on the point of ripeness, gathering over-ripe or wet fruit is the recipe for disappointment.

Handling: Pick soft fruit with a tiny length of stalk where possible, so that you have something to hold on to other than the fruit itself. Too much handling easily bruises the fruit, making it deteriorate more quickly.

Storage: On the way back from the farm or market, keep the fruit in the shade, not on the back window ledge of the car in full sunshine. When you get home spread the fruit on trays or keep them in the basket, covered and cool in the refrigerator if they have to be kept overnight before making the jam.

Washing soft fruit: Do not wash soft fruit until just before making the jam. Put the fruit in a colander and lower it gently into a bowl of cold water, drain it thoroughly.

Natural pectin: Pectin is a gel-like substance which is present in all fruits but in varying quantities. It helps jams to set.

Commercial pectin: With fruits that are low in natural pectin this can save the day. Instructions for use come with each bottle. As well as ensuring a set, less boiling is required therefore the yield is better and the flavour very fresh.

284

The right container: Choose a pan which will hold your chosen quantity of fruit and allow room for it to boil vigorously. The pan should be large enough for the jam to treble in volume as it bubbles up the sides after the sugar has been added. The wider the surface of the pan, the quicker the evaporation, which raises the temperature of the jam. This explains why old-fashioned preserving pans were usually so wide rather than deep and are ideal if you make a lot of jam.

Testing for the Setting Stage
This applies to all jams, jellies and marmalade.

Sugar thermometer method: Jam must reach a temperature of 105-106°C/220-222°F before it will set. Always put the thermometer into the jam after the sugar has dissolved to allow it to heat slowly. Take the reading at eye level as accuracy is important, be patient until it reaches the correct degree.

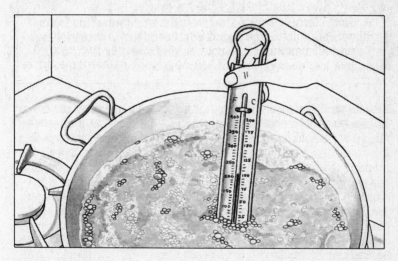

Saucer method: Drop a small spoonful of the jam on to a saucer. When the jam is cold, draw your finger through it and if it is ready, the surface will wrinkle quite thickly. Remember to draw the pan away from the heat while you test the contents. To speed up the cooling process, you could cool the saucer in the refrigerator before dropping the jam on to it.

Homely method: Dip a clean wooden spoon into the jam, lift it with a little jam, cool it slightly while you count to ten, then turn it sideways above the pan. The setting stage is reached when a clinging, flake-like drop forms on the edge of the spoon before it falls off sharply and cleanly.

PROBLEMS

Clearing the surface: Strawberry jam, in particular, throws up a lot of scum, but a little bit of butter does the trick. As soon as the heat is turned off, stir in a good knob of butter and the scum will magically disappear. This is quicker than skimming, less wasteful and it gives the jam a shine.

Adding a large quantity of sugar to the simmering fruit lowers the temperature of the mixture and can lead to overcooking. To prevent this warm the sugar beforehand either in a baking tin in a low oven or in your warming drawer.

Bicycle jam: This was the name given to soft set jam by my father because it free-wheeled off the bread. The fact that it goes a lot further is dubious comfort! The cause is often lack of fast boiling after the sugar has been added. This is done to evaporate the natural liquid in the fruit, thus bringing up the temperature of the jam until the setting stage is reached. It should boil all over the surface.

Too thick with a granular texture: Return the jam to the pan, add a little water and stir it over a gentle heat until all the crystals have dissolved, then bring it up to the boil and re-pot. This may be done as each jar is required.

CARE OF THE FRUIT

Strawberries: The fruit should be fully matured and nicely coloured as this is when the pectin content is highest. Choose fairly small strawberries.

Frozen fruit: Use frozen fruit in the same way as freshly picked fruit. It is useful to freeze gluts of fresh fruit for jam-making. Weigh and label the fruit before freezing, ready to follow your recipe.

Strawberry jam: For strawberry jam do not add water but put in some lemon juice while the fruit simmers before adding the sugar. This helps to extract the natural pectin. Add the juice of one lemon to every 450 g (1 lb) of strawberries.

JAM JARS

Filling the jars: Stand warm jars on a tray covered with newspaper, this not only catches the drips but will also contain the spill should a jar break. To avoid the risk of cracking the glass, put a teaspoon into the jar as you fill it, then lift it out and put it in the next one. Fill the jar up the neck well above the shoulder, as the jam will shrink as it cools. While still hot, wipe off any drips with a damp cloth.

Covering the jam jars: Put waxed paper discs on the jam as soon as the jars are filled. The cellophane jam pot covers can then be fixed either immediately or when the jam is completely cold. Moisten the cellophane top with a slightly damp cloth and stretch it, moist side uppermost, over the jar before stretching round the elastic band.

JAM MAKING GUIDE

Pectin and setting: Fruits which are low in pectin have little or no water added but often have extra lemon juice. The pectin content of fruit varies according to the seasons, which in turn affects the quality of the fruit. Over-ripe fruit has less pectin. Even different varieties of the same fruit can vary in their suitability for jam-making. Lemon juice is sometimes added, as acid helps to extract the pectin. Blending fruits of high and low pectin content can be useful and a great success for example, gooseberry and strawberry. Generally the acid fruits contain more pectin. This is why they are sometimes mixed with sweeter fruits, for example blackberry and apple.

Note to chart: The yield depends on the pectin content of the fruit. Where more water can be added, the yield will be greater. Also good setting properties mean there is less boiling to bring the fruit to the setting stage and therefore less evaporation.

JAM-MAKING GUIDE

When available	FRUIT	QUANTITY kg	QUANTITY lb	PREPARATION	ADDITIONS	WATER litres	WATER pints	SIMMER minutes	SUGAR kg	SUGAR lb	RAPID BOIL (approx.) minutes	YIELD kg approx.	YIELD lb approx.
SPRING													
Mar.–June	RHUBARB and GINGER	1.75	4	Remove leaves and cut into inch pieces. Put ginger in plastic bag and bruise with rolling pin	Grated rind and juice of 2 lemons. 50g (2 oz) bruised root ginger	0.3	½	25–30	1.75	4	15–20	2.75–3	6–7
SUMMER													
Early June–July	GOOSEBERRY	2.75	6	Top and tail berries. Small scissors are good for this	–	1.2	2	20–30	2.75		10	5.5	12
End June–July	GOOSEBERRY and STRAWBERRY	1.5 / 0.5	3 / 1	As above. Hull strawberries	–	–	–	15	1.75		10	2.75–3	6–7
End June–July	STRAWBERRY (not over-ripe)	1.75	4	Hull the fruit	The juice of 4 lemons	–	–	10–15	1.75		10	3	7
End June–July	APRICOT	1.75	4	Quarter and remove stones	The juice of 1 lemon. 25g (1 oz) split almonds, added after rapid boiling	0.45	¾	20–30	1.75		20	3	7
July	BLACK CHERRY and RED CURRANT	1.75 / 0.22	4 / ½	De-stalk and stone cherries. Sieve red currants	–	2.25	4	20	1.75		10–15	3	7

July–Aug.	RASPBERRIES or LOGANBERRIES (not over-ripe)	1.75	4	Hull the fruit	–	–	–	15–20	1.75	4	5	3	7
July	CHERRY (Morello) RASPBERRY and RED CURRANT	1 / 0.5 / 0.5	2 / 1 / 1	De-stalk and stone / Hull / De-stalk	The juice of 1 lemon	–	–	25	1.5	3½	7–10	2.25–2.75	5–6
July	BLACK CURRANT	1.5	3	De-stalk	–	1.25	2¼	20–30	1	2	5	4	9
Aug.	BLAEBERRY (soft set)	0.5	1	As above	–	–	–	10	0.5	1	3	0.75	1½
Aug.	PEACH (not over-ripe)	1.75	4	Pour water over peaches, leave 20 seconds, replace with cold. Skin, halve and quarter	The juice of 1 lemon. 25g (1 oz) split almonds, added after rapid boiling	0.45	¾	20–30	1.75	4	20	3	7

AUTUMN

Aug.–Sept.	GREENGAGE or PLUM	1.75	4	De-stalk, halve and quarter and remove stones. If preferred, skim off stones after boiling	The juice of 1 lemon if fruit is ripe	–	–	20–30	1.75	4	15	2.75	6
Aug.–Sept.	PLUM and RUM (just under-ripe)	1	2	As greengage and plum	4 tablespoons rum. Use demerara sugar	–	–	20–30	1	2	5	1.5	3½
End Aug.–Sept.	DAMSON	2	4½	De-stalk. Halve and remove stones or skim off after boiling	–	0.9	1½	20–30	2.25	5	10	4	9

JAM - MAKING GUIDE

When available	FRUIT	QUANTITY kg	QUANTITY lb	PREPARATION	ADDITIONS	WATER litres	WATER pints	SIMMER minutes	SUGAR kg	SUGAR lb	RAPID BOIL minutes (approx)	YIELD kg approx	YIELD lb approx
Sept.	ELDERBERRY	1.75	4	De-stalk by drawing through prongs of a fork	The juice of 3 lemons	—	30	1.5	3½	20	2.25	5	
Sept.	TOMATO and LEMON (not over-ripe)	2.75	6	Cover tomatoes with boiling water, replace with cold after 20 seconds. Skin and quarter	The grated rind and juice of 3 lemons	—	35	2.75	6	45–60	4	9	
Sept.	GREEN TOMATO and ORANGE	1	2	As above	Grated rind and juice of 1 orange	—	20	0.75	1½	15	1.25	2½	
Sept.	ORCHARD PEAR, APPLE and PLUM	0.5 0.5 0.5	1 1 1	Peel, slice and core Peel, slice and core Halve and de-stone	The juice of 1 lemon. 1 piece of bruised root ginger	0.3	½	30	1.5	3	5–7	2	4½
Sept.–Oct.	PUMPKIN and APPLE	1 0.5	2 1	Fruit weighed after peeling and removing pips. Core and slice	Grated rind and juice of 1 lemon. 1 level teaspoon tartaric acid	1.2	2	30	1.5	3½	20	2	4½

WINTER

When available	FRUIT	QUANTITY kg	QUANTITY lb	PREPARATION	ADDITIONS	WATER litres	WATER pints	SIMMER minutes	SUGAR kg	SUGAR lb	RAPID BOIL minutes (approx)	YIELD kg approx	YIELD lb approx
Nov.–Dec.	CRANBERRY and APPLE	0.5 0.5	1 1	De-stalk, thaw if frozen. Peel, core and slice	—	0.6	1	10	1	2	5	1.75	3¾

STORING JAM

Long storage: If the jam is being stored for very long periods, cut out greaseproof paper circles and brush each one with a little lightly beaten egg white before using as covers, moist side uppermost. Tie them with string as elastic bands are apt to perish in a few months.

Storing: A cool, dark, dry cupboard is ideal for keeping the jam. Label the jars clearly with type and date, so that each batch can be identified quickly.

Whiskery tops: This happens when softly set jam is stored. The cause is too low a proportion of sugar or insufficient boiling. Storing in a damp or steamy cupboard can set up mould. Metal covers, even on top of cellophane are also apt to encourage mould.

STARTING OFF

Speedier jelly: Seedy or stalky fruit is often used because of the ease of preparation. There is no need to stalk currants or top and tail gooseberries when making jelly, which saves a lot of time.

Jellies are made with just the juice of fruit. Choose fruits which have a good, strong flavour. Soft fruits such as redcurrants, blackcurrants and raspberries are excellent and plums, damsons and crab apples also make very good jelly. Choose fruit which is slightly under-ripe. Do not use over-ripe fruit.

Home-made jelly bag: Not many households have a flannel jelly bag. I use doubled muslin or a clean tea towel. Scald it with hot water then use to line a large bowl, letting it overlap the sides. Pour the boiled pulp into it and gradually gather it up round the sides. Tie it securely in the centre with a long piece of string. To suspend it to drip into the bowl overnight, put a kitchen stool or chair on to the kitchen table, the bowl underneath. Take the ends of the string up either side of the seat, gradually lifting the bag of pulp until it is suspended above the level of the bowl.

To squeeze or not to squeeze: Overnight straining extracts almost all the juice from the pulp, the resulting jelly should be sparkling and crystal clear. As fruit is expensive the pulp in the bag can be squeezed to extract the last drop but the jelly will not have quite the sparkle, though you will get about 150 ml (¼ pint) more juice.

Wild fruit: Remember wild fruit when jelly-making: it gives a deeper concentration of flavour and colour.

JELLY-MAKING GUIDE

Note to chart: As with jam-making the yield depends on the pectin content of the fruit. Amounts made are generally smaller than for jam as only the juice of the fruit is used, not the pulp.

JELLY-MAKING GUIDE

When available	FRUIT	QUANTITY kg	QUANTITY lb	PREPARATION	ADDITIONS	WATER litres	WATER pints	SIMMER minutes	SUGAR	RAPID BOIL minutes approx	YIELD kg	YIELD lb approx	SERVE WITH
SUMMER													
Early June–July	GOOSEBERRY	1.5	3	–	–	0.45	¾	20	0.5kg(1lb) to 0.6 litres (1 pint) strained juice	4–5	1.5	3	Lamb, duck or pheasant
July	RASPBERRY	1	2	–	–	–	–	10	As above	3–4	0.75	1½	Use as jam
July	RED CURRANT	1	2	–	–	0.3	½	15	As above	4–5	1.25	2¾	Lamb, jugged hare, game, turkey
July	BLACK-CURRANT	1.5	3	–	–	1.5	2½	30	As above	5	2	4½	Use as jam
AUTUMN													
End Aug.–Sept.	DAMSON	2.75	6	–	–	1.5	2½	30	As above	15–20	2	4½	Use as jam
Sept.	BLACKBERRY and APPLE	1 / 0.5	2 / 1	Chop roughly	–	1.5	2½	20–30	As above	20–30	1.75	4	Duck, pigeon
Sept.–Oct.	APPLE or CRAB APPLE	2.75	6	Quarter	Drop of pink food colouring	1.2	2	30	As above	20–30	2.25	5	Pork, duck, goose

293

JELLY-MAKING GUIDE

When available	Fruit	Quantity kg	Quantity lb	Preparation	Additions	Water litres	Water pints	Simmer minutes	Sugar	Rapid boil minutes (approx)	Yield kg (approx)	Yield lb approx	Serve with
Sept–Oct.	CRAB APPLE (spiced)	1.25	2½	As above	As above. 20g (¾ oz) pickling spice and 300ml (½ pint) cider vinegar	0.3	½	20	0.5kg (1lb) to 0.6 litres (1 pint) strained juice	10	1.25	2½	As above
Sept–Oct.	MINT and APPLE	1 large handful / 1.25	2½	Strip stalks. Chop roughly	Drop of green food colouring	0.3	½	20	As above	10	1	2	Lamb
Oct.	QUINCE and APPLE	1 / 1.25	2 / 2½	Chop roughly	Finely grated rind and juice of 2 lemons	2.75	5	30–40	As above	20–30	1.75	4	Cold ham, smoked mackerel, lamb
Oct.	ROSEHIP (ripe and red)	1.75	4	Mince	1 level teaspoon tartaric acid	1.75	3	30	As above	15–20	1	2	Milk shakes
Oct.	ROWAN and APPLE	0.5 / 1	1 / 2	Chop roughly or mince	Juice of 1 lemon	0.6	1	30	As above	8–10	0.25	½	Venison, game

WINTER

When available	Fruit	Quantity kg	Quantity lb	Preparation	Additions	Water litres	Water pints	Simmer minutes	Sugar	Rapid boil minutes (approx)	Yield kg (approx)	Yield lb approx	Serve with
Nov.–Dec.	CRANBERRY	1	2	–	–	0.3	½	30	As above	8–10	1.25 / 1.5	2½ / 3	Turkey, chicken, ham

MARMALADE

▓STARTING OFF

Sweet success: Preserving sugar, granulated and demerara sugar can all be used. The reason for using preserving sugar is that it dissolves more quickly but the other two varieties are cheaper to buy. It is important to stir whichever sugar you use over a gentle heat until it is dissolved.

Gordon Bleu

TIPS

Any skimming of the fruit mixture should be done towards the end of the cooking time. It is wasteful to do it throughout the cooking and is, in any case, not necessary.

Frozen Seville oranges: Because of the shortness of the season and the fact that they arrive in the shops just after Christmas when everyone is busy, try freezing the fruit whole to make the marmalade at a more convenient time. When thawed, the frozen oranges are much easier to chop. If space is limited in the freezer, chop the peel and mince the fruit before packing it in polythene containers for the freezer. Remember to label the quantity of fruit.

Dark and delicious: Add a small quantity of black treacle to the boiled marmalade, just before potting. This darkens the marmalade and gives it a subtle mellow taste. Use 1 level teaspoon of treacle to 450 g (1 lb) of marmalade.

Whisky special: The time to add a little whisky to flavour the marmalade is after the setting stage has been reached.

Variations: Lemons, oranges, tangerines, mandarins, satsumas, lime and grapefruit can all be used to make marmalade. Tangerines, mandarins and satsumas are apt to be too sweet, so are best mixed with lemons, grapefruit or Seville oranges. The important thing is to keep the correct proportions of citrus fruit, water and sugar as the recipe guides you.

A taste of ginger: A little chopped preserved ginger can be added to the boiled fruit. Grated fresh ginger also adds a good flavour. Try it out on a small quantity first. Pot most of the marmalade, but leave a little in the pan. Add the ginger and bring it up to boiling point again before potting.

Extra special: If they are available at the time you are making marmalade, rhubarb or pears are a nice addition. Add up to a quarter of the weight of the citrus fruit but it is not necessary to adjust the quantity of water or sugar.

▓ PROBLEMS

Runny marmalade: Sometimes there is no time to re-boil a batch of runny marmalade to rectify this problem. The flavour, however, is not affected, so try some of these ways of using it up.

For puddings: Flavour custard or milk puddings with soft set marmalade or serve it with sponge or steamed puddings. Substitute runny marmalade for the syrup in an open tart. Cook a little of this marmalade with stewed apples or use to flavour an apple pie instead of sugar. Serve it over ice cream, try flavouring it with whisky for a special occasion. For another win, try it with pancakes: sprinkle the pancakes with lemon and sugar, roll them up then coat them with marmalade before warming them in the oven.

Tough peel: This is caused by undercooking the fruit at the first stage before the sugar is added. Try pre-soaking the chopped fruit overnight before boiling, though this is not essential. The trick is to give the fruit a long, slow simmering until the skins are absolutely tender. Do not add sugar until this point is reached.

For baking: Gingerbread or tea loaves are very good with marmalade added to the mixture, reduce the syrup or treacle accordingly. My favourite is a banana loaf; I like to brush marmalade over the top when it is hot from the oven.

Time saver: Small batches of marmalade can be made with a tin of ready-chopped and cooked oranges. Follow the instructions on the label. This ready-prepared fruit is also useful if storage space is limited, as you can make a batch just when you like. A jar or two of marmalade is a great attraction for fund-raising sales, especially during the summer and before Christmas when most home-made marmalade has run out.

Floating fruit: Provided the marmalade has reached the setting stage, the fruit should not float towards the top of the jars. However, it is a good idea to cool the marmalade for a few minutes before potting it, then give it a good stir and you will ensure that the fruit stays in suspension.

CHUTNEY

▦ STARTING OFF

Choice of pan: Use aluminium or unchipped enamel pans for making chutney or pickles. Copper, brass or iron pans must not be used for vinegar mixtures as they will become corroded.

Spices: Whole spices are better than ground ones. They can be bought separately if required by the recipe but mixed pickling spice is readily available. The spices should be loosely tied in a piece of muslin for easy removal after cooking. As a guide use 25-50 g (1-2 oz) pickling spice to each 600 ml (1 pint) of vinegar.

Sugar: Demerara or soft brown sugar give a good flavour and colour. I find it best to cook all the minced ingredients without the sugar to avoid risk of burning. When they are nicely tender and soft, add the sugar and simmer very gently, stirring all the time, until the chutney is sufficiently reduced to be thick and glossy, without pools of liquid on the surface.

Vinegar: Vinegar is added to help preserve the chutney and add its characteristic flavour. Malt vinegar gives the chutney a richer colour. Cider vinegar is good for some chutneys, especially apple-based ones.

Doubling a recipe: Remember if you wish to make double the quantity of a particular recipe, the cooking time will be longer and therefore only one and a half times the spices in the original recipe will be needed, as the longer cooking will extract more flavour.

STORING AND USING

Covering the bottles: Unlined metal tops should never be used as vinegar will corrode them. Paper covers are not sufficient to prevent evaporation over long storage. Jam jars with plastic lined tops are good but cover them with polythene first. Bottling jars with glass lids are ideal.

Storage: Chutney is best eaten two months after it is made. The storage allows it to develop a good mellow blend of flavours. Use it within one year, kept beyond this, it is apt to thicken and dry out which overemphasizes the spice flavours.

Chutney mix: Ends of jars can be mixed and reboiled to make your own individual flavour. If the chutney has gone very stiff, add a little more vinegar or water.

Using surplus chutney: In a glut year it is tempting to make more chutney than can be used, so try it in some of the following more unusual ways.

For flans and sausage rolls: Spread the pastry base of a cheese or egg and bacon flan with a thin coating of chutney before adding the filling. Sausage rolls have extra zest if the pastry is spread with chutney before forming the rolls.

Meat loaf: Add two tablespoonfuls of chutney to a meat loaf mixture, it will give an individual flavour. Use a sharp green tomato chutney in preference to a sweet one.

Barbecue baste: Mix equal quantities of chutney, tomato ketchup and oil together and use it to brush over the food before it is grilled or barbecued.

Better bacon: Brush the barbecue baste (above) over the fat of a bacon joint once the dark skin has been taken off, for added interest and flavour. This should be done ten to fifteen minutes before the end of the baking time in a fairly hot oven.

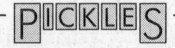

MAKING AND USING

Salt first: Pickling is a method of preserving fruit or vegetables in spiced vinegar. To do this successfully, they must first be brined (i.e. steeped in a salt and water solution) to extract some of their natural liquid and enable them to absorb the spiced vinegar. If the fruit and vegetables are not brined, the natural liquid will dilute the vinegar and lessen its preserving quality.

Dry brine: Allow 50 g (2 oz) salt to each 450 g (1 lb) vegetables. This is used for vegetables which are high in liquid content, such as marrow and cucumber. Sprinkle the salt in layers between the sliced vegetables. Leave overnight. Next day squeeze out all the liquid which has formed.

Wet brine: Allow 50 g (2 oz) salt for each 600 ml (1 pint) water. Dissolve the salt in the water in an earthenware or polythene bowl large enough to hold the vegetables as well. This brine is used for onions, sprigs of cauliflower, shredded pepper, cabbage, runner or French beans. Cover the vegetables with a plate to keep them below the surface. Soak in brine overnight, drain and dry them before packing into jars and covering with spiced vinegar.

Spiced vinegar: Use 25 g (1 oz) pickling spice to 1.2 litres (2 pints) vinegar. Bring the mixture to the boil, turn off the heat and leave for two hours for the flavour of the spices to be extracted, then strain. A larger quantity of spiced vinegar can be made than is required for immediate use. Keep it tightly covered until needed.

Pickled beetroot: As beetroot is boiled and sliced before pickling there is no need to brine it. Simply cover it with vinegar.

Fresh relishes: These are used immediately, though if they contain salt, vinegar and sugar they will keep for a day or two in the refrigerator. A simple relish is a mixture of chopped, deseeded tomatoes, cucumber and a little onion, which makes a nice cool and crunchy contrast to serve with a hot curry.

Delayed action: It is best not to use pickles immediately they are made as the flavours need a little time to mellow. However, if stored for too long the texture of the vegetables will soften. Pickled onions for example are best used within three to six months.

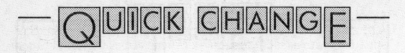

▦RETHINKING

Calm and flexible: If you are suddenly faced with important business guests for dinner, stay calm. Either consider buying a complete meal from a delicatessen or make your favourite familiar recipes which you can cook at speed and be confident that they'll be successful.

Thought for the morrow: If you have started to prepare a dinner party and it is suddenly cancelled, go ahead, cook the meal and give the family a treat, and freeze any that is over. An alternative is to freeze it all and then you have a ready-prepared dinner party for unexpected guests another day.

Loaves and fishes: When extra guests are suddenly sprung on you, try to treat it as a stimulating challenge. If possible avoid shopping again and use the time to make additional dishes from things you have in the store cupboard. Even a duck can be stretched from four to six if you add extra vegetables and make a richer stuffing (see page 314).

A warning in the morning: Provided you have a little advanced warning here are ideas for increasing a main course which you have already planned for family or guests.

▦STARTERS

Extend with a starter: A first course will make a slender main course more satisfying.

Canned or packet soup: Make this more interesting by mixing different kinds, such as tomato and green pea – lentil and tomato – asparagus and chicken – mushroom and cream of leek – Scotch broth and vegetable – consommé and Bovril.

Cream of tomato soup using tomato purée: Thin a basic white sauce with stock and add a small can of concentrated tomato purée.

Cream of mushroom soup: Thin a basic white sauce with stock and add chopped or sliced mushrooms which can be liquidized for speed. If you are really desperate use a can of mushrooms, although they don't have quite so much flavour as fresh ones.

Variation: A little pasta or rice can be added and cooked in the soup. Add extra stock and whisk in a little instant potato powder to thicken it.

Baked eggs: Break eggs into greased individual ramekin dishes, top with a tablespoon of top milk or single cream and season with salt and pepper. Bake in a moderate oven until the whites are just set. A small slice of pâté in the base of each dish is a nice addition.

Egg mayonnaise: Fill a small bowl with mayonnaise, put it in the middle of a plate and surround it with half hard-boiled eggs, cut-side downwards to prevent the yolks drying. Encircle with water-cress or cress. Allow at least one hard-boiled egg for each person.

Tomato fingers: Choose even-shaped fairly large tomatoes, skin and slice them and lay the slices neatly down on fingers of thinly sliced brown bread. Sprinkle with salt and freshly ground pepper and a pinch of sugar. Scatter the top with chopped basil or marjoram.

Sardine starter: Nestle a sardine into a curly lettuce leaf. Spoon a little potato salad beside it (you can use canned potato salad) and sprinkle with chopped chives.

Apple, carrot and nut salad: Slice an apple and turn the slices in lemon juice to keep them a good colour. Grate a carrot, mix it with the rest of the lemon juice and add a tablespoon of sultanas. Arrange next to the apple and sprinkle a few chopped nuts on top.

Pâté with olives or gherkins: Chill a tin of pâté for a few minutes in the freezer before opening to make it cut more easily. Arrange small slices on plates with gherkins and olives. Serve with crisp-bread or pains grillés (French toasts), which are easier than making toast at the last moment.

A quick pâté: Beat together 100 g (4 oz) liver sausage and the same amount of cream cheese with a teaspoon of curry powder and a tablespoon of sherry. Pack into a small dish. If you have a roll of pâté, arrange slices in little pots and cover with melted butter.

Mackerel or tuna pâté: Mash canned mackerel or tuna with a fork and beat in enough melted butter to make a spreading consistency. Season carefully with salt, freshly ground black pepper, a little lemon juice and half a teaspoon of horseradish sauce.

Citrus cocktail: Mix a tin each of grapefruit and mandarin segments and add a few quartered maraschino cherries. Add a few drops of Kirsch if you have it.

Avocado starter: To make two avocados enough for six, skin and stone and slice the flesh and divide it between small plates before adding a few sliced skinned tomatoes and lettuce. Lightly brush the avocado and tomato slices with French dressing.

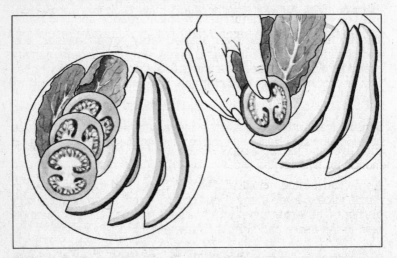

Mushrooms on toast: Wash and dry the mushrooms and cut the stalks straight, but do not remove them. Don't peel cultivated mushrooms. Slice or quarter large ones but leave button mushrooms whole. Cook them briefly in a little butter and lemon juice and heap on lightly buttered toast or serve with melba toast. Canned mushrooms can be used.

Dips: Make a quick dip – liquidize a can of baked beans and add a little extra tomato purée and lemon juice. Serve with pieces of raw vegetable if there's time or with savoury or cheese biscuits.

▦ MAIN MEALS

Grilled steak: To make four steaks enough for six, grill each steak and then cut into slanting slices which can be arranged on one side of a hot serving dish with vegetables on the other. Extra vegetables will help pad out the meal, such as a tin of sweetcorn or vegetables from the freezer, and potato crisps. A good accompaniment would be pats of parsley butter or a little made mustard beaten into butter and formed into a roll inside a sheet of wet greaseproof paper and left to chill before being sliced.

Emergency puff pastry: If you have no frozen puff pastry you can create something similar by using just over half hard margarine to flour and grating the margarine into the flour insteading of rubbing it in as you would for shortcrust pastry. The margarine needs to come straight from the refrigerator. Mix it lightly with water, avoid too much kneading and roll it out about 1 cm (½ inch) thick. It's a good idea to leave the pie in the refrigerator for an hour before putting it in the oven as this will prevent it shrinking from the sides of the pie-dish. Bake the pie for about two hours – begin with 20 minutes in a hot oven to set and start browning the pastry, and then on a low heat. If the top browns too quickly put a damp paper bag on top.

Fried liver and bacon: To make four slices of liver and four of bacon enough for five, lay the slices of liver in a deep dish, side by side, cover them with boiling water and leave for up to 15 minutes. Then lift out the slices, dry them carefully and cut them in 1 cm (½ inch) strips before frying in a little butter with a teaspoon of oil. Just stir for a few minutes before adding a few drops of Worcestershire sauce or soy sauce and salt and pepper. Make the bacon go further by stretching the rashers on a board under the blade of a heavy knife and grill them briskly before cutting them into 2.5 cm (1 inch) lengths. Heap the liver on a dish, put the bacon on top and serve some of the vegetables on the same hot dish or surround it with grilled half tomatoes. *An alternative:* The liver 'chips' can be coated with seasoned flour to make them go further but they will need a little more fat for frying.

Steak and kidney pie: Make one more helping by buying the steak in one piece and slicing it yourself. Begin by rolling a little piece of ox kidney into each strip of steak and coating this lightly with seasoned flour. Make more rolls in the same way and arrange them loosely in the pie dish, leaving space between the pieces of meat to allow the gravy to circulate. Surround the pie funnel with a second row to give the pie a nice domed shape before filling it three-quarters full with stock or water. Use puff pastry as shortcrust tends to become 'chippy' with long cooking.

Chinese chicken-in-a-wok: To make three quarter pieces of chicken enough for five, cut the skin and bones from the flesh and chop the chicken into small cubes. Stir fry the chicken with a finely chopped onion and two tablespoons of oil over a strong heat for two or three minutes before adding a finely chopped green pepper and two finely chopped celery stalks. Don't let the vegetables lose their crispness by overcooking; add some nuts and serve with plenty of boiled rice and a salad.

Chicken casserole: To make three pieces enough for four, cut the chicken pieces in half at the joint and casserole them together with a can of condensed mushroom soup flavoured with ½ teaspoon curry powder. No extra liquid is needed. Cover and cook in a moderate oven for about 1½ hours. Give the guests one and a half pieces each.

Turkey pieces: These can be cooked the same way as chicken but will probably require 2 hours in a slightly slower oven.

Sausage hot pot: To make eight sausages (450 g (1 lb)) enough for five or six, thinly slice a large onion and 750 g (1½ lb) potatoes and combine the onion and half the potatoes with a can of tomatoes and a sliced leek or half a shredded cabbage in a casserole. Season and start to cook in a fairly hot oven with the sausages in a roasting pan on the shelf above. Once the sausages are nicely browned they can be cut in slanting pieces and added to the hot pot with the remaining potato slices and cooked as usual.

Lamb or pork patties: To make three chops enough for five, mince or grind the meat finely and work in enough cold water to make a soft consistency which will just hold its shape. Season, cook as usual and serve with slices of red or green dessert apple, and baked beans or broad beans in parsley sauce.

Minced beef plait: To make minced meat go further make a bolognaise sauce with half the specified amount of liquid and combine with a can of minced steak and enough brown bread-crumbs to make a soft handling consistency. Place the mixture down the centre of a rectangle of puff pastry on a backing sheet. Snip either side of the pastry with slanting cuts to within 2.5 cm (1 inch) of the meat. Moisten the sides and ends of the pastry with water then cross the slit edges of pastry, joining them firmly and tucking the ends inside. Brush the top with beaten egg mixed with a good pinch of salt to give it a shine. Bake in a hot oven for about 30 minutes.

Shoulder of lamb: To make a small half shoulder serve an extra two, cut out all the bones and fill the meat with a lemon and thyme stuffing mix. Press the joint into shape and tie it with string before roasting in the usual way. Serve carved in straight neat slices. (See also page 314 for the stuffing.)

Ham salad: To make three or four slices of ham go a long way, boil a little pasta and toss it in French dressing while it is still hot. Cut the ham in strips and toss with the pasta; the dressing helps to keep the ham a good colour. Add peas, chopped pepper, diced celery, tomato quarters, sliced raw mushrooms, and cubes of cheese and finish with a sprinkling of fresh herbs.

Shepherd's pie or cottage pie: To make a pie for four stretch to five, add a thick layer of leeks in white sauce between the meat and the potato top. A little beaten egg brushed over the potato gives it a golden top.

Lamb, pork or beef casserole: To make a casserole for four into enough for six or seven, cut up the meat quite finely and serve on top of freshly cooked spaghetti. Sprinkle with Parmesan cheese, if you have it, and top each helping with a knob of butter.

Curried eggs: These can be made quickly – hard-boil the eggs, cover them with canned or packet curry sauce and serve with boiled rice.

Roast duck: To make a duck for four feed six, cut the roasted duck into six joints and arrange them on a hot dish garnished with orange wedges. Serve with sage and onion stuffing balls, apple sauce, potatoes and two vegetables or a green salad. Green peas are the traditional accompaniment, or add sliced carrots if they are at hand. (See also page 314 for the stuffing.)

To crisp duck skin: Pierce the skin with a sharp fork before roasting and rub over with salt. Ten minutes before the duck is ready melt a tablespoon of clear honey and brush over the surface; it will brown very quickly. It is better to err on the side of well-cooked rather than undercooked, especially when it is necessary to get every bit of flesh off the bones.

Goujon of fish fillets: To make four fillets enough for five or six cut the fillets in strips lengthways and tie a single knot in the larger ones. Dip the fish pieces in egg and breadcrumbs and fry them in deep fat, but twist the pieces in your fingers just before frying to give them a more interesting shape. Serve with lemon wedges, tartare, parsley or tomato sauce and potato crisps.

Home-made tartare sauce: Add chopped gherkins, capers, parsley or a little apple chutney to home-made or bought mayonnaise.

Fillets of fish in batter: To make three fillets enough for four, cut each fillet in three, making triangular pieces. For a quick batter, mix four tablespoons of self-raising flour with a little lemon juice and enough

310

water to make a thick coating consistency. Serve the battered, fried fillets with chips. (The same batter is excellent for making fritters with pieces of cooked vegetable, apple or banana slices, or cooked and drained dried fruit.)

Fish in a parcel: To make two frozen cod or haddock steaks enough for four, top them with butter, salt and pepper and wrap them in a large rectangle of puff pastry. Place the parcel seam side down on a baking sheet and score the top lightly with a sharp knife and brush with beaten egg. Bake in a hot oven for about 30 minutes, slightly less if the fish has been thawed.

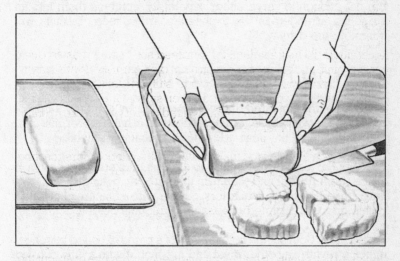

Fish cakes: To make eight fish cakes out of four fillets, poach the fillets in milk and then flake the fish, removing any bones or skin. Use the fish, milk, and water if necessary to make up a medium packet of instant mashed potato, before mixing thoroughly into the fish with some salt, pepper, a touch of ground mace and plenty of finely chopped parsley. Cover with egg and breadcrumbs and cook in the usual way.

A cheesy filling: Make fish cakes more satisfying by moulding a thin triangle of processed cheese into the centre of each one before rolling in egg and breadcrumbs. It's best to shallow fry as they may split in deep fat.

▓DESSERTS

Fruit extra: To make a rice pudding, sweet soufflé or custard cream go further serve with a can of fruit or with a quick fruit sauce made by heating some jam.

Salad for all: A few pieces of fresh fruit can be extended by chopping them up to make a fruit salad and adding a tin of lychees or strawberries.

A good appearance: If you have a little cheese and a little fresh fruit but not enough to serve either separately, combine them into an attractive arrangement on a cheeseboard. Cheese biscuits will complete the display.

▓THE TOTALLY UNEXPECTED GUEST

Cheese soufflé for three: Increase a soufflé by bringing a cup of freshly made white breadcrumbs to the boil in half a pint of milk and, after taking it off the heat, add it to the usual ingredients.

Fish pie: For a quick meal, boil two or three packets of frozen fish in sauce (from frozen) and then turn them into an oven dish with two hard-boiled eggs cut in quarters. Scatter with a mixture of crushed potato crisps and grated cheese and grill until golden.

Potted meat: Spin out the leftover end of a piece of boiled bacon by mincing it with any other meat and mashing it with a little cooked creamed potato or some fresh breadcrumbs. It will need moisture and seasoning so add some stock and a little ground mace before packing into a straight-sided dish and running a little melted butter over the surface. Top with bay leaves and serve with toast, hot rolls or crispbread.

Croque Monsieur: To make a variation of a toasted sandwich, spread two slices of bread with butter. Cover one with a thin slice of cheese, melt it under the grill and top with a slice of ham. Add the second slice of bread and butter and toast the top. Turn it over, sprinkle with grated cheese and brown under the grill. *Croque Madame* is made with cold sliced chicken instead of ham.

Supper special: Put a thick slice of French bread or half a split roll for each person in an ovenproof dish. Moisten with well flavoured stock which can be made with a stock cube. Top the slices with thinly sliced cheese, then a slice of ham and, finally, grated cheese. Bake in the oven to heat thoroughly. For extra big appetites top each with a fried egg.

Ratatouille plus: Turn a can of ratatouille into a pie dish, heat it in the oven, pour uncooked scrambled egg mixture on top and scatter with grated cheese. Bake in the oven until the egg is set.

Pancakes: Make the batter a little thicker for hearty appetites. Add a thinly sliced apple or a few raisins or both. Fry large pancakes in a frying pan as it is sometimes easier to cut them in half before turning them. Sprinkle with sugar or serve with syrup.

Hot waffles: Toast the waffles in a toaster or under the grill. Dust with icing sugar and serve with any canned or stewed fruit and ice cream. They also make a good base for bacon and eggs; use potato waffles for this if you have them in the freezer.

ACCOMPANIMENTS AND SAUCES

Worthy extenders: Pastry, sauces, batters, bread, pasta, rice, potatoes and other vegetables, and salads will all extend a meal.

Working in a hurry: If you're short of time try to use the same piece of kitchen equipment for different jobs and reduce washing-up. For example, make breadcrumbs in the liquidizer before liquidizing soup; chop parsley in the liquidizer with bread cubes to start off the breadcrumbs for a meat or chicken stuffing.

Speedy crumble topping: This is really the first stage of making shortcrust pastry but it is much quicker as it is sprinkled over the fruit and involves no rolling out. Rub in half the quantity of fat to flour as you do for pastry, then mix in the same amount of soft brown sugar as fat. It is useful to keep in the refrigerator or freezer. Add a little ground cinnamon to make a crispy top for tray bakes.

Accompaniments and stuffings: Serving the traditional accompaniments, such as stuffing or stuffing balls, helps to stretch the meal. Stuffings can be bought in a packet but add lemon juice and a few chopped fresh herbs.

Parsley, lemon and thyme stuffing: This is easy to make and can be used for chicken, fish, veal, lamb and turkey. For duck, pork and ham change the herbs to sage and parsley. Blend 100 g (4 oz) crustless white bread in the liquidizer with a good handful of washed and dried parsley and three sprigs of thyme, stripped off the stalks, then add the finely grated rind and juice of half a lemon, salt and freshly ground pepper, 50 g (1 oz) melted margarine and one beaten egg. Mix well and use for stuffing or roll into small balls and fry in shallow fat.

White sauce: This is very adaptable and quickly made, but make sure the butter and flour form a fairly soft mixture so that the sauce can be kept smooth. The heat can be turned off at this stage and the sauce left for several hours if necessary – a useful way of cutting time at the last moment and often better than trying to keep the sauce hot. While it is coming to the boil the sauce must be stirred vigorously as this is the chance for the butter to melt and absorb the flour, making a velvet smooth sauce. If milk is short add up to half the quantity of vegetable liquid, stock or fish stock.

Keep it smooth: If a white sauce develops lumps beat it well with a whisk, or blend in the liquidizer for a few seconds or sieve it.

Uses for plain white sauce: Coat vegetables or fish in smooth white sauce and grate a suspicion of nutmeg into the melting butter to extract the full flavour. It's especially nice for coating cauliflower and vegetable marrow, a boiled chicken or boiling fowl.

Additions to white sauce: Vary a plain white sauce by adding finely chopped *parsley* – delicious on fish, vegetables and hot boiled ham or bacon.

Add chopped *hard-boiled egg* and pour over steamed, poached or baked fish, and baked potatoes. The easiest way to chop a hard-boiled egg is to put it on a board and press the potato masher down on it, cutting it into chunky pieces.

Add 50 g (2 oz) *grated cheese* with half a teaspoon of French mustard. Beat the cheese into the sauce after it has boiled. Never reboil after adding the cheese. Good with fish dishes, pasta, vegetables and for coating hard-boiled eggs.

Add enough *English mustard* to give the sauce a tang. Good with a boiled ham or bacon joint, also with grilled mackerel.

Shallots are generally specified in recipes where only a delicate flavour of onions is required. However they only appear in autumn and winter. At other times pickling or button onions can be used instead and if these are not available use a quarter to half a medium onion as a substitute for one shallot.

Tomato sauce: Add concentrated tomato purée to white sauce to give the strength of flavour you like. Good with some vegetables, nice with butter beans, pasta, chicken and fish.

Onion sauce: Make this either by adding a finely diced cooked large onion or onion purée to white sauce. It is often served with lamb, mutton or hot ham.

Caper sauce: Make by adding three teaspoons of drained capers to a white sauce. Traditionally this is used for coating boiled mutton but it is also excellent with hard-boiled eggs and potato dishes.

Anchovy sauce: This is mainly served with fish. Make by adding pure anchovy paste (which is very strong, so add it carefully) to white sauce. Anchovy essence can also be used but is less strong so requires more to flavour.

Moussaka topping: Beat one egg into the white sauce, pour it on to a dish and bake in a moderate oven until it is puffed up. Ideal for topping fish or vegetable pie.

White sauce for a savoury flan base: Beat two eggs into the basic sauce then add any nice titbits which are at hand, such as a tin of salmon, flaked, sliced mushrooms or grated cheese.

Savoury soufflé: This requires a thicker sauce base so use half the milk normally needed to make a white sauce and then add vegetable purée (a small packet of chopped frozen spinach is excellent, so are swede, parsnips or Brussels sprouts), minced ham or cheese (Stilton is good). Beat in two egg yolks then beat the whites, not too stiffly, and fold them into the mixture. Bake in a greased soufflé dish in a fairly hot oven for about 30 minutes.

Sweet white sauce: Add a little sugar and a few drops of vanilla essence to white sauce and serve over puddings as a change from custard. It can be made very special with a little brandy, rum or sherry added instead. Excellent with Christmas pudding and mince pies as well as fruit pies, sponge puddings or baked apples. Finely grated orange, lemon or tangerine rind all give a citrus flavour, and a tablespoon of marmalade beaten into the sweetened sauce gives it texture.

PASTA AND RICE

Pasta: Add a little cooked pasta to a salad to give it more substance and a small quantity of freshly cooked pasta to scrambled egg just before it sets. This can be finished with crisply fried bacon, crumbled and scattered over the top.

Lasagne: This is a good standby but if minced beef is not available make twice the amount of white sauce and stir a can of chopped asparagus spears into half of it. Add a little chopped ham if you have it. Layer this with the lasagne keeping the plain white sauce for the top and covering it liberally with grated cheese before baking.

Cook lasagne in plenty of boiling water in a large pan. If you find you have a problem with the lasagne sticking together, next time try putting the sheets in one by one and allowing the water to come back to the boil after each addition.

Smoked haddock lasagne: Cook diced carrot, celery and leek in a little stock with a knob of butter and spread over the base of the dish. Add a layer of lasagne then flaked smoked haddock stirred into half the cheese sauce. Cover with lasagne then add another layer of sauce and top with grated cheese before baking. Lasagne need not be precooked. When using it dry, make the white sauce thinner as the lasagne absorbs liquid while it is cooking. Make sure all the pasta is thickly covered with sauce.

Macaroni cheese: Make it more interesting and substantial by slipping a few sliced tomatoes on the base of the dish with a little diced corned beef or cooked sausage or some fried onions before adding the macaroni and cheese sauce.

Rice: Accompany any stew, goulash, ragoût or curry with rice. A little cooked rice is useful for making kedgeree, risotto and pilaff or for mixing with nuts and raisins to stuff peppers.

317

Boiled noodles: Toss cooked noodles in melted butter and add plenty of freshly ground black pepper. Served as an accompaniment to a meat course, they make a change from potatoes. Always keep packets of noodles in the store cupboard – they make excellent standby meals and a substitute when potatoes run out.

Cheesy rice: Make a quick and easy emergency meal by combining 100 g (4 oz) freshly boiled long-grain rice with two beaten eggs, a pint of milk and 225 g (8 oz) of grated cheese, plenty of salt and pepper and half a teaspoon of Hungarian paprika. Pour into a buttered ovenproof dish and cook in a moderately hot oven for about 30 minutes until it is set. The texture should remain moist. Serve with mango chutney or tomato ketchup. A crisply cooked green vegetable is a good addition.

Rice salad: Add French dressing to hot rice as soon as it has been drained. Leave to cool then stir in cooked sweetcorn, mixed diced vegetables, green beans, and chopped chives or spring onions. If you like yellow rice add half a teaspoon of turmeric to the water as the rice is cooking. This rice salad is good to serve with cold meat to make a satisfying meal.

PANCAKES

Pancakes or crêpes: Pancakes are one of the most versatile foods; they can be made quickly and are equally good sweet or savoury. One leftover pancake can be snipped with a pair of scissors into clear soup. Larger strips can be deep-fried, tossed in cinnamon sugar and served as a pudding with jam sauce.

More uses for batter: Pancake batter can also be used for Yorkshire puddings and Toad-in-the-hole. Fry some onion rings and put them into the tin before the sausages and batter, or use cider instead of water for the batter to make it more interesting.

Savoury fillings for pancakes: Use a quantity of white sauce and add any of the following: fried sliced mushrooms, cold chopped chicken with some green peas, flaked smoked haddock or flaked fresh or tinned salmon with chopped parsley, or chopped cooked vegetables. When the pancakes are filled, they can be folded in halves, quarters or loosely rolled. Brush them with melted butter and heat in a moderate oven for 15 to 20 minutes. The surface can be sprinkled with grated cheese before baking provided that the flavour blends with the filling.

Sweet fillings for pancakes: Jam or lemon juice rolled into each pancake is a traditional favourite and small bananas or half bananas wrapped with the jam are good fillers. Apple purée sweetened with brown sugar and chopped nuts or sultanas is especially good. Stack the pancakes with the filling spread between each then heat some apricot jam and brush it over the pancake stack. Heat them in the oven. Slice like a cake to serve. Fruit pie fillings are good for filling pancakes. Add a little finely grated lemon or orange rind as they are inclined to be rather sweet. (See also 'runny marmalade', page 296.)

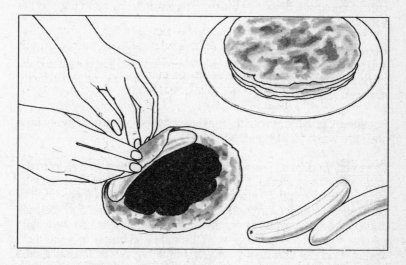

SALADS AND VEGETABLES

A green salad: This need not contain a wide range of vegetables. A green salad does make much more of a main course and can be served instead of a cooked vegetable thus saving preparation, cooking time and fuel. Either arrange the salad on individual plates to serve with grilled, roast or fried meat or chicken, or serve a green salad, lightly tossed in French dressing, after the main course and before the pudding.

Quick French dressing: Choose a jar with a wide neck and a tight fitting plastic lid. Put two teaspoons of French mustard, salt and freshly ground pepper into the jar, add the vinegar, screw on the lid and shake well to mix in the mustard. Add the oil and shake again. The contents will settle but can easily be shaken again before use. Cider or wine vinegar gives a nice mild flavour.

Curdled mayonnaise: This can happen if the eggs and oil are at different temperatures, so eggs for mayonnaise should be left out of the refrigerator. When you see it just starting to curdle, beat in a few drops of hot water which may smooth the mayonnaise, or tip it into another bowl, wash the first bowl or blender goblet and break another egg into it. Beat this well then very gradually add the curdled mixture. If you are making mayonnaise by hand use just the yolk of the egg.

Vegetables: Short speedy cooking helps vegetables to go further and keep their flavour. Cut them in even slices so that they will cook at the same rate, and undercook rather than overcook them in order to retain texture.

Potatoes: Cook them with their skins on when you can; it saves time and any wastage of potatoes.

Creamed potatoes: These need a lot of milk and butter to make them really tasty. Hot milk with butter melted into it makes a smooth, much lighter and fluffier texture, see page 180. If you are short of time, after you have drained the potatoes tip the pan, add the milk and butter and carefully heat the milk. When it boils use the potato masher to beat the potatoes with the milk and butter to a soft fluffy cream. Add salt and freshly ground white pepper to season. Add a touch of grated nutmeg to make them really special.

TIME AND FUEL SAVERS

Baked potatoes: These are great favourites and sure fillers. To speed the cooking bring them to the boil in a saucepan on top of the cooker, drain them after five minutes and put them in the oven. They can be cooked quickly in a hot oven (45 minutes to 1 hour at 400°F, 200°C, Gas Mark 6) or for hours in a slow one.

Baked onions: Cut off the root end but do not peel them, simply put them in a moderate oven and cook until they are soft and tender when tested with a skewer. To remove the skins, simply squeeze the tops and the cooked onion will slip out.

Toppings and fillings: To make a meal from a large baked potato cut it in half, rub a knob of butter over the cut sides and heap with a hot or cold filling. One suggestion is grated cheese and a spoonful of chutney topped with an onion ring. For a cold filling try chopped hard-boiled egg in mayonnaise.

Roast potatoes: To make the outside of roast potatoes crisp and keep the insides fluffy, par-boil peeled potatoes for five minutes. Drain off the water, replace the lid and give the pan a sharp shake so that the surface of the potatoes is roughened a little. Put the potatoes in hot dripping, baste them and roast fairly briskly.

Roast parsnips: Peel them only if they are old or the skins are marked, cut into chunks and roast as for artichokes.

Roast Jerusalem artichokes: These are one of the nicest additions to roast beef, only bettered by roast parsnips. Scrub the artichokes, there is no need to peel them, and bring to the boil on top of the cooker. Drain and finish them off round the beef.

Roast root vegetables: Large root vegetables, e.g. turnips, swedes, parsnips, are difficult to cut. Use a large chopping knife to cut the vegetables into four or eight pieces, then peel each piece with a small knife.

Roast pumpkin: Do not peel pumpkin. Cut it in large chunks, removing all the seeds, arrange round the roasting meat (beef, lamb or ham), baste and roast it. There is no need to par-boil pumpkin as it cooks quite quickly. Always serve with the skin on. This is quite easy to cut off and holds the pumpkin pieces together, thus making it much easier to serve.

Frozen vegetables: If the oven is being used, wrap frozen vegetables in foil with a knob of butter and place them on a spare part of the oven shelf instead of boiling them on top of the cooker. This will save space and fuel.

Cooking beetroot: Cook the leaves of beetroot like spinach. Boil beetroot with two inches of stalk and the root intact and without skinning. This keeps the colour bright and the skins rub off easily with the stalks and root.

Cordon Bleu Tips

The easiest way to skim fat from stocks without waiting for the liquid to get cold is first to take off as much as you can with a metal spoon. Next cut a piece of kitchen towel into strips and draw each strip gently across the surface of the liquid. You can then turn the paper over and use the other side in the same way. Carry on until all the fat has been absorbed.

Freezing herbs: Pick herbs, such as parsley, chives, thyme, sage, tarragon and basil, when they are at the height of growth. Wash and dry them well. Chop finely, pack into small cartons, put on the lids and freeze. Scrape off the amount you want with a teaspoon and put the cartons back in the freezer. Alternatively, pack in ice cube trays, see page 272.

A quick chop: Sieve mushrooms through the coarse grid of a Mouli vegetable mill.

To store mushrooms for instant use: Chop the mushrooms finely. Melt a knob of butter in a frying pan, add the mushrooms and cook them slowly, stirring occasionally, until the liquid is driven off. Pack them into small pots and store in the refrigerator for up to 4 weeks or in the freezer for up to 3 months. They are ready for instant use for a quick sauce (white sauce base) or for cream of mushroom soup (add extra stock and milk to the white sauce and finish the soup with a tablespoon of cream).

Washing spinach: Washing spinach can be a tedious job but here's a way to save a little time and let the spinach rinse itself. Put it into a large bowl in the sink, cover with a cake cooling tray and run cold water through the leaves until they are clean. The wire tray prevents the leaves from floating away.

Pickling beetroot: If you pickle your own beetroot in vinegar, once the beetroot has all been used up, keep the vinegar and use it again for the next batch of beetroot pickling. The vinegar can also be used for making French dressing; the slight colouring can be attractive with some dishes.

Ratatouille: This is a delicious blend of tomatoes, onions, red and green peppers, aubergine and courgettes, simmered gently in oil with herbs and garlic. The proportions of the vegetables can be varied according to what you have available. An added advantage is that it freezes beautifully. It makes a useful first course, topped with grated cheese, or can be served as a supper dish with a fluffy moussaka top made with thick white sauce, or with a creamed potato top browned in the oven.

A quick dry: A salad spinner not only dries lettuce but also herbs and mushrooms quickly.

Freezing tomato purée: It is much more economical to buy large cans of concentrated tomato purée. To store it, freeze the purée in an ice cube tray, then remove the cubes from the tray and pack in the freezer in a polythene bag. They are now readily available for instant use in small amounts.

EMERGENCY STORES

—In the storecupboard—

1 can baked beans	1 can luncheon meat
1 can red kidney beans	or corned beef
1 can flageolet beans	1 carton long life milk
1 can butter beans	1 carton long life cream
2 cans soup	or topping
1 can condensed	1 can minced steak
mushroom soup	1 can tuna or mackerel
1 packet soup	1 packet instant mashed
1 packet croûtons	potato powder
1 can tomatoes	1 packet potato crisps
1 can concentrated	1 can sweetcorn
tomato purée	1 can ratatouille

—In the Freezer—

1 small loaf sliced bread
White breadcrumbs ⎫
Grated cheese ⎬ these run freely after being stored in polythene bags
Crumble topping ⎭
Puff pastry
Stack of 12 pancakes, separated by greaseproof paper for use singly
Scones or drop scones

DIVERSIONS

▨ SAVOURIES

About turn: If a stew or casserole boils dry, do not stir the contents but tip them out into a clean saucepan, leaving the burnt pieces in the bottom of the original pan. Make up the quantity with a tin of appropriately flavoured soup.

Overcooked chicken: If the chicken has become unattractive through being cooked for too long, carve it in the kitchen and arrange it on a serving platter with a vegetable garnish.

A watching brief: Watch rice and pasta carefully as it is cooking to make sure it doesn't dry out and burn. A tablespoon of oil added to the cooking liquid will help keep the grains or strands separate.

General improvement: Undercooked green vegetables will have a better colour, are more nutritious and will actually go further.

Powerful pepper: There is no way to counteract a gravy or stock which has been over-peppered. You will have to reject half the liquid and make up the rest with a stock cube and water or vegetable cooking liquid.

Cordon Bleu

TIPS

Both leftover egg yolks and egg whites can be stored for a few days but are often then discarded. It is preferable to use them straightaway in another recipe. Egg yolks can be used up in custards, mayonnaise, rich pastry or with cream as a liaison for puréed vegetable soups. Leftover egg whites are easily made into meringues.

Salt saver: If you've forgotten to put salt in your shortcrust pastry mix, sprinkle a little over the base of the prepared flan before cooking.

Seasonal advice: Both salt and pepper can be added to dishes once they're cooked, so season lightly when cooking and provide condiments for guests to help themselves.

Read all about it!: Always read all the way through a recipe before deciding whether or not to cook it. You can then be sure that you have the time, the ingredients and, most important, the containers needed for that particular recipe.

▦ BAKING

Stubborn brandy snaps: Brandy snaps are unwilling to curl when they get too cool. Replace in the oven for a moment or two to make them flexible again. It is best to bake a few at a time.

Sunken cake: When a cake sinks or domes in the centre, cut out the centre with a round cutter to make a ring cake. This is easy to cut and ice and can be dusted wth sieved icing sugar.

Flat Victoria sandwiches: This can happen when the wrong size tin has been used. Always use the size given in the recipe. If the tin is too big the cake will be thin, biscuity and overbaked, while too small a tin will make the cake too thick and it may overflow and be undercooked in the centre. The flat sponge is good for trifles.

Whisked fatless sponges: Have the oven at the correct temperature ready to bake the sponge the minute the mixture is in the tin, otherwise it will lose air and therefore volume. Always tip the tin to level the mixture, never spread it as this breaks the air bubbles.

Test for readiness: A sponge must be baked for the correct length of time or it will fall when it is taken out of the oven. To test if it is ready press the centre with your finger; it should be resilient. Also the sponge should be slightly shrinking away from the sides of the tin.

Dry sponges: If a sponge has overcooked, turn it upside down on to a wire tray but leave the tin over it until it is cold to keep it moist.

Dry fruit cake: Moisten the fruit with sherry or fruit juice overnight before making the cake. The fruit will absorb it and be much more flavoursome, moist and mellow.

Unwilling egg whites: No matter how much you beat, sometimes egg whites will only produce a few bubbles instead of fluffy volume. Newly laid eggs will not whisk easily; they are much better after four or five days. A scrupulously clean bowl and whisk are essential as the smallest speck of grease or egg yolk will prevent the whites whisking properly. A pinch of salt increases the volume.

Using unbeatable egg whites: Don't waste them, use them brushed over pastry and sprinkled with caster sugar before baking sweet pies – this makes a lovely crispy glaze.

The well kept egg white: An unbeatable egg white will keep in a covered container in the refrigerator, see page 86. Add to any egg dishes where a rise is not required, such as scrambled eggs.

Weeping meringues: If meringues are not successful, check that you are using 50 g (2 oz) of sugar for every egg white. Less sugar will cause weeping and the meringues may go sticky during storage. Try a slightly hotter oven but watch the meringues carefully. This will dry out the moisture more quickly and therefore help to prevent them from sticking to the tin. Bake meringues on flat trays or upturned baking sheets so that you can easily run a sharp knife under them to loosen them. Using non-stick silicone paper solves the problem of sticking.

327

Meringues in poor shape: This could be for the same reason as above, that is too little sugar, but it is possible the egg whites were not beaten stiffly enough. They really must stand up in straight peaks before any sugar is added. Then add a third of the measured sugar and beat again to the same stiff consistency before folding in the rest of the sugar.

Broken meringues: Meringues do break easily so save the broken ones for a special ice pudding. Whisk 300 ml (½ pint) of double cream and lightly stir in 300 ml (½ pint) of sweetened fruit purée (raspberry, blackcurrant, blackberry and damson are all excellent). Add three handfuls of roughly crushed meringues, fold in quickly and turn the mixture into a bowl to freeze. Take the ice pudding out of the freezer an hour before it is needed and put in to the refrigerator. Turn on to a pretty plate for serving, accompanied by sweet curly wafer biscuits.

Singed meringues: If the meringue topping is slightly burnt on top, you can improve the appearance and to some extent the flavour by dusting it with icing sugar.

Hard pastry: This means too much water. Surprisingly little extra water can become too much. Add it by hand so that you can feel the texture of the pastry. The rubbed in mixture should knead together into a firm dough. Adding more flour just upsets the proportions.

Rub it better: The only way to correct a hard pastry mix is to rub in a little more flour and fat of the same proportions and knead this into the original mixture.

Crumbly pastry: This means too little water. The pastry will be difficult to handle and break very easily as you use it. This is one of the reasons why flan mixtures leak through the pastry. When patching pastry make absolutely certain the splits are firmly joined with water.

Rising pastry: When pastry rises through the flan filling this means there is not enough filling to weight the pastry. To counteract this next time it is best to use plain flour for the pastry and always try to allow time for the pastry-lined tin to rest in the refrigerator for at least 10 minutes before filling and baking.

Moist flan bases: Just before putting the flan into the oven slip it on to a hot baking sheet and stand it on top of the cooker for just a few seconds to start the heat cooking the base. Then slip it into the oven and bake in the normal way.

Avoid overcooking: If the flan filling is an egg-based mixture, overcooking it will tend to moisten the base if the egg separates.

Dropping the tart: If a tart is dropped it can often be rescued by cutting slices from the undamaged part and arranging them round a plate. Sliced tomatoes or watercress can be arranged between slices of savoury tart.

BAKING

Cutting a round cake: Cut the cake in half, then quarters, then each quarter in two or three depending on the size of the cake and how large the slices are required. For easy serving, slip each slice into a paper cake case and reassemble the cake in a circle.

Cutting cakes from the freezer: Cut cakes, tray bakes, fruit loaves or gingerbread while still partly frozen. The slices will be much neater than if cut when fully thawed.

Icing a frozen Victoria sandwich: Ice the cake when it is semi-frozen for a really speedily-set icing.

Tray bakes: These are so much more convenient than little cakes. Use a tin with straight corners and sides to achieve even slices and deep enough to hold the thickness of the mixture. They freeze well, too, as they can be wrapped separately and stacked.

Scones: Cool scones between two clean teatowels to keep the surface soft and moist.

Coats on: When coating foods with sauces or icings stand the food on a cooling rack and then place the rack on a large tray. Pour the sauce or icing over the food and then scrape up the excess from under the rack to use again. Stand freshly washed racks in the oven while it is still warm to ensure they are not put away damp.

Biscuits: Instead of rolling out and cutting each biscuit, form the mixture into a long roll, wrap it in waxed paper and freeze it. When you want to make the biscuits simply cut slices from the roll and bake as normal.

Spreading drop scones: These are good with butter, jam, syrup or honey but very sticky to handle if they are overlapped on a plate or tray. Spread the drop scones with butter then put the jam etc., over half of the top of the scone, overlapping the butter side to make them easier to lift, and less sticky to eat.

▓SANDWICHES

Speedy spread: Allow about 225 g (8 oz) of butter for a large sliced loaf. Where possible mix the butter with the filling, such as pâté or egg. For example, soften the butter in a bowl, add shelled, hot hard-boiled eggs and mash them down with a potato masher. Add mayonnaise and salt and pepper to taste.

A good grip: Stacks of sandwiches are apt to tip over and spill out their fillings. To prevent this put them between the ends of the loaf or between pieces of cardboard and grip them together with elastic bands. This keeps them moist until they are ready to cut for serving.

Dainty sandwiches: These are nice for smaller numbers or for a cocktail party. To serve them, cut off the top of a large loaf lengthways and scoop out the centre crumb leaving only the crust. Fill the empty loaf with little sandwiches and put on the loaf lid. This will keep the sandwiches beautifully moist, instantly ready to serve and the outside crust can be frozen afterwards and used again. The centre can be left to go stale and used for breadcrumbs.

IDEAS TO HELP WITH SUNDAY COOKING

Easy carving: To make a shoulder of lamb easy to carve, use a small sharp knife to loosen the flat shoulder blade bone all the way round, as far down as the joint. Leave it attached. Roast the meat in the usual way. Before carving hold the blade bone tightly with a piece of kitchen paper towel and give it a sharp twist to remove it. The meat can now be carved into neat slices which will look better on the plate and will go further.

Yorkshire puddings: To save a little time when making Yorkshire puddings to serve with roast beef, add hot water instead of cold to the batter just before it is poured into the hot dripping. Yorkshire puddings need a hot oven so take the meat out when it is ready and increase the oven heat to cook the puddings while making the gravy and finishing the vegetables. The meat will be easier to carve and be more tender if it is allowed to rest for 10-15 minutes after cooking.

The gravy: Make the gravy before dishing up and pour it into a vacuum flask. This saves time and the gravy will be hot for first, and even second, helpings.

One extra helping: If there is only one helping of meat left, carve it and, using the rest of the vegetables and gravy, make up a meal for one and freeze it on a plate. Reheat it in a hot oven from frozen, or quicker still in the microwave oven next time one of the family comes home late.

No waste: If there is any gravy left, boil it rapidly without a lid to reduce the liquid and strengthen the flavour, and then freeze in the ice cube tray. Store the frozen gravy cubes in a polythene bag in the freezer ready to add to stews or gravy for extra flavour.

Kneaded butter: A useful thickening can be made by working together two tablespoons of plain flour and 25 g (1 oz) of softened butter (generous weight) to a paste. Keep it in the refrigerator to use as a thickening for soups, gravy and stews. Add just a small knob at a time, letting it run down the sides of the pan to melt the butter while whisking it into the liquid. Simmer for a few minutes.

DAIRY TIPS

Piping cream: Use a large nylon piping bag and a medium star pipe. Place the pipe in the bag, turn the top edge of the bag outwards over your hand and fill the bag with cream. Unfold the top of the bag, gather it up to enclose the cream and give it a twist above the cream to hold it inside. Pipe with the pressure from above the cream so that none of it can escape.

Small hands: If you have a small hand it is helpful to drop the piping bag into a jug or round grater, with the top of the bag folded over the edge, before filling.

Fair distribution: To pipe cream round a trifle, start with four stars, marking the surface in quarters. Fill in alternate spaces evenly so that if you run out of cream the decoration will not be lopsided.

Emergency cream: Melt 100 g (4 oz) unsalted butter in a pan with 150 ml (¼ pint) milk. Bring to the boil and simmer for one minute. Liquidize the mixture for 30 seconds at full speed and pour into a bowl to finish cooling. This makes a thick coating cream.

A cheese board: This is an after dinner luxury. Try serving a small portion for each person of a very special cheese, nicely arranged with biscuits, a little bunch of grapes or quartered apples. Either rub the edges of apples with lemon juice or cut at the last moment.

Liptaur cheese: This is an interesting blend of flavours. Any leftover cheese can be used. Grate the cheese then beat in enough hot milk and butter to make a spreading consistency. Season with salt, paprika pepper and a little tomato purée. Add a few capers and two or three chopped gherkins or a little chopped pickle or chutney. Heap on to a dish and sprinkle the top with caraway seeds if liked. This is useful for packed lunches, is good on baked potatoes or will add a little sparkle to a ploughman's lunch. It keeps well in a covered container in the refrigerator.

CHARTS

#

▓ *LARDER OR STORE CUPBOARD*

Cool and fresh: Ideally the temperature should not exceed 10°C (50°F) and there should be some ventilation. Any outlets or windows should be closely covered with gauze or a perforated sheet of zinc to keep out insects and possible vermin.

Shelf cover: The shelves should be covered with easy-clean materials such as ceramic tiles, self-adhesive or laminated plastic etc., and any spills should be mopped up immediately.

Up-to-date food: Perishable foods should be checked regularly to make sure they have not become stale or bad. Store cupboard cans and packets should be used in rotation with the new acquisitions always put at the back of the shelves. A good way to keep a check is to date packets as you buy them, if not already date-stamped.

Storage containers: It is safe to store in the original packets until opened after which the contents are best stored in containers or storage jars with tight fitting or airtight lids. Strong smelling commodities, such as coffee, herbs, spices etc., must be kept in really airtight containers for they easily and quickly lose their aroma and flavour when exposed to the air. Airtight storage is vital for dry ingredients such as salt and baking powder which absorb moisture easily and can become caked.

Unwelcome visitors: All cereal products store well but need frequent checking to make sure no insects have got into the packets or containers. If insects are discovered, immediately discard the product and make a thorough search of everything else close by.

Life in the can: Canned fish in oil (not tomato sauce) and canned meats keep for several years provided the cans are not damaged. Cans of ham need a little extra care. Those which are over 900 g (2 lb) and pasteurized should not be kept for longer than six months and are best stored in the refrigerator, to make them easier to slice. Sterilized hams of 900 g (2 lb) or less can be safely stored for two-three years. Canned fruits are best used within a year as the fruits may begin to discolour after this time although they are quite safe to eat. Condensed milk begins to discolour after six-nine months. Dried full-cream milk will keep for a few weeks after opening and will then go rancid.

Always discard immediately any cans which have 'blown', that is have bulging ends and leaking or rusty seams.

HOW LONG WILL IT KEEP?

Extra long keepers
ideal for emergency meals

Canned fish in oil and canned meats (not ham)	5 years
Sugar – cubed, granulated and caster	2 years
Canned vegetables	2 years
Canned soups	2 years
Canned cook-in sauces	2 years
Canned sponge puddings	2 years
Canned pasta foods in sauce	2 years
Canned meat and vegetable meals	2 years

Long keepers
(up to 1 year) – Provided the packets and/or containers, cans etc. are unopened and/or kept airtight.

Blancmange powder	Icing sugar
Canned fish in tomato sauce	Instant coffee
Canned fruit juices	Instant desserts
Canned milk	Jams
Canned milk puddings	Malted milk
Chutneys	Marmalades
Cocoa	Most canned fruit
Cornflour	Oils
Custard powder	Packet soups
Dehydrated foods	Pasta and rice
Drinking chocolate	Treacle and syrup

Other foods

Flour, plain	up to 6 months
Flour, self-raising	2-3 months
Baking powder, bicarbonate of soda etc.	2-3 months

Dried yeast	up to 6 months
Cake mixes	6 months
Pastry mixes	6 months
Biscuits – according to variety	3-12 months
Brown sugars	up to 3 months
Glacé cherries, angelica	3-4 months
Cake decorations	up to 1 month
Block chocolate	up to 2 months
Liquid food colourings	indefinitely
Essences	up to 12 months
Breakfast cereals	up to 1 month
Oatmeal, rolled oats	3-4 months
Nuts, coconut	up to 6 weeks
Ground almonds	up to 1 month
Dried peas, beans and lentils etc.	6-12 months
Dried fruits	2-3 months
Canned prunes and rhubarb	up to 9 months
Instant low fat/skimmed milk powder	2-3 months
Evaporated milk	6-8 months
Condensed milk	4-6 months
Carbonated drinks in cans	6-12 months
Tea, loose coffee	up to 1 month
Vinegars	up to 9 months
Anchovy essence, gravy browning	up to 12 months
Dry and bottled mustard	up to 9 months
Salad creams, mayonnaise and ketchups	up to 9 months
Herbs, spices, seasonings	up to 6 months
Canned ham – over 900 g (2 lb)	6 months (keep refrigerated)
Jellies, gelatine	up to 12 months

▓ REFRIGERATOR STORAGE

Temperature: The average refrigerator maintains a temperature of 2-7°C (35-45°F) which is sufficiently low to stop micro-organisms developing but it will not kill any already present before the food is put into the cabinet.

Fresh is a must: Make sure only fresh perishable foods are bought to store in the refrigerator – second best is not good enough.

Keep it shut: Try to open the refrigerator as little as possible and make sure the door is properly shut after each visit.

Under cover: All food should be covered before it is put in to the refrigerator. If food is just cooked then allow it to cool before putting it into the refrigerator.

Reduce frost: It is hot or uncovered food which makes the frozen food compartment become frosted up and this makes an insulating layer which prevents the refrigerator from working efficiently.

No spills: Wipe up all spills so they don't have time to solidify; and watch that small items don't get hidden behind something larger – either eat up quickly or discard.

Regular cleaning: Defrost the refrigerator regularly unless it does this automatically. Clean it with a weak solution of bicarbonate of soda dissolved in warm water, using a clean cloth, and dry it well. Soap or detergent should not be used, it will leave a strong smell which may permeate the foods.

Time to refresh: Remove cooked foods and cheese from the refrigerator about 30 minutes before required so they can 'come to' and will be served at their best with fullest flavour.

Correct places: Do try to store foods in the correct place in the refrigerator:
Raw foods such as meat, bacon, poultry and fish should go in the coldest part. This is usually directly under the frozen food compartment, but check in the manufacturer's handbook.
Cooked meats and made-up dishes on the middle shelves.
Vegetables and salads should go at the bottom of the refrigerator in the salad crisper drawer, if there is one.
Butter should be put in the butter compartment which is often on the door where the temperature is warmer, and thus prevents butter from becoming too hard; otherwise store fats a little lower down than the meats etc.

Star rating: Refrigerators have a Star Rating given by manufacturers as a useful guide as to how long you can keep commercially frozen food in the frozen food compartment of a fridge or freezer section of a fridge/freezer. Check the star markings both on the commercially frozen food packets and those on your own refrigerator.

Maximum temperature of frozen compartment	Maximum Storage Time for a) Frozen foods	b) Ice Cream
* − 6°C (21°F)	Up to 1 week	1 day
** −12°C (10°F)	Up to 1 month	Up to 2 weeks
*** −18°C (0°F)	Up to 3 months	Up to 3 months

STORING PERISHABLE FOODS IN THE REFRIGERATOR

Milk and Milk Products

Fresh milk	In bottle or covered container	3-4 days
Milk desserts, custards, etc.	In covered dish	2 days
Cultured milk (e.g. buttermilk)	In original container	7 days
Fats	In original wrapper (butter in the door compartment)	2-4 weeks
Cheese	In original pack, polythene, greaseproof or foil	1-2 weeks
Cream cheese	In covered container, polythene or foil	5-7 days

Poultry

Whole fresh	Prepare and wrap in polythene or foil. Remove wrappings from ready-to-cook birds	2-3 days
Cooked poultry	Cool and chill straight away. Remove stuffing, wrap or cover with polythene or foil	2-3 days
Frozen birds	Leave in original wrapping. Chill straight away in the frozen food compartment or leave to thaw slowly at the bottom of the fridge – up to 36 hours depending on size	Depends on star rating for freezing. 2-3 days in main fridge
Cooked and made-up poultry dishes	Cool and chill in covered dish or container	1 day

Meat

Joints	Refrigerate straight away	3-5 days
Steaks	Wipe off any excess blood	2-4 days
Chops	Cover with polythene or foil	2-4 days
Stewing meats		2-4 days
Smoked ham		1 week
Offal and mince		1-2 days
Bacon rashers	Wrap tightly in foil or plastic film or put into a polythene container	7-10 days

Cooked meats

Joints	Wrap in foil or polythene or	3-5 days
Casseroles	leave in the covered dish in	2-3 days
Made-up dishes	which they were cooked – or any other container	2-3 days

Fish

Raw	Covered loosely in polythene or foil	1-2 days
Cooked	Covered loosely in polythene or foil; or in a covered dish	2 days
Frozen	In original pack in frozen food compartment	Depends on star rating

Eggs

Fresh in shell	Small end downwards	2 weeks
Yolks	Covered with water if whole	2-3 days
Whites	Covered container	3-4 days
Hard-boiled eggs	Uncovered	2-3 days

Yeast

Fresh	In loosely tied polythene bag	Up to 1 month

Fruit and vegetables

Soft fruit	Clean and chill in a covered container	1-3 days
Hard and stone fruits	Lightly wrapped	3-7 days
Bananas	Never refrigerate unless in a fruit salad	

| Salad vegetables | Clean and drain thoroughly, store in salad drawer or lightly wrapped in polythene or in a plastic container | 4-6 days |
| Greens and other vegetables | Prepare ready for use and wrap lightly or place in the salad drawer | 3-7 days |

Pastry items

Made-up pastry	Wrap lightly	2-3 days
Pastry crumbs	In polythene bag	2 weeks
Cooked pies	Covered	1-2 days

STORAGE IN THE FREEZER

Vegetables

Most vegetables store well for up to 12 months provided they have been properly blanched, drained, packed and fast frozen. The exceptions are as follows:

Avocado purée	1-2 months
Beetroot – small whole, sliced or diced	6 months
Cabbage – braised	6 months
Cauliflower	6 months
Cooked and prepared vegetable dishes	3 months
Florence fennel	6 months
Herbs	6 months
Jerusalem artichokes	3 months
Leeks	6 months
Mushrooms – cooked	3 months
Onions or shallots	6 months
Potatoes – whole, new and boiled	3 months
Duchesse	3 months
baked in jackets, roast	3 months
Croquettes	3 months
chipped	6 months
Raw mushrooms	1 month
Unblanched vegetables	4-6 weeks
Vegetable purées	6-12 months

Fruits

These can either be frozen in dry packs, packed with dry sugar or packed in syrup. All fruits will vary slightly from year to year and with the quality.

Fruit in sugar or syrup	6 months
Fruit without sugar or syrup	2-12 months
Fruit purées	12 months
except apple purée	6 months
apricot purée	4 months
Fruit juices	6 months
Marmalade oranges (Sevilles)	6 months

Meats (raw)

Beef	Joints	8-12 months
	Steaks	6 months
	Mince	2 months
	Sausages	2 months
Lamb	Joints	6-8 months
	Chops and cutlets	6 months
Pork	All joints (any size)	3 months
	Chops	3 months
	Sausages	2-3 months
Bacon	Joints (smoked)	6 weeks
	Joints (unsmoked)	3 weeks
	Rashers (smoked)	6-8 weeks
	Rashers (unsmoked)	3 weeks
	All vacuum-packed joints and rashers	up to 4 months
Veal	All cuts of veal	6 months
Tongue	All types	6 months
Poultry (raw and unstuffed)	Chicken	12 months
	Turkey	6-12 months
	Duck	6-9 months
	Goose	4-6 months
	Giblets (packed separately)	2 months
Game	Rabbit and Hare	6-9 months
	Venison	12 months
	Birds – pheasant, grouse etc.	12 months

Cooked Meats

Bacon joints	3-4 weeks
Roast meat and poultry, whole	2 months
Sliced meat and poultry	1-2 months
Meat pies	3-4 months
Meat loaves, pâtés etc.	1-3 months
Ham, sliced	1 month
Tongue, sliced	1 month
Cooked casseroles	2 months
Cooked casseroles including ham, bacon or pork	6-8 weeks
Offal (raw or cooked)	1 month
Cured meats, smoked meats and smoked sausages	1 month

Fish (raw)

Oily fish –salmon, trout, herring, mackerel etc.	2-3 months
White fish – cod, haddock, plaice, sole, etc.	3-6 months
Crab and lobster	1 month
Mussels	1 month
Scallops and oysters	1 month
Raw shrimps and prawns	1 month

Fish (cooked)

Cooked fish dishes	1 month
Cooked prawns and shrimps	1 month

Breads

Baked bread – brown or white	4-6 months
Unbaked bread – brown or white unrisen	2 months
risen	3 weeks
enriched risen	4 weeks
Baked crusty loaves and rolls (otherwise crust crumbles and falls off)	1 week
Breadcrumbs	up to 6 months
Sandwiches	1-2 months
Yeasted rich buns and pastries, croissants	1 month
Yeasted teabreads	3 months
Pizzas (depending on toppings)	1-3 months
Pizzas without toppings	4 months
Pitta bread	3 months
Muffins and crumpets	2 months

Cakes

Undecorated cakes	4-6 months
Decorated cakes	3 months
Rich fruit cakes*	6-9 months
Unbaked cake mixture	1 month
Scones	6 months
Shortbreads	3 months
Cheesecakes	1-2 months
Biscuits – unbaked or baked	6 months
unless highly spiced when only	2 months

*It is not necessary to freeze rich fruit cakes, as they can be wrapped and kept in an airtight container. However, freezing extends their life.

Pastries and puddings

Mousses	3 months
Soufflés	3 months
Ice cream – commercial	1-2 months
Ice cream – home-made	2-4 months
Baked pies	6 months
Unbaked pies	3 months
Baked flan cases, unfilled	6 months
Baked and filled flan cases	2 months
Unbaked flan cases, unfilled	3 months
Pastry – shortcrust, puff, flaky, unbaked	3 months
Pastry – shortcrust, puff, flaky, baked	6 months
Baked puddings	3 months
Steamed puddings	3 months

Dairy produce

Butter, salted	3 months
Butter, unsalted	6 months
Lard	5 months
Margarine	5 months
Rendered dripping	5 months
Cheese, hard or blue	4 months
Grated cheese	6 months
Cream – 40% butterfat and over	3 months
Homogenized milk	1 month
Eggs, separated	6 months

Miscellaneous

Pancakes, unfilled	4-6 months
Pancakes, filled ·	2 months
Pancakes, filled with fish	1 month
Cooked pasta (plain)	1 month
Pasta dishes	2-3 months
Stuffing mixtures	2 months
Soups	3-4 months
Stocks	3-6 months
Sauces – tomato, apple etc.	12 months
highly flavoured or spiced	2-3 months
Commercial yogurt	4-6 weeks
Commercially frozen foods	up to 3 months or as directed on the package

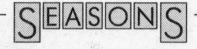

WHEN TO FREEZE

A Calendar of Freezing: This is a guide to help plan a year of freezing to ensure a good turnover of items in the freezer. It also states when is the best time to freeze down the items. The seasonal availability will, however, vary according to the weather in any one year.

The following are available all the year although prices fluctuate throughout so do pick your best time and price.

All types of meat	Grapes	Peppers
Cabbages	Lemons	Potatoes
Carrots	Mushrooms	Rabbit
Cauliflowers	Onions	Tomatoes
Chicken	Oranges	Turkey
Ducklings		

WHEN TO FREEZE ░GAME

JANUARY
Hare
Partridge
Pheasant
Snipe
Venison
Wild duck

FEBRUARY
Hare
Venison
Wild duck

MARCH
Venison

April, May, June and July no game as such although venison, hare, pigeons and rabbits will be available.

AUGUST
Black game
Grouse
Snipe
Venison

SEPTEMBER
Black game
Grouse
Hare
Partridge
Snipe
Venison
Wild duck and geese

OCTOBER
Black game
Grouse
Hare
Partridge
Pheasant
Snipe
Venison
Wild duck and geese
Woodcock

NOVEMBER
Black game
Grouse
Hare
Partridge
Pheasant
Snipe
Venison
Wild duck and geese
Woodcock

DECEMBER
Hare
Partridge
Pheasant
Snipe
Venison
Wild duck and geese
Woodcock

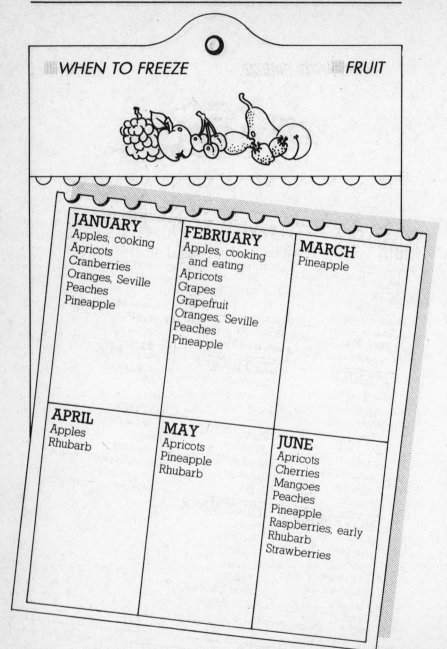

WHEN TO FREEZE FRUIT

JANUARY
Apples, cooking
Apricots
Cranberries
Oranges, Seville
Peaches
Pineapple

FEBRUARY
Apples, cooking
   and eating
Apricots
Grapes
Grapefruit
Oranges, Seville
Peaches
Pineapple

MARCH
Pineapple

APRIL
Apples
Rhubarb

MAY
Apricots
Pineapple
Rhubarb

JUNE
Apricots
Cherries
Mangoes
Peaches
Pineapple
Raspberries, early
Rhubarb
Strawberries

WHEN TO FREEZE FRUIT

JULY
Apricots
Blackcurrants
Cherries
Fresh figs
Gooseberries
Grapes
Limes
Loganberries
Mangoes
Nectarines
Peaches
Raspberries
Strawberries

OCTOBER
Apples, cooking
Cranberries
Damsons
Melons
Nectarines
Pears
Plums
Pumpkins
Quinces
Raspberries, late

AUGUST
Apricots
Cherries
Cultivated
    blackberries
Currants, black, red
    and white
Figs
Gooseberries
Grapes
Greengages
Limes, Loganberries
Peaches, Plums
Raspberries

NOVEMBER
Apples, cooking
Cranberries
Mandarins
Pears
Tangerines

SEPTEMBER
Apples, cooking
Bilberries
Blackberries
Damsons
Figs
Greengages
Melons
Peaches
Pears
Plums
Raspberries, late

DECEMBER
Apples, cooking
Apricots
Cranberries
Grapes
Pineapple

WHEN TO FREEZE VEGETABLES

JANUARY
Aubergines
Broccoli
Celery
Horseradish
Kale
Onions

FEBRUARY
Aubergines
Beetroot
Broccoli
Cabbage
Celery
Horseradish
Jerusalem artichokes
Leeks
Parsnips
Peppers, green
Potatoes
Spring greens
Swedes, Turnips

MARCH
Aubergines
Horseradish
Kale
Parsnips

APRIL
Aubergines
Carrots
Cauliflower
Kale
Spinach

MAY
Asparagus
Broccoli
Carrots
Cauliflower
Courgettes, early
Kale
Peppers, green
Potatoes, new

JUNE
Asparagus
Broccoli
Carrots
Cauliflower
Courgettes
Herbs
Peas
Peppers – green
  and red
Potatoes, new
Spinach
Tomatoes

WHEN TO FREEZE VEGETABLES

JULY
Artichokes, globe
Beans – broad
    early runner
    French
Beetroot
Broccoli
Cauliflower
Courgettes
Marrow, Peas
Peppers – green
  and red
Spinach
Tomatoes

AUGUST
Artichokes, globe
Beans – broad
    French
    runner
Beetroot,
Cabbage, red
Courgettes
Horseradish
Marrow
Peas
Spinach
Tomatoes

SEPTEMBER
Artichokes, globe
Aubergines
Beans, runner
Beetroot, Broccoli
Cabbbage, red
Courgettes
Leeks, Marrow
Onions
Peppers – green
  and red
Spinach, Swede
Tomatoes
Turnip

OCTOBER
Aubergines
Beetroot
Celery
Chestnuts
Horseradish
Leeks
Onions
Parsnips
Peppers, green
Spinach
Sprouts
Tomatoes

NOVEMBER
Avocado purée
Broccoli
Cabbage, red
Celery
Leeks
Onions
Peppers, green
Sprouts
Swede

DECEMBER
Avocado purée
Broccoli
Cabbage, red
Celery
Jerusalem artichokes
Onions
Parsnips
Peppers, green
Sprouts
Swede

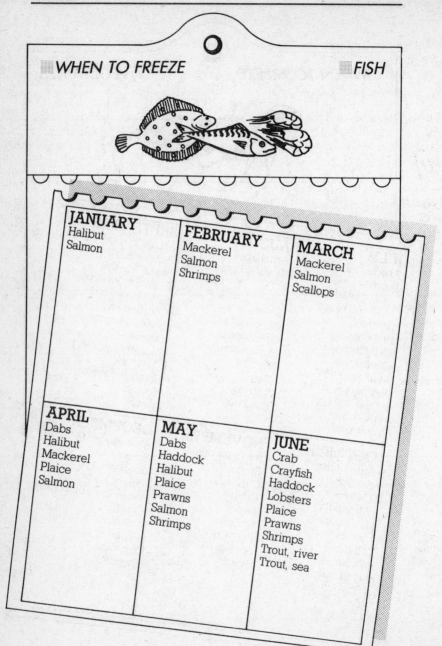

WHEN TO FREEZE   FISH

JANUARY
Halibut
Salmon

FEBRUARY
Mackerel
Salmon
Shrimps

MARCH
Mackerel
Salmon
Scallops

APRIL
Dabs
Halibut
Mackerel
Plaice
Salmon

MAY
Dabs
Haddock
Halibut
Plaice
Prawns
Salmon
Shrimps

JUNE
Crab
Crayfish
Haddock
Lobsters
Plaice
Prawns
Shrimps
Trout, river
Trout, sea

WHEN TO FREEZE FISH

JULY
Crayfish
Dabs
Haddock
Lobster
Plaice
Prawns
Shrimps
Trout, river
Trout, sea

AUGUST
Crab
Crayfish
Dabs
Lobster
Plaice
Prawns
Shrimps
Trout

SEPTEMBER
Mackerel
Prawns
Shrimps
Trout, river
Trout, sea

OCTOBER
Mackerel
Prawns
Salmon
Shrimps

NOVEMBER
Halibut
Salmon

DECEMBER
Halibut
Prawns
Shrimps

353

▓SEASONAL FRUIT CHART

Fruits in store: Fruit is perishable and best bought in usable amounts. This really means the softer fruits; apples and pears which are hard are bought for storage for the winter. Only buy blemished or soft fruits, which will be cheaper, to make into purées or sauces or fillings. Store all fruit in a cool place and do not pile it up high in a bowl for it will easily fall out and bruise.

Treat with care: Great care is taken in the distribution of fruit because of its perishable nature and it should arrive in the shops in very good condition. It is then up to you to transport it carefully, store it carefully and eat as quickly as possible while it is in prime condition, see pages 76 to 79.

▓AVAILABILITY OF HOME-GROWN FRUITS

Apples, cooking – January-June, August-December
Apples, dessert – January-May, August-December
Blackberries – July-September
Blackcurrants – July, August
Cherries – June, July
Gooseberries – June, July
Loganberries – July
Pears – January-April, September-December
Plums – August-October
Raspberries – June-October
Redcurrants – July
Rhubarb – January-May
Strawberries – May-October

▓AVAILABILITY OF IMPORTED FRUITS

Apples – all year
Apricots – January, April, May-August, November, December
Avocados – all year
Bananas – all year
Cherries – January, April, May, July, August, November, December
Clementines – January, February, November, December
Coconuts – all year
Cranberries – January, November, December

Dates – January-May, July, August, October-December
Figs – January, June, July-December
Gooseberries – June
Grapefruit – all year
Grapes – all year
Greengages – July-September
Kiwifruit – all year
Lemons – all year
Limes – all year
Lychees – January-June, August, November, December
Mandarins – April
Mangoes – all year
Melons – all year
Nectarines – January-March, June-September, December
Oranges – all year
Passion Fruit – all year
Paw Paws – all year
Peaches – January, May-September, December
Pears – all year
Persimmons – January, February, November, December
Pineapples – all year
Plums – January, February, March, June-November
Pomegranates – September-December
Raspberries – November
Satsumas – January, February, March, October-December
Seville oranges – January, February
Strawberries – January-August, October-December
Ugli fruit – January-May
Watermelons – May-September
Wilkings – January-March

SEASONAL VEGETABLE CHART

Wise buying: It is wise always to buy your produce fresh from a reputable greengrocer, stall, supermarket or farm shop. Inferior produce may be cheaper but it is not worth the effort and the result. Buy regularly and do not store fresh vegetables for longer than necessary.

Correct storage: Store vegetables in a cool, dry, well ventilated atmosphere – preferably in a rack as this ensures air circulation. If vegetables are bought in polythene bags, either take out or make large holes in the bag for ventilation. Remove vegetables from cling film or punch holes in it. Paper bags are excellent for storage.

Staying fresh: Root vegetables should stay fresh for five-six days with proper storage and green vegetables for two-three days. Certain items, such as lettuce, are good stored in the crisper drawer of the refrigerator or at least at the bottom of the refrigerator. Keep any blemished vegetables separate from the rest as they will turn the good produce bad too, and very quickly.

▓AVAILABILITY OF HOME-GROWN VEGETABLES

Asparagus – April-June
Aubergines – July-November
Beansprouts – all year
Beetroot – all year
Broad beans – June-August
Broccoli – March, April
Cabbage – all year
Calabrese – January, February, March, June, July,
          August-December
Carrots – all year
Cauliflower – January, February, March, April, May-September,
          November, December
Celeriac – January, November, December
Celery – January, February, May, June, July, August, September
        November, December
Chicory – April, May
Chinese leaves – January, June, July, August, September,
          November, December
Courgettes – June-September
Cucumber – March-September
Curly kale – February-March, December
French beans – July, August
Garlic – January-April, September-December
Globe artichokes – May
Greens – January-July, October-December
Jerusalem artichokes – January-April, December
Leeks – August-May
Lettuce – all year

Marrows – June-October
Mushrooms – all year
Onions – all year
Parsley – January-March, May-October, December
Parsnips – January-May, August-December
Peas – June-August
Peppers – October
Pickling onions – September-December
Potatoes – all year
Pumpkin – October, November
Radishes – April-November
Runner beans – July-October
Spinach – all year
Spring onions – all year
Sprouts – January, February, March, September, October,
            November, December
Swede – January-April, June-December
Sweetcorn – August-October
Tomatoes – April-November
Turnips – January-April, July-December
Watercress – all year

▓AVAILABILITY OF IMPORTED VEGETABLES

Asparagus – April-July, September-December
Aubergines – all year
Batavia – January, February
Beetroot – May-August
Broad beans – March-June
Broccoli – March
Cabbage – January-May, July, September-December
Calabrese – January-March, May, June, November, December
Carrots – January-March, May, June
Cauliflower – January-March, July, December
Celery – all year
Chicory – January-May
Chillies – all year
Chinese leaves – January-September, December
Courgettes – all year
Cucumber – all year
Endive – January, March

Fennel – January-May
French beans – January-May, November, December
Garlic – all year
Ginger – all year
Globe artichokes – all year
Leeks – April
Lettuce – all year
Mangetout – February
Okra – all year
Onions – all year
Parsley – January-May, October-December
Parsnips – March, April
Peppers – all year
Pickling onions – September-December
Potatoes – January-May, December
Radishes – all year
Salsify – January-April
Spinach – March, April
Spring onions – February-August
Sweet potatoes – all year
Sweetcorn – May-August
Tomatoes – all year
Turnips – May-August

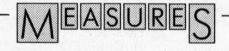

MEASURES

Measuring without scales

Butter, lard etc.	25 g (1 oz) = 2 level tablespoons
Cheese, grated cheddar	25 g (1 oz) = 3 level tablespoons
Cocoa	25 g (1 oz) = 2¾ level tablespoons
Cornflour, custard powder	25 g (1 oz) = 2½ level tablespoons
Curry powder	25 g (1 oz) = 3½ level tablespoons
Desiccated coconut	25 g (1 oz) = 5 level tablespoons

Dried breadcrumbs	25 g (1 oz) = 3¼ level tablespoons
Dried yeast	25 g (1 oz) = 1½ level tablespoons
Dry mustard	25 g (1 oz) = 3½ level tablespoons
Fresh breadcrumbs	25 g (1 oz) = 7 level tablespoons
Grated chocolate	25 g (1 oz) = 1¼ level tablespoons
Ground almonds	25 g (1 oz) = 3¾ level tablespoons
Ground coffee	25 g (1 oz) = 4 level tablespoons
Ground ginger	25 g (1 oz) = 3½ level tablespoons
Instant coffee powder	25 g (1 oz) = 6½ level tablespoons
Medium oatmeal	25 g (1 oz) = 2½ level tablespoons
Powdered gelatine	25 g (1 oz) = 2 level tablespoons
Salt	25 g (1 oz) = 1¾ level tablespoons
Semolina, ground rice	25 g (1 oz) = 3 level tablespoons
Sugar – caster	25 g (1 oz) = 2 level tablespoons
Sugar – granulated	25 g (1 oz) = 2 level tablespoons
Sugar – icing	25 g (1 oz) = 2½ level tablespoons
Sugar – soft brown	25 g (1 oz) = 1½ level tablespoons
Sultanas, currants	25 g (1 oz) = 2 level tablespoons
Syrup, unheated	25 g (1 oz) = 1 level tablespoon
Uncooked rice	25 g (1 oz) = 1½ level tablespoons
Unsifted flour	25 g (1 oz) = 3 level tablespoons

OVEN TEMPERATURES

This is the standard guide used in most cookery books. If your cooker varies from this chart then consult the handbook which came with the cooker.

	Electricity	Gas Mark
Very cool	110°C (225°F)	¼
	120°C (250°F)	½
Cool	140°C (275°F)	1
	150°C (300°F)	2
Moderate	* 160°C (325°F)	3
	180°C (350°F)	4
Moderately hot	190°C (375°F)	5
Fairly hot	200°C (400°F)	6
Hot	220°C (425°F)	7
	230°C (450°F)	8
Very hot	240°C (475°F)	9

*In some cookery books this temperature is stated as 170°C.

Boiling point for liquids is 100°C (212°F)
Simmering point for liquids is approx 96°F (205°F)
Blood heat (or tepid or lukewarm) is approx 37°C (98°F)
Freezing point is 0°C (32°F)

▓TEMPERATURE SCALES

To convert Centigrade temperatures to an approximate Fahrenheit, multiply by 9, divide by 5 and then add 32. Conversely, to turn a Fahrenheit temperature into an approximate Centigrade, subtract 32, multiply by 5 and then divide by 9.

▓SOLID MEASURES

The true metric equivalent, rounded up to the nearest whole number, is given in brackets up to 450 g.

Metric	Imperial	Metric	Imperial
10 g	¼ oz	425 g (425 g)	15 oz
15 g	½ oz	450 g (454 g)	16 oz (1 lb)
20 g	¾ oz	500 g	1¼ lb
25 g (28 g)	1 oz	750 g	1½ lb
40 g	1½ oz		1¾ lb
50 g (57 g)	2 oz	1 kg	2 lb
65 g	2½ oz		2¼ lb
75 g (85 g)	3 oz	1¼ kg	2½ lb
90 g (100 g)	3½ oz		2¾ lb
100 g (113 g)	4 oz	1½ kg	3 lb
120 g	4½ oz		3¼ lb
150 g (142 g)	5 oz		3½ lb
165 g	5½ oz	1¾ kg	4 lb
175 g (170 g)	6 oz		4¼ lb
185 g	6½ oz	2 kg	4½ lb
200 g (198 g)	7 oz		4¾ lb
225 g (227 g)	8 oz	2¼ kg	5 lb
250 g (255 g)	9 oz		5¼ lb
275 g (284 g)	10 oz	2½ kg	5½ lb
300 g (312 g)	11 oz		5¾ lb
350 g (340 g)	12 oz	2¾ kg	6 lb
375 g (369 g)	13 oz	3 kg	7 lb
400 g (397 g)	14 oz	3½ kg	8 lb

Metric	Imperial	Metric	Imperial
4 kg	9 lb	7¼ kg	16 lb
4½ kg	10 lb	7½ kg	17 lb
5 kg	11 lb	8 kg	18 lb
5½ kg	12 lb	8½ kg	19 lb
6 kg	13 lb	9 kg	20 lb
6½ kg	14 lb	9½ kg	21 lb
6¾ kg	15 lb	10 kg	22 lb

MEASUREMENTS

3 mm	= ⅛ inch	10 cm	= 4 inches
5 mm	= ¼ inch	13 cm	= 5 inches
1 cm	= ½ inch	15 cm	= 6 inches
2 cm	= ¾ inch	18 cm	= 7 inches
2½ cm (2.5 cm)	= 1 inch	20 cm	= 8 inches
4 cm	= 1½ inches	23 cm	= 9 inches
5 cm	= 2 inches	25 cm	= 10 inches
6 cm	= 2½ inches	28 cm	= 11 inches
7½ cm (7.5 cm)	= 3 inches	30 cm	= 12 inches
9 cm	= 3½ inches	33 cm	= 13 inches

LIQUIDS

Standard spoon measures are available in sets usually marked both in Metric and Imperial quantities; although just one or the other measurements can be found on some. Recipes often state spoon measurements only in Imperial to avoid confusion.

1.25 ml (or a pinch)	= ¼ teaspoon
2.5 ml	= ½ teaspoon
3.75 ml	= ¾ teaspoon
5 ml	= 1 teaspoon
10 ml	= 2 teaspoons
15 ml	= 3 teaspoons = 1 tablespoon
150 ml	= 8 tablespoons = ¼ pint = 5 fl oz
25 ml	= 1 fl oz
50 ml	= 2 fl oz
65 ml	= 2½ fl oz
85 ml	= 3 fl oz
100 ml	= 3½ fl oz

120 ml	= 4 fl oz
135 ml	= 4½ fl oz
150 ml	= ¼ pint = 5 fl oz
175 ml	= 6 fl oz
200 ml	= ⅓ pint = 7 fl oz
250 ml	= 8 fl oz = 1 American cup
275 ml	= 9 fl oz
300 ml	= ½ pint = 10 fl oz = 1 British cup
350 ml	= 12 fl oz
400 ml	= 14 fl oz
450 ml	= ¾ pint = 15 fl oz
475 ml	= 16 fl oz = 2 American cups
500 ml	= 18 fl oz
600 ml	= 1 pint = 20 fl oz = 2 British cups
750 ml	= 1¼ pints
900 ml	= 1½ pints
1 litre	= 1¾ pints
1.2 litres	= 2 pints
1.25 litres	= 2¼ pints
1.5 litres	= 2½ pints
1.6 litres	= 2¾ pints
1.75 litres	= 3 pints
2 litres	= 3½ pints
2.25 litres	= 4 pints
2.5 litres	= 4½ pints
2.75 litres	= 5 pints

But milk is always measured exactly 568 ml = 1 pint.

4.55 litres = 1 gallon =	8 pints
1 decilitre	= 3½ fl oz
5.6 decilitres	= 20 fl oz = 1 pint
1.8 centilitres	= 1 tablespoon = 15 ml
0.6 centilitre	= 1 teaspoon = 5 ml

CUP MEASURES

The majority of American recipes give the quantities of ingredients in American standard cups and spoons. Anyone who does not possess these measures should be able to convert the figures into British measures with the aid of the following information:

1 American cup holds 250 ml or 8 fl oz but an English or Imperial cup holds 300 ml or ½ pint (10 fl oz).

1 American teaspoon = approx 1/6 fl oz (a little smaller than ours).

1 American tablespoon = 3 teaspoons or ½ fl oz.

16 American tablespoons = 1 American cup.

An American tablespoon holds exactly 10 g (0.35 oz).

It is possible to find a British dessertspoon which holds exactly this amount and can be kept for American conversions.

All the following measurements are the same as 1 American cup.

Butter, margarine and lard	225 g (8 oz)
Chopped walnuts	110 g (4½ oz)
Condensed milk	295 g (10¾ oz)
Cornflour	120 g (4½ oz)
Currants	150 g (5 oz)
Dry breadcrumbs	100 g (4 oz)
Flour	100 g (4 oz)
Fresh breadcrumbs	25 g (1 oz)
Glacé cherries	200 g (7 oz)
Golden syrup, treacle	325 g (11½ oz)
Grated cheddar cheese	100g (4 oz)
Honey	350 g (12 oz)
Icing sugar	110 g (4½ oz)
Long grain rice	185 g (6½ oz)
Mixed chopped peel	185 g (6½ oz)
Oil	225 g (8 oz)
Peanut butter	225 g (8 oz)
Powdered gelatine	160 g (5⅓ oz)
Pudding rice	200 g (7 oz)
Seedless raisins	170 g (6¾ oz)
Shredded suet	110 g (4½ oz)
Sugar – soft brown, caster, granulated	200 g (7 oz)
Whole blanched almonds	165 g (5½ oz)

▓GUIDE TO SUGAR SYRUP TEMPERATURES

Smooth: 102-104°C (214-218°F)
Dip a spoon into the syrup and allow it to cool for a moment or two. Once it is cooler, rub a little syrup between the thumb and forefinger. The fingers should slide smoothly but the syrup should cling to the skin.

Thread: 107°C (225°F)
Using a small spoon remove a little of the syrup and allow it to fall from the spoon on to a dish. The syrup at this stage should form a fine thin thread.

Soft ball: 113-118°C (235-245°F)
Drop a small amount of the syrup into iced water. Mould the sticky syrup into a soft ball with the fingers. Remove the ball from the water. It should immediately lose its shape.

Firm ball: 118-121°C (244-250°F)
Drop a little syrup into iced water, then using the fingers mould into a ball. Remove the ball from the water. It should feel firm but pliable and fairly sticky.

Hard ball: 120-130°C (248-266°F)
Drop a little syrup into iced water, then using the fingers mould into a ball. Remove the ball from the water. It should feel resistant to the fingers and still feel quite sticky.

Soft crack: 132-142°C (270-286°F)
Drop a little syrup into iced water. Remove from the water and gently stretch it between the fingers. It should form hard but elastic strands, and only feel slightly sticky.

Hard crack: 149-154°C (300-310°F)
Drop a little syrup into iced water. Remove from the water. It should form brittle threads which snap easily between the fingers, and no longer feel sticky.

Caramel: 160-177°C (320-350°F)
Using a small spoon remove a little of the syrup and pour it on to a white saucer. The syrup should be a light golden brown colour.

▓QUICK TEMPERATURE GUIDE

Thread	107°C (225°F)
Soft ball	115°C (238°F)
Firm ball	119°C (246°F)
Hard ball	125°C (256°F)
Soft crack	138°C (280°F)
Hard crack	151°C (304°F)
Caramel	168°C (336°F)

A sugar thermometer is a great help when making sugar syrups and the above temperatures will give you a quick guide to the stage the syrup has reached.

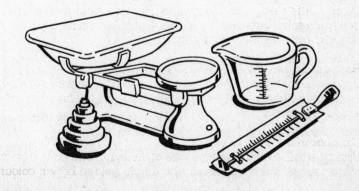

proving dough 138, 220;
rye 56;
too salty dough 172;
covering with seeds 202;
slicing thinly 244;
storing 105-6;
thawing 281;
warming 252;
white 56;
wholemeal and wholewheat 56;
yeast 201, 202
Bread and butter pudding 178, 210
Breadcrumbs: and egg coating
  138-9, 149;
  freezing 269, 344;
  making 213
Brie 90, 91. *See under* Cheese
Brining: dry 300; wet 300-1
Brioche dough 202
Broad beans 44; savory and 197
Broccoli 45; and almonds 236;
  cooking 185
Buffet parties 24-30.
  See also Canapés *etc.*
Bulk buying 34, 36-8
Butter 206; buying 51, 52;
  clarifying 150;
  freezing 170, 264, 345;
  frying with 149;
  refrigerating 95-6, 340;
  savoury 237;
  unsalted 51, 203
Butterbeans: storing 93; uses 110
Butter cream, freezing 265
Buttermilk 203

▓ *C*

Cabbage 45; quantities 19;
  freezing 342;

leaves for Dolmas 185;
red 184;
salad 186, 249;
storing 84;
wet brining 300-1
Cakes: almond paste to cover 22;
  baking 134-5, 165-7;
  baking in microwave 221, 225;
  custard filling 173;
  cutting 329;
  decorations 248,
  see also Icing, Piping;
  using food processor 123, 124;
  freezing 215, 268, 269, 275, 345;
  freezing mixture 174, 269;
  lining cake tins 136-7;
  mixing bowls for large 141;
  recipe basics 20;
  storing 103-5, 210;
  storing mixture 338;
  sunken 326;
  tins for 132;
  useful ingredients to have 95
Camembert cheese 91
Canapés 177; quantities 23-4
Candied peel: softening in
  microwave 225;
  storing 95
Canned food, storage life of 336-8
Caper sauce 316
Caramel, making 172-3, 364
Caramel custard 173
Caraway seeds 197
Cardamom 199
Carrots 45; estimating quantity 19;
  scraping 180;
  serving 184, 236;
  storing 80
Carving knives, electric 126
Casseroles 118, 135, 158-60;
  when boiled dry 325;

I

J

K

wet brining 300-1
Pet food: and hygiene 112
Pheasants: estimating quantity 18
Pickles, storing 97-8
Pickling 300-1
Picnics 238; ice-pack bags for 252;
    plates and glasses for 25
Pies: frozen 280;
    moulds 132-3, 140, 141
Pigs' trotters 67
Pineapples 42-3, 78;
    and gelatine 200;
    coring slices 189;
    serving 242;
    for tenderizing meat 157
Pine nuts 110
Piping icing 247, 248;
    improvised bags 142
Piping cream 332-3
Pitta bread 56; thawing 281
Pitta pockets 17
Pizza: bases 202;
    freezing 344;
    frozen 215
Planning meals 10, 11-13, 135-6
Plates, improvised 30
Plums 43; freezing 261;
    halving 190;
    poaching 161;
    removing stones 190;
    ripening 79, 188.
    See also under Fruit
Poaching 160-2
Poppadoms 233
Pork (see also under Meat): and
    fried apple 237;
    and spiced fruit 237;
    buying 66-7;
    keeping crackling crisp 239;
    freezing 262, 263;
    patties 309;

roasting 155, 157;
    storing 87;
    stretching quantities 309;
    'Wienerschnitzel' 229
Porridge 214
Port, storing 101
Potatoes 48;
    baked 180, 203, 320, 321;
    barbecuing 153;
    boiling 180;
    cooking in microwave 220;
    creamed 320;
    home-made crisps 122;
    estimating quantity 19;
    freezing 342;
    frying chips 148, 149;
    mashed 180;
    peeling 180;
    for picnics 238;
    preparing 134;
    roast 110, 321;
    salad 250;
    sauté 186;
    serving 239;
    steaming 163;
    storing 83, 134;
    keeping warm 252
Poultry: barbecuing 153;
    boning 210;
    buying 59-61;
    freezing 215, 263, 343;
    frozen 278;
    frying 151;
    packaging 59;
    refrigerating 340;
    roasting 155-7;
    sewing up 171, 212;
    storing 87-8
Poultry shears 117
Praline 168
Prawns (frozen): improving

wet brining 301

S

Safflower oil 69
Salad 249-50; American 226, 227;
  apple, carrot and nut 305;
  cabbage 186;
  garlic flavour 183;
  green 319;
  pasta and 317;
  preparation 184;
  to prevent wilting 249;
  ready-made 69;
  serving 250;
  using up old 109-10
Salad dressings 251; storing 338.
  See French dressing
Salami: buying 68;
  storing 89-90
Salmon (smoked), storing 89
Salsify 48; cooking 170
Salt 70, 111; keeping dry 208
Sandwiches 23, 330-1;
  flavoured butter for 243;
  freezing 270-1, 344
Sardines 111; as starter 305
Satsumas 41
Sauce 169; anchovy 316;
  brown 196;
  caper 316;
  cheese 205;
  estimating quantity 18, 19;
  fish 177;
  freezing 169, 170, 216, 271, 346;
  onion 316;
  peach 189;
  to prevent skin forming on 169,
  174, 177;
  using processor 123;

raspberry 189;
separation 195;
simple 22;
soy 111;
for steamed puddings 238;
for stewed fruit 238;
straining 212;
strawberry 189;
sweet 316;
tomato 316;
white 314-15, 316
Saucepans: care of 211;
  essential 117-18;
  storing 145
Sauerkraut 229
Sausage rolls: freezing 268;
  making 20, 171, 178
Sausages: barbecuing 153;
  cold 108;
  freezing smoked 344;
  frying 171;
  grilling 152;
  smoked 69;
  stretching quantities 309.
  See Frankfurters
Savory 197
Scales, kitchen 119
Scissors, kitchen 116
Scones 173, 203, 329; freezing 345;
  spreading 330
Scorzonera 48; cooking 170
Seakale 48
Sea salt 70, 111
Seasoning 70-1, 243, 326.
  See Salt *etc.*
Sell-by dates 37
Serving dishes, improvised 30
Sesame oil 69, 228
Sesame seeds 110
Shallots 315; freezing 342;
  storing 82

T

U

V